**COMMUNITY COLLEGE OF
PHILADELPHIA**
Philadelphia, Pennsylvania

Achebe the Orator

Recent Titles in
Contributions in Afro-American and African Studies

African Settings in Contemporary American Novels
Dave Kuhne

The Harlem Renaissance: The One and the Many
Mark Helbling

Willis Richardson, Forgotten Pioneer of African-American Drama
Christine Rauchfuss Gray

Critical Essays on Alice Walker
Ikenna Dieke, editor

Education and Independence: Education in South Africa, 1658–1988
Simphiwe A. Hlatshwayo

African American Autobiography and the Quest for Freedom
Roland L. Williams, Jr.

The White Image in the Black Mind: A Study of African American Literature
Jane Davis

Black Leadership for Social Change
Jacob U. Gordon

Mythatypes: Signatures and Signs of African/Diaspora and Black Goddesses
Alexis Brooks De Vita

African Visions: Literary Images, Political Change, and Social Struggle in
Contemporary Africa
Cheryl B. Mwaria, Silvia Federici, and Joseph McLaren, editors

Voices of the Fugitives: Runaway Slave Stories and Their Fictions of Self-Creation
Sterling Lecater Bland, Jr.

Meditations on African Literature
Dubem Okafor

Achebe the Orator

The Art of Persuasion in Chinua Achebe's Novels

Chinwe Christiana Okechukwu

Foreword by Chinyere Grace Okafor

Contributions in Afro-American and African Studies, Number 202

GREENWOOD PRESS
Westport, Connecticut • London

Library of Congress Cataloging-in-Publication Data

Okechukwu, Chinwe.
   Achebe the orator : the art of persuasion in Chinua Achebe's novels / by Chinwe Christiana Okechukwu.
     p. cm.—(Contributions in Afro-American and African studies, ISSN 0069–9624 ; no. 202)
   Includes bibliographical references and index.
   ISBN 0–313–31703–8 (alk. paper)
   1. Achebe, Chinua—Technique. 2. Politics and literature—Nigeria—History—20th century. 3. Literature and society—Nigeria—History—20th century. 4. Achebe, Chinua—Political and social views. 5. English language—Nigeria—Rhetoric. 6. Political oratory—Nigeria. 7. Nigeria—In literature. 8. Persuasion (Rhetoric) I. Title.
II. Series.
PR9387.9.A3Z849   2001
823'.914—dc21   00–064054

British Library Cataloguing in Publication Data is available.

Library of Congress Catalog Card Number: 00–064054
ISBN: 0–313–31703–8
ISSN: 0069–9624

First published in 2001

Greenwood Press, 88 Post Road West, Westport, CT 06881
An imprint of Greenwood Publishing Group, Inc.
www.greenwood.com

Printed in the United States of America

The paper used in this book complies with the
Permanent Paper Standard issued by the National
Information Standards Organization (Z39.48–1984).

10 9 8 7 6 5 4 3 2 1

Dedicated
to my Father,
the late Patrick Obisie Okonkwo
and my mother,
Elizabeth Nonyelum Okonkwo

Contents

Foreword

In an age when literary criticism is dominated by postmodernist and postcolonial theorizing that often relegates social contextualization and in-depth analysis, one is stimulated by Chinwe Christiana Okechukwu's contextual engagement of Achebe's novels as well as her incisive scrutiny of aspects of Achebe's creative impulse and power of oration. She bends down to such basics as the dynamics of imagery in Achebes's texts. The mechanics of metonomy in constructing the name "Umuofia" and the use of hyperbole in representing the collision of two arrogant patriarchies in *Things Fall Apart* are explained with an insider's perception and a critic's logistics. Achebe's portrayal of the crushing of African patriarchy by the colonial one through local imagery is examined as an oratorical art that elevates the prose. No doubt, the author's perception as an Ogidi woman from the same traditional Igbo village as Achebe empowers her insider's knowledge of the "crevices" and nuances of symbols and images derived from Ogidi locality. This insight not only links her with other insiders of Igbo critiquing space such as Kalu Ogba, who used his comprehension of Igbo folklore to examine Achebe's novels in *Gods, Oracles and Divinations,* but gives her work a special place on the insiders' pedestal because of her positionality in Ogidi creative space and tradition which she shares with Achebe.

Okechukwu studied English in universities in Great Britain and Nigeria, has a Ph.D. in Rhetoric from Catholic University of America in Washington DC, taught English language and literature in various institutions in Nigeria, and is at present a Full Professor at Montgomery College in Rockville, Maryland, where she teaches English, Literature, and Writing. From this educational background in language she examines Achebe's syntactic choices in the novels and comes up with interesting findings. Subject and object structures, contrasting sentences, pauses, semicolons, coordinating conjunctions, and coordinated clauses are analyzed for their contribution in denoting meaning. The author's language and linguistic skills are also employed in analyzing the use of pronouns in creating communal and individual experiences--a device that hastens Achebe's depiction of the movement from homogeneity to disintegration of the clan. She sees the dramatic pauses, rhetorical questions, sentence structures, participial phrases, sentence length, and contrast as part of Achebe's rhetorical style. Her explanation of the impact of the clash of African language with the invading colonial culture connects with D. E. S. Maxwell's examination of the relationship between language and place, while her idea that "oratory changes to meet with the demands of a changing audience" intersects with the notion of the influence of setting on an invading language explained by Bill Aschcroft, Gareth Griffiths, and Helen Tiffin in *The Empire Writes Back.*

These connections denote the author's argument in the ongoing debate about the encounter between indigenous settings and colonizing processes and also lead to her singular contribution in filling of a gap in the criticism of Achebe's works— that is, the oratorical analysis of the novels. Equipped with her knowledge of an African albeit, Igbo-Ogidi worldview, dialectics, and rhetoric as well as her study of English language and rhetorical pattern, she examines Achebe's art of persuasion and shows how traditional African rhetoric and the changing rhetorical patterns encode meaning and portray different levels in the transition of African society from traditional to colonial, postcolonial, and militarized conglomerates. The first chapter provides an overview of Achebe's background, works, and intentions as a writer. The second chapter deals with Achebe's first novel, *Things Fall Apart.* Relying on the force of her argument about change in oratory which, she sometimes endorses with the ideas of Perelman and Olbrecht-Tyteca on the role of audience in argumentation, she examines the movement of the society from a homogenous one through confusion and infiltration to adulteration and fragmentation. In the third chapter, she refers to Aristotle's, Quintilian,'s and Cicero's characterization of rhetorical pattern in her discussion of dialectics, sophistry, and persuasion in *Arrow of God.* When possible, she employs classical allusions to explicate rhetorical moves. For example, the *agon* between Nwaka and Ezeulu is compared with that of Brutus and Mark Antony in Shakespeare's *Julius Caesar.* She goes into detail in analyzing the rhetorical tools of the characters and expressing the dialectics of role and pragmatism of change in Ezeulu. She explores the flawed rhetoric of the colonizer whose name, Winterbottom, is symbolic of the confusion and comatose state he initiates in the society. She examines Ezeulu's inadequate use of dialectics and rhetorical skills in his internal inquisition of his inner self and sees it as detrimental in his management of the people he leads. Achebe's depiction of the power of ethics and values in the art of persuasion is best illustrated by the Christian oratory in the novel which draws inspiration from Saint Augustine's teaching.

In the fourth chapter, the bombarded theme of corruption in *No Longer at Ease* is given a new touch through the author's exploration of the influence of the postcolonial landscape on rhetoric. Oratorical pieces are used to examine the incompatibility of Western education and African tradition in the modern postcolonial landscape of the city with multiple *ethos* and *logos*. A complex of social forces revealed through rhetoric is seen as the *raison d'être* of the hero's malaise. The fifth chapter, which is based on *A Man of the People*, oratorical techniques for acquiring and manipulating power are examined and shown to constitute a sophisticated weapon in the hands of politicians. The rhetoric of cohesion in *Things Fall Apart* has receeded while monlogism of the media replaces dialogue in *A Man of the People*. The author contends that this movement illustrates the fact that societal evolution affects rhetorical strategies. In the sixth chapter, which is based on *Anthills of the Savannah*, the rhetoric of the military is seen as comparable to that of the politician, except that the former has that component of power which Mao Tse-Tung located "in the barrel of the gun." Through skillful use of persuasive art, Achebe convinces the reader that the problem lies in the intrusion of the military and the academia in political governance.

Chinwe Christiana Okechukwu seems to be at her best in these chapters that describe Achebe's use of the epistemic power of oratory to advance his argument about the African encounter with the West. The chapters constitute her major contribution to the scholarship on Achebe because of their pioneering position, depth of analysis, and new insights they bring. This explication of Achebe's use of oratory in delineating homogeneity, transition, and flux of Igbo/African society in its colonial encounter is perhaps one of the greatest tributes criticism has paid to the father of African literature. Being a creative writer nurtured in the same Ogidi-Igbo creative space as Achebe gives her an insider's knowledge of Achebe's metaphoric engineering. One also gets the impression that as a scholar, she is a fan of her country-village man and deftly conveys her appreciation of how the teacher not only "writes back to the empire" but with great empathy represents the African view for his people so as to salvage their mutilated ego from the depth of inferiority and subordination where the colonial process has confined it.

This pioneering study of Achebe's writings from a rhetorical stance is a welcome contribution to literary criticism. It is a sign of more erudite scholarship from this burgeoning scholar.

Chinyere Grace Okafor

Acknowledgments

First and foremost, my thanks go to my late father, Patrick Obiesie Okonkwo, who had all the patience a parent could have for one's offspring--he needed it, seeing the child he brought forth into the world. I thank him for all the encouragement when he was alive, all the confidence he had in me and all the tolerance he exhibited. All these gave me the tremendous courage to dare life and take on challenges that seemed insurmountable. My thanks go to my mother, Elizabeth Nonyelum Okonkwo, who sometimes took my rebellion calmly and sometimes marched forward to tether and arrest it yet was gentle and tender enough not to snuff it out; who although she found my rebellious nature excruciating and infuriating, recognized it as pregnant with greater things to smile about and threaded softly at times, while resigning to God to channel this torrent she had given birth to. Mama, you rightly nicknamed me the animal that never failed to leave its footprints on any soil it treaded. I hope this very footprint on the soil of literary criticism will reward you for all those years of trepidation for my fate. I saw your bewilderment, and I felt your confusion and pain. I hope this ultimate fruit of those rebellious days is enough to assuage your anguish at a child who refused to be tethered to the homestead. To you I say thank you.

I thank my late husband, Mr. Frank Nnaji Okechukwu, who loved and cherished me for the seven years we were married, before a ghastly motor accident snatched him away from us. Thanks for the beautiful children we made together. "Iyom, Omeka Nwanyi," I hope you are enjoying eternal peace.

I also thank my husband, Engineer Bona Umeaku, who as a boyfriend in those schooldays posed the challenge that kept spurring me on to higher things. I did not study Electrical Engineering as you did (I had wanted to do just that in order to challenge your supremacy), but in the words of Jide Obi, my townsman and a great musician, "I love this place I found." Thanks for loving me and caring about me all those years. Thanks for not giving up. Thanks for eventually making us realize that we belong together. You are still the one.

My gratitude also goes to my children, Cassandra, Vanessa, and Elvira, for their much-valued support. To them I say, may their children give them all that I enjoyed from them. I would not have survived the excrutiating days of studying for a Ph.D. degree in America if not for them. Their patience while I was getting my Masters degrees in Nigeria and in Britain was tremenduous. I will never forget their support.

I also thank my brother, Anthony Okonkwo, who has given his solid support when needed. May he get tenfold all that he has given. He and my other siblings, Osita, Augustine, Ebele, Vincent, the late Ambrose, Oby, Ogoegbunam, and the late Chinedu have parts in my achievement.

I give a great thanks to Dr. Mary Owens, my friend and at present my department chair, at Montgomery College, Rockville, Maryland, for her support both academically and otherwise. To her, I give the name *Oyi ka nwanne*, a friend who surpasses a sibling.

Next, I thank Dr. Jean Dietz Moss, Professor of Rhetoric and Director of the Rhetoric Program at Catholic University of America in Washington D.C., my teacher, mentor, and supervisor, who not only encouraged me to explore the academic field of rhetoric, but exercised great patience and showed a great amount of caring throughout the duration of putting this work together. I call her *Odi uko na-mba*, one whose qualities are rare to find in any part of the world. My thanks also go to Dr. Joseph Sendry, Professor of English and Director of the Graduate Program, English Department, Catholic University of America, my able supervisor, for his kindness at those times when other matters external to writing this book threatened to eclipse the matter at hand; and to Dr. Emmanuel Obiechina, for taking the time to read my work and give valuable suggestions. My immense thanks go to Montgomery College for its support all through the period of writing this book. I also thank Catholic University of America, for providing the conducive academic atmosphere that enabled me to go through a program in rhetoric in the institution.

I thank also the following people who have in one way or the other given me their support: Dr. Chinyere Okafor; Dr. Samual Asein, Dr. Dubem Okafor, Dr. Tanure Ojaide, Professor Caroline Terry, Dr. William Soderberg, Professor Helen Youth, Mrs. Mary Kay Hinkle, Mrs Jo-Anne Caisse, Dr. Maryrose Winslow, Dr. Sarah Pickert, and many other people, all of whom I will not be able to acknowledge individually. For those I have omitted to mention here, I am not minimizing your contributions. Rather, I am constrained by the principle of selection to express my thanks in the words of the Old Man from Abazon in Chinua Achebe's *Anthills of the Savannah:* "To everyone his[/her] due."

Introduction

Chinua Achebe is a Nigerian novelist whose writings abound in rhetorical representation. He has harnessed the power of oratory to show how his society has responded to the exigencies of its encounter with the West. Achebe's main purpose for writing, as he has stated in various interviews and essays, is to set straight the records about his people and his culture and to show his people "where the rain started to beat them" because Igbo people have a saying that "a man who can't tell where the rain began to beat him cannot know where he dried his body."[1] He decided to use the novel form to educate his people. He uses oratory and other rhetorical elements to achieve this purpose in his novels, which encapsulate the history of Nigeria, focusing on the African colonial encounter and its aftermath. Thus Achebe's novels are great sources for learning about discourse in the Igbo community as well as the larger Nigerian community. These novels show a society that has been fragmented and a people who are striving to reconstruct a society they lost during their encounter with the West. Achebe foregrounds the role of discourse, for the indigenous as well as for the invading people's, vividly illustrating the clash of cultures that took place during this period in history and the lingering aftermath of this collision.

The interrelationship of rhetoric and literature sheds considerable light on Achebe's use of the novel genre to persuade. The historical trajectory of rhetoric and literature aids Achebe's artistry since Achebe has successfully woven the two genres into the fabrics of his novels, making these novels great arguments for his stated mission. Although Aristotle did not directly equate rhetoric to poetics in *Rhetoric*, some of his pronouncements in *On the Art of Poetry* (*Poetics*)[2] do link the two disciplines. In *Poetics*, where Aristotle deals with thought, he asserts that thought belongs to rhetoric and also manifests in poetic speeches. Thought, which Aristotle sees as the third property of tragedy, is "the ability to say what is possible and appropriate in any given circumstance; it is what, in the speeches in the play, is related to the art of politics and rhetoric."[3] In Chapter 19 where he deals specifically with "Thought and Diction," Aristotle sees thought to include "all the effects that have to be produced by means of language; among [which] are proof and refutation, the awakening of emotions such as pity, fear, anger, and the like, and also exaggeration and depreciation."[4] He also notes the characteristic of rhetoric to teach and delight. Literature and rhetoric come together in Achebe's novels. In *The Rhetoric of Fiction*, Wayne C. Booth rejects the idea that good fiction should be "pure," devoid of rhetoric. As he sees it, "if recognizable appeals to the reader are a sign of imperfection, perfect literature is impossible to find."[5] His argument is that fiction has a rhetorical function whether it is overtly persuasive or not. He recognizes that great literature and drama work rhetorically to build and strengthen communities.[6] Simon Gikandi expresses the same view while discussing Achebe's political vision in his novels. Gikandi contends that Achebe chose the novel form to propagate his views and educate his audience because Achebe recognized the function of the novel, not solely as a mode of representing reality, but one which had limitless possibilities for inventing a new national community.[7] In effect, poetics uses rhetoric as part of the elements of an effective composition. More importantly, literary artists have, sometimes, used their fiction as a forum for defending their theses. Chinua Achebe is one of such literary artists. Thus he uses oratory not only to advance the themes of the novels but also to delineate his characters, and to portray the impetus and the temper of the times.

Taken together, Achebe's five novels--*Things Fall Apart* (1958), *No Longer at Ease* (1960), *A Man of the People* (1966), *Arrow of God* (1967), and *Anthills of the Savannah* (1988)--encompass the entire sociohistorical and political experiences of Nigeria, from precolonial times to the present. *Things Fall Apart* deals with the impact of the Western *ethos* on traditional Igbo communal life. The novel, set partly in the precolonial days and partly at the moment of contact with Western culture, recreates and interprets the Igbo past just before the conquest and colonization of that society by the British and, dispassionately, anatomizes the consequences of that incursion. *No Longer at Ease*, set partly in Lagos, the then Nigeria's capital, and partly in the village of Umuofia, enacts the temptations confronting a young educated Nigerian man when burdened with enormous social and financial responsibilities in his country. It describes the oppressive demands made on the educated elite in a transitional society battling with the crumbling of old values under the pressures of new ones. *Arrow of God* returns to the theme of the conflicts of Western and Igbo traditional worldviews. It shows the struggle for the power to possess the African soul which followed the intrusion of the West on the African soil, dramatizing why the West was able to "seize the initiatives in the organization of the African society."[8] *A Man of the People*, set in the city, deals with politics, exposing the abuses that emanate from the imposition of an alien sociopolitical system on a collection of different ethnic groups, each of which has its own peculiar sociopolitical culture. *Anthills of the Savannah* deals with military rule in Nigeria and shows what happens when soldiers leave their barracks and decide to take on the rulership of a country. It also shows that the acquisition of power and what use the powerful make of this acquisition depend on the type of officials with which the ruler surrounds himself, especially in a heterogenous country filled with intellectuals who are busier lining their pockets and tripping each other in their bid to get close to power than they are with advising the ruler properly.

Chapter 1 of this book deals with Achebe's view of the novel genre, emphasizing his background, why he wrote his novels, and his views of the African novel. This chapter presents an overview of Achebe's writing and examines his published interviews and essays to throw light on his intentions in the novels and on his views of African literature with respect to its mission, its practice, and its audience. Chapter 2 examines the arguments in *Things Fall Apart* in relation to its intended audience. It also assesses the impact the change in the composition of the audience has on the language of the oratory within the text. Achebe uses oratory to expose the subtle movement from a homogeneous society to a hetrogeneous one by making the orators accommodate the changes experienced during the historical conjuncture of the society of the novel. Chapter 3 treats Achebe's portrayal of the failure of dialectics and empty rhetoric as means of persuasion in *Arrow of God* and reveals the effectiveness or ineffectiveness of the major characters' oratory. The effect of locale on oratory in *No Longer at Ease* provides the focus of Chapter 4. Chapter 5 focuses on *A Man of the People* as a meditation on the specious argumentation deployed by the corrupt indigenous politicians to justify a decadent system, while Chapter 6 examines the duplicitous manipulation of argumentation by military dictators in *Anthills of the Savannah* to rationalize their entry into politics and to persuade the populace of their salvific role. Finally, the Conclusion recapitulates the salient findings of the book, elaborating on Achebe's rhetorical praxis.

NOTES

1.   Chinua Achebe, "The Role of the Writer in a New Nation," *Nigeria Magazine* 81 (1964): 157.

2.   Aristotle, *On the Art of Poetry (Poetics)*, trans. T.S. Dorch, *Classical Literary Criticism: Aristotle: On the Art of Poetry, Horace: On the Art of Poetry, Longinus: On the Sublime* (London: Penguin, 1965). All subsequent reference to this text will be documented as *Poetics*.

3.   Ibid., 40.

4.   Ibid., 57-58.

5.   Wayne C. Booth, *The Rhetoric of Fiction* 2nd ed. (Chicago: University of Chicago Press, 1983), 99.

6.   Ibid., 17.

7.   Simon Gikandi, *Reading Chinua Achebe: Language and Ideology in Fiction*, (London: James Currey, 1991), 3.

8.   Ibid., 5.

Chinua Achebe and the African Novel

CHINUA ACHEBE AND WHY HE WROTE

Chinua Achebe was born in 1930 to a Christian evangelist and church teacher in Ogidi in what was then Eastern Region of Nigeria (now Anambra State). He was christened Albert Chinualumogu, as he informs the reader in his essay, "Named for Victoria, Queen of England."[1] Because his neighbors, as well as his uncles and cousins, practiced the Igbo traditional religion while his father followed the ways of the church, Achebe found himself pulled by two cultures.[2] As he vividly states in this essay, the confusion of the times of his growing up is not amenable to a simplistic explanation.

By virtue of his birth, Achebe went to a mission school, part of the British colonial system of education. He went on to study at Government College, Umuahia, and University College, Ibadan. At first he had enrolled to study medicine at the University but changed to the arts program, majoring in English, history, and religion. There, he was exposed to the works of Shakespeare, Milton, Wordsworth, as well as to the novels about Africans by Graham Greene, Joseph Conrad, and Joyce Cary. The educational curriculum projected Western values, religion, and culture as superior to those of the colonized people. The colonized people were even said to be without history or culture. Values, where they were recognized to have existed in the colonized region, were perceived as inferior or chaotic, unfathomable, incomprehensible, irrational, and illogical. The literature written in English at this time about Africa and Africans did nothing but reinforce this idea of illogical, unintelligent, irrational, childlike, and primitive people by caricaturing the people and the continent. Joseph Conrad's *Heart of Darkness* and Joyce Cary's *Mister Johnson* are examples of such literary caricaturization of the colonized people and their societies.

Achebe was a student at the University College, Ibadan at a time when the Nationalist Movement for Independence was at its peak. Africans had begun questioning the European presumption of superiority and the cultural assumptions behind the British rationalization of and justification for its imperialization of Africa. On graduation from Ibadan, Achebe worked as a broadcaster. During this stint at the Nigerian Broadcasting Coorporation, in the External Affairs Division, he wrote his first novel, *Things Fall Apart*.

Apart from his five novels, Achebe has published two collections of short stories: *The Sacrificial Egg and Other Stories* (1962) and *Girls at War* (1972); two books of children stories, *Chike and the River* (1966) and *How the Leopard Got Its Claws* (1972); and two collections of poems, *Beware Soul Brothers and Other Poems* (1971) and *Christmas in Biafra* (1973). In addition, he has published two books of essays, *Morning Yet on Creation Day* (1975) and *Hopes and Impediment* (1988 and 1989), both of which treat a variety of subjects: literature, literary criticism, language, colonialism, cultural imperialism, war, personal travels, and Igbo cosmology. He has also published a book of social-political commentary, *The Trouble with Nigeria* (1983), and co-edited with Dubem Okafor, *Don't Let Him Die: A Memorial Anthology* (1978). With Obiora Udechukwu, he composed a collection of poems, *Akaweta* (1982), in the Igbo language.

Achebe's novels are seen as fora for arguing his theses and for disseminating knowledge to his audience. Having studied English literature at a time when his people, as well as his native culture, were denigrated in such novels as Conrad's *Heart of Darkness* and Cary's *Mister Johnson*, he was in no doubt that the image of Nigerians, even Africans for that matter, presented in these much undeservedly praised novels was extremely superficial and warped. Therefore, he "thought if" *Mister Johnson*, with its warped and most superficial picture of both the country and the Nigerian character "was famous, then someone ought to try and look at this from the inside"[3] and in this way present an accurate picture of both the country and the people. *Things Fall Apart*, therefore, becomes an avenue for debunking *Mister Johnson*.

The major problem Achebe saw occurring all over the world, before he wrote his novels, and which he voiced in his presentation at the Nigerian Library Association Conference in 1964, was the debate between white and black over black humanity. In the 1990s, he showed that he still resented this state of affairs as much as he resented it even before he wrote his first novel in the 1950s. I believe he still does in this new millenium. He has not made any counterstatement on that issue yet. Not only does Achebe have problems with the image of the African in colonialists' literature, he vehemently attacks the arguments used by the colonizers to rationalize and justify their presence in Africa. In his essay, "African Literature as Restoration of Celebration," presented at the South Bank Show in 1990, he still focuses greatly on arguments that nullified the legitimacy of his people as humans. In the essay, he frowns at colonization for its practice of not just denying the "presence of a man standing before" it but also for its "questioning" the man's "very humanity."[4] In Achebe's view, this state of mind is possible among the colonizers because every aspect of the black man has been questioned throughout European education. European education, he points out, has taught its people that the African has "no soul, no religion, no culture, no history, no human speech, and, as a reader of John Buchan's *Prester John* will discover, no sense of responsibility." The literary tradition, he insists, has presented African characters which are hardly humans. Shakespeare created Caliban, whose only attribute was that he "wouldst gabble like a thing most brutish." Conrad's Caliban was more monstrous than Shakespeare's. Where Shakespeare was able, at the end of *The Tempest*, to give Caliban one attribute of humanity, the power of speech, Conrad's Caliban only made "a violent babble of uncouth sounds and continued to make it until the end of the novel." Achebe's essay, "An Image of Africa: Racism in Conrad's *Heart of Darkness,*" says much of what he thinks of Conrad's enterprise in that novel.[5] Chantal Zubus' description of *Heart of Darkness* as portraying Conrad's "jaundiced vision of man-eating Africans"[6] gives credence to Achebe's conclusions about that novel.

Achebe also castigates the church for raising doubts about Africans' humanity. In his view, because the African body was fetching money for the European market, the church could only indulge in endless, equivocating debates about whether the African had a soul or not.[7] Achebe cites Philip D. Curtin's book, *The Image of Africa: British Ideas and Actions*, which validates Achebe's contention on the church's role in wreaking havoc on the African image. Curtin, Achebe points out, divulges that children's books, Sunday school tracts, and the popular press were avenues for fostering this negative image of the African.[8] Achebe strongly believed that this subject of African humanity presented the African writer with a great challenge which should be addressed first before dealing with contemporary political issues, and he took up the challenge through the novel medium. He insists that no serious writer "could stand aside from this debate or be indifferent to this argument which calls his full humanity into question."[9]

Achebe sees himself as a teacher who uses his novels to teach his people to recognize the source of their problem in order for them to stop accepting the notion of racial inferiority. His theses are that his society had a substantive and valid culture before the advent of the European and that the people had dignity before the society's contact with Europe. According to Achebe, his people must regain this dignity which they had lost, for "[t]he worst thing that can happen to any people is the loss of their dignity and self-respect."[10]

Because of this avowed pedagogic use of his novels, Achebe carved out a clear audience for them. His audience was the Nigerian schoolboy who, to Achebe's utter irritation, would rather write about the winter than about the harmattan, one of Nigeria's seasons, for fear of being called a bushman. In his essay, "The Novelist as

Teacher," he wonders how anybody could feel that there was anything shameful about his weather. Therefore, he saw it as part of his duty to purge this blasphemy. As a teacher, Achebe made his mission clear. He would help to purge the blasphemy that African objects are things to be ashamed of and instill in Africans pride in their culture and objects as materials fit for poetry.[11]

Achebe reminds those who criticize his use of the novel form to educate instead of concentrating his attention on art *qua* art, and even shows by the themes he has chosen for his novels, that using his art to control the society's articulation of issues had been part of the traditional African concept of the artist's role in the society.[12] Therefore, he has to use his art to expose the fact that even though there were some gains that accrued from Africa's encounter with the West, Africa suffered terribly from that encounter in terms of human dignity and human relation as that "encounter has warped the mental attitudes of both black and white."[13]

ACHEBE'S VIEW OF THE AFRICAN NOVEL

Achebe's views of the African novel are found in his various pronouncements on the concerns of African writers given their peculiar relationship with history. He states categorically that those who strive to define African literature without taking cognizance of the complex nature of Africa of the period being depicted are bound to fail.[14]   Here Achebe is reacting against critics like Kolawole Ogungbesan, Sunday Anozie, and Sam Asein who argued totally against Achebe's use of the novel form to educate. Such a critic as Ogungbesan, thinks that authors should separate literature from politics[15] and sees such use of the novel genre to educate as "a betrayal of art."[16] Anozie attacks Achebe's idea of using the novel form for other purposes. [17] In his own part, Asein, quoting extensively from an earlier interview given by Christopher Okigbo, frowns at the same issue.[18]

Such critics as these three are of great concern to Achebe. Hence Achebe, in one of his essays, pleads that African novels should not be be subjected to strictures.[19] In this essay, Achebe laments the Europeans' and the misguided Africans' efforts to transfer the critical criteria used for evaluating European novels to the African novel. In Achebe's eyes, only Africans can legitimately write on African experiences, and as long as these experiences dictate the vision of the artist, the novelist is free to use the novel form to educate. Achebe sees Africa as both "geographical expression" and "a metaphysical landscape."[20]   However, he concedes to the penalties of being an African[21] As he sees it, the historical fact of Africa's occupation by the Europeans justifies the African writer's obsession or preoccupation with the themes of colonialism, domination, and exploitation. This preoccupation may take the form of protest, absolving Europe of its guilt, and showing that Africa was bound to violence even before its occupation by Europe. Nevertheless, Europeans are not justified in clutching at the illusion that Africans should aim at literary objectivity.

According to Achebe, what European criticism is asking for when it speaks of objectivity is tantamount to commiting suicide for the pleasure of another. The European calls this illusion of objectivity "universality," while Achebe calls it an affliction with a warped vision: "A vision which creates a false polarity between an object and its abstraction and places its focus on the abstraction."[22] Achebe seriously objects to Eldred Jones' application of universalist categories in his evaluation of Wole Soyinka's novel, *The Interpreters* in *The Essential Soyinka*.[23] For a critic to insist, as Jones does, that African novelists should strive for universality, is to ask the novelists to renounce their visions, to discredit those visions and the absolute validity of their experiences. The implication of this is that Nigerian writers, for example, who are dissatisfied with the state of affairs of their society may not write about them unless they check to see if similar things occur in the capitals of the West and if the critics there would approve.[24]

The other issue is that African writers are accused of being overly political in their novels. Achebe cites a discussion with a Professor Snyder, who reminded him that politics has always been present in literature and gave examples ranging from Dante to Eliot. Achebe objects to literary legistlators dictating to African writers what role their art should play. For one thing, he says, African writers are late starters; therefore, they need to hold all the literary debates that had been held prior to their arrival to the literary arena. The African writers should ignore the European critics' habit of decreeing what subject matters have literary merits and what form the African writers should choose for their art.[25] As for the Europen concept of "universality," Achebe sees it is as a eurocentric term, coined by colonialist critics to denigrate African literature and set European literature up as a standard to strive for. He reminds the critics that "[m]ost African writers write out of an African experience and commitment to an African destiny. For them that destiny does not include a future European identity for which the present is but an apprenticeship."[26] Wayne C. Booth's opinion on the issue of "pure art" validates Achebe. In *The Rhetoric of Fiction*, Booth asserts that great literatures contain rhetorical intrusions.[27] George Orwell also offers a strong opinion on the issue of making art "pure," devoid of politics when he observes: " no book is genuinely free of political bias. The opinion that art should have nothing to do with politics is itself a political attitude."[28]

As for the language in which a novel should be written before it qualifies as an African novel, Achebe believes that such a language must be one of the languages spoken by the African people on the African soil.[29] Since many European languages are spoken on African soil, they qualify as the language of African novels. However, he insists that the user of the European language who wishes to extend the frontiers of the language being used must do so out of his or her expertise of the language and not out of ignorance.[30] The issue of the language of the African novel has been important to Achebe. In October 1996, at a conference on "Languages Across Cultures and Boundary," hosted by West Chester University in Pennsylvania, Achebe vehemently declared that he did not ask the Europeans to come to his country and leave their languages carelessly in his backyard. He charged the owners of the English language with carelessness because, according to him, they should have realized how potent a thing language could be. Since they made such a careless mistake, they should not complain that he had begun "to do marvelous things" with their language. Indeed, he had in an earlier essay promised to do "unheard of things" with the English language.[31] And Achebe has done so in his novels.

Achebe has been mostly acknowledged in his innovative use of the English language to depict non-English experiences. Lekan Oyeleye examines how transference of meaning in *Things Fall Apart* and *Arrow of God* is used to achieve literary excellence. He asserts that Achebe uses transference to overcome the limitation imposed on him by the language medium, English, when he tries to convey an African culture. Transference in the hands of Achebe becomes a process in the domestication and Africanization of English.[32] Adrian Roscoe, in spite of his quarrel with Achebe for employing the novel genre in the service of education, recognizes the effectiveness of the use of proverbs in the novel. As Roscoe sees it, the proverbs represent a "versatile device" used to guide conduct, to instruct, and to keep people united. They are also used as weapons of debate and as a buttress for oratory.[33]

Achebe spares neither the African critic who emphasizes the fact that European languages are second languages to African writers and, as such, constitute an impediment to creative writing. Nor is he soft on the European critic whose arrogance, he believes, is an attempt to deny him the much-needed vision to see what new boundaries are being broken by the new impetus given the European languages. He is irked by Obi Wali's "Dead End of African Literature," which insists that "until these writers and their Western midwives accept the fact that any true African literature must be written in African languages, they would be merely pursuing a dead end, which can only lead to sterility, uncreativity and frustration."[34] Achebe in reply cites Christopher Okigbo's and J. P. Clark's poems, *Limits* and *Night Rain,* respectively, and asserts that instead of sterility these works exhibit accomplishment and hopes that no African should strive to write English like the native speakers; it is neither necessary nor desireable.[35]

For the group of critics who have said that because the novel was invented in England, the African novel does not exist, Achebe's replies that he does not need to be a descendant of Henry Ford to drive a car expertly.[36]

Achebe's background and his published essays throw light on his intention in his novels and on his views about African literature with respect to its mission, its practice, and its audience. However, since his avowed intention has been to use his novels as an avenue for instruction, his novels have benefitted from the age long established historical trajectory of rhetoric and literature and have given the reader instructions on the art of persuasion in Achebe's fictional society. Achebe as the orator who sought to persuade the reader of these novels on the issues of their concerns has also effectively tapped into the rhetorical elements in his society to ferry his argument accross the literary river. *Things Fall Apart* is thus seen as an argument woven around the idea of the audience as the pivot of argumentation.

NOTES

1.   Chinua Achebe, "Named for Victoria, Queen of England," *Morning Yet On Creation Day* (New York: Doubleday, 1975), 116-124; *Hopes and Impediments: Selected Essays* (New York: Doubleday, 1989), 30-39. The essay is contained in both books. Subsequent references to the above books will be documented as *Morning Yet* and *Hopes,* respectively.

2.   *Morning Yet,* 119; *Hopes,* 35.

3.   Lewis Nkosi, Cosmos Pieterse, and Dennis Duerden, eds., *African Writers Talking: A Collection of Radio Interviews* (London: Heinemann, 1972), 4.

4.   Achebe, "African Literature as Restoration of Celebration" (South Bank Show, 1990). Also in Kirsten Holst Petersen and Anna Rutherford, eds., *Chinua Achebe: A Celebration* (Portsmouth, NH: Heinemann, 1991), 5.

5.   Achebe, "An Image of Africa: Racism in Conrad's *Heart of Darkness,"* *Hopes,* 1-20; Achebe's essay "Impediments to Dialogue Between North and South,"*Hopes,* 21-29, also discusses his view on Europeans' denial of Africans' humanity.

6.   Chantal Zubus, "The Logos-Eater: The Igbo Ethno-Text," in Petersen and Rutherford, *Chinua Achebe,* 19.

7.   Achebe, "African Literature as Restoration of Celebration," 5.

8.   Philip D. Curtin, *The Image of Africa: British Ideas and Actions* (Madison: University of Wisconsin Press, 1964), vi. Quoted in Achebe, "African Literature as Restoration of Celebration," 5.

9.   Achebe, "The Role of a Writer in a New Nation," *Nigeria Magazine,* 8(1964), 157.

10.   Ibid., 157.

11.   Achebe, "The Novelist as Teacher," *Morning Yet,* 71-72.

12.   Achebe, "Colonialist Criticism," *Morning Yet:* 23.

13. ˙ Achebe, "The Black Writer's Burden," *Presence Africaine* 31, 59 (1966) : 135.

14.   Achebe, "The African Writer and the English Language," *Morning Yet:* 93.

15.   Kolawole Ogungbesan, "Politics and the African Writer," in Innes and Lindfors, eds., *Critical Perspectives on Chinua Achebe,* (London: Heinemann, 1979), 7.

16.   "The Modern Writer and Commitment," in Donatus I. Nwoga, ed., *Literature and Modern West African Culture,* (Benin, Nigeria: Ethiope, 1978), 7.

17.   Sunday Anozie, *Christopher Okigbo: Creative Rhetoric* (New York: Evans, 1992), 17.

18.   Sam O. Asein quoted Christopher Okigbo in his essay. "Literature as History: Crisis, Violence and Strategies of Commitment in Nigerian Writing," ed. Nwoga, *Literature and Modern West African Culture,* 105.

19.   Achebe, "Thoughts on the African Novel," *Morning Yet,* 89.

20.   Ibid., 83.

21.   Ibid.

22.   Ibid., 84-85.

23. Ibid., 85-86.

24. Ibid., 87.

25. Ibid., 88-89.

26. Ibid. 10.

27. Wayne C. Booth, *The Rhetoric of Fiction*, 2nd ed. (Chicago: University of Chicago Press, 1983), 99.

28. George Orwell, *A Collection of Essays* (Garden City, New York: Doubleday, 1957), 316.

29. Achebe, "Thoughts on the African Novel," *Morning Yet*, 83.

30. Achebe, "African Literature and the English Language," *Morning Yet*, 99.

31. Achebe, "Colonialist Criticism," *Morning Yet*, 10.

32. Lekan Oyeleye, "Transference as a Stylistic Strategy: Inquiry in the Language of Achebe's *Things Fall Apart* and *No Longer at Ease*," *Odu* 32 (July 1987), 160-169.

33. Adrian Roscoe, *Mother Is Gold: A Study in West African Literature* (London: Cambridge University Press, 1977), 124.

34. Originally in *Transition* X, 1963; quoted in "The African Writer and the English Language," *Morning Yet*, 99.

35. Achebe, "The African Writer and the English Language," *Morning Yet*, 99-100.

36. Achebe, "Thoughts on the African Novel," *Morning Yet*, 89.

Chapter 2

Audience and Oratory:
Things Fall Apart

AUDIENCE AS A PIVOT OF ARGUMENTATION

Woven around the audience as the mainstay of successful argumentation, Achebe's *Things Fall Apart* is a great argument for the merits of the Igbo culture. Achebe's arguments are clear and he handles them superbly. He argues that his people had a culture that was as good as, if not better than, the Western culture, which came to destroy it. He also argues that the Europeans misconceived the Africans. Because the Europeans lacked knowledge of the people's language, they could not have a real insight into the African worldview. He insists that the composition of the audience affects the *topoi* of the oratory in the novel.

Achebe makes it clear that the audience for his pedagogic argument is the Nigerian schoolboy who would rather write about winter than write about the harmattan for fear of being called a bushman.[1] Achebe, who was himself once a schoolboy, used *Things Fall Apart* to purge the kind of blasphemy he perceived in this schoolboy's fear. Perelman and Olbrechts-Tyteca contend that if a speaker, or a writer for that matter, knows his or her audience, he or she knows how to condition it and achieve contact of minds.[2] In their opinion, a writer can achieve contact of mind through "such factors as membership in the same social class, ... and other social relations."[3] As a cultural insider who belongs in the culture he is trying to defend, Achebe appeals to the logic of the experience he shares with this schoolboy, his primary audience. As an insider, he is qualified to speak for the culture. Hence, he makes it clear that he is only appealing to the youth in his society and not to the

Westerner, who does not share the same worldview as his society.

The colonizers, whose ideology Achebe is obviously trying to debunk, have a different order of hierarchy, given their education and historical backgrounds. In discussing hierarchies, Perelman and Olbrechts-Tyteca assert that people begin to think of hierarchies when they need to defend them. In their book, *The New Rhetoric*, they divide hierarchies into concrete and abstract and point out that one may not have to justify concrete hierarchies. However, abstract hierarchies require a transcendence, not a simple preference of one thing over another but a systematized hierarchy that has the power to establish the whole system of values. It may thus become the criterion for the hierarchical structure of a society's values, with every other thing being ordered according to its governing principle. The audience may accept the same values but may rank them differently quantitatively and qualitatively.[4]

For the most part, Achebe's argument in defense of his culture hinges on a qualitative hierarchy; it will be ineffectual to appeal to the colonizers whose superiorist binarity has made them see the colonized's culture as inferior to Western culture. As Perelman and Olbrechts-Tyteca rightly prescribe, for an arguer to use qualitative hierarchies, there must be assumptions of both the arguer and the audience on what is higher on the hierarchy than others.[5] Achebe shares the same assumptions with his society, but these are not those of the Western audience. Hence, in using the literary medium, he tries to establish a sense of communion centered upon particular values of those hierarchies recognized by his audience. When a rhetorician does this, usually in epidictic rhetoric, "the speaker turns educator."[6] And that, precisely, is what Achebe has done in *Things Fall Apart*.

The argumentative techniques employed by Achebe to achieve "adherence of minds" to his thesis—that the white man destroyed what was good in his culture— exposes the effect of audience on argumentation. Arrangement of material is one rhetorical art that Achebe exploits to the fullest in *Things Fall Apart* in order to argue its thesis successfully. Plato is strict about his prescription on arrangement in rhetoric. The orator, according to Plato, should divide the subject carefully into its component parts, and the points of the speech should not be mechanically assembled. This is because every discourse must be organized, like a living being, with a body of its own, as it were, so as not to be headless or footless, but to have a middle and members, composed in fitting relation to each other and to the whole[7] Achebe is very conscious of arrangement as a rhetorical technique.

The argument that African people did not hear of culture for the first time from the Europeans and that the encounter with the West did not augur well for African culture is successful because of Achebe's power of arrangement of materials. Achebe's *Things Fall Apart*, as the embodiment of this argument, propounds a thesis and uses a convergence of the "opinionables," very strongly and artistically arranged to induce the minds of the readers to its adhesion. It thus uses a convergence of proof and syllogistic arrangement of materials to great effect.

Achebe exposes Umuofia culture with all its imperfections. Part One of the novel is devoted to a presentation of the culture as it was before the coming of the white man. In this part, Achebe sets out the values that are cherished by that society. These values are fame (which rests on solid personal achievement), honor (the bringing of it to one's village through sports like wrestling), and through exhibitions of valor, courage, and bravery in wars. Ironically, these are the same values that westerners also valued. In European history and European literature, these values have been celebrated and lauded. In "Beowulf," as in the rest of Old-English literature, valor and vengeance are twin virtues that underlie the society's privileging of vengeance of a friend's death (*wergild*) over obsequies.[8] Achilles' fate in *The Iliad* is as a result of his quest to avenge his friend Patroclus. In Aristotle's *Ethics*, courage is sought after because it is believed to benefit others rather than the possessor.[9] Achebe seems to be saying that these are also the values of his people. He seems to be saying, *You people, my Nigerian schoolboy audience, who have studied European history and literature must recognize that the white man who thinks that our values are inferior to his own also possesses the same values. Why then should you be ashamed of your own values?*

Selection and presentation of material is an important argumentative technique that Achebe exploits effectively to defend his culture. Successful persuasion selects appropriate materials and creates a "presence" that moves an audience. The selection and presentation of materials make the materials important and pertinent. Not only that, the materials thus selected and presented act directly on the audience's sensibility and force the audience to react to them because, as Perelman and Olbrechts-Tyteca insist, "[i]t is not enough indeed that a thing should exist for a person to feel its presence. Accordingly, one of the preoccupations of a speaker is to make present, by verbal magic alone, what is actually absent ... to enhance the value of some of the elements of which one has actually been made conscious."[10] By selecting data and weaving them around his chosen "presence," Okonkwo, Achebe makes the audience empathize with this "presence," thereby making the audience accept his thesis. This technique is used effectively in *Julius Caesar* when Mark Antony shows his audience Caesar's cloth covered with blood.[11]

By presenting Okonkwo's journey from birth to death, Achebe has achieved adherence of minds to his thesis that colonialism destroyed what was good in his culture. In showing the values in Umuofia culture, Achebe creates a conscious reality in which these values inhere and makes the reader focus on them. Okonkwo manifests these values, imbuing them with *energia*. The reader is made to admire that living manifestation of the indigenous culture for its beauty, and at the same time, to condemn its excesses. The reader can recognize these values through a flesh-and-blood human being, who exhibits courage, fear, and other human emotions. Achebe makes the reader admire the positive values in the culture through Okonkwo's rise from abject poverty to the highest but one rank in the society. While setting out Okonkwo's virtues—courage, industry, valor, and strength—Achebe is careful to show his vices—short temper, impatience, and inflexibility. Achebe does this to caution the audience that this man, like any other man, is not perfect, just as his culture, like any other culture, is not perfect. Okonkwo has emotional, psychological, and physical defects, which at times lead him to commit acts of violence. When he stammers and cannot get out his words fast enough, he strikes his opponent. Therefore, instead of speech or rhetoric, he sometimes resorts to *ad baculum*, just as the white man does when he cannot get out his words fast enough. In a parallel incident in Abame, when rhetoric failed to subjugate the people, the white man proceeded to slaughter, or "pacify," the people. Both Okonkwo and the white man, thus, exhibit the beautiful, the harsh, and the ugly parts of the human nature and culture.

The first chapter of this novel shows the beautiful and admirable in both Okonkwo and his culture. Okonkwo is first seen at the height of his fame as a youth when he throws Amalinze, the cat, a young wrestling champion who had been undefeated for many years. By this feat, Okonkwo brings great honor to his village. Achebe uses this incident to make the reader admire Umuofia as it cherishes honor brought to it through sports. Before Achebe unfolds to the reader what Okonkwo later becomes, he stops to acquaint the reader with the obstacles Okonkwo had to overcome before achieving greatness. Okonkwo had to bring himself out of abject poverty, pull himself up by his bootstraps, as it were. Achebe portrays Unoka, Okonkwo's father as a poor role model, full of demerits. But in an undisguised tribute to the natural virtue of Okonkwo's culture, Achebe raises Okonkwo above these demerits and remarks: "Fortunately, among these people a man was judged according to his worth and not according to the worth of his father" (6; ch. 1) [all quotes in this chapter are from the 1994 Doubleday edition of *Things Fall Apart*]. Through "dissociation"[12] argumentation technique, Achebe depicts this culture as benevolent. Valorizing achievement as it does, the culture does not pin one down to one's inherited status. This culture does not brand its members. After revealing the father's demerits, Achebe reiterates Okonkwo's merits to reinforce the argument for Okonkwo and his achievements. Achebe seems to be saying: *Look at this man. Look at his father. Look at what the man has become.*

Achebe argues that Okonkwo's deficiencies should be excused. Achebe locates Okonkwo's deficiencies in his background and in the allowances given them by the culture. He seems to be saying that given the kind of background Okonkwo has had, he is bound to be different from other villagers, emotionally and psychologically. He compares both Okonkwo and his father with others in the village. He portrays a character, Obierika, Okonkwo's best friend, who does not possess Okonkwo's vices but does not have his virtues either, at least not in the degree to which Okonkwo possesses them. He portrays Ezeudu as a wise old villager, who possesses Okonkwo's virtues, even has a higher title, and is more astute than Okonkwo, but whose background is not given and so cannot really be compared with that of Okonkwo.

Then the reader sees Nwakibie, the man who gives Okonkwo his start as a householder by lending him seed yams for planting. Nwakibie is rich, has three wives and treats his wives and children more leniently than Okonkwo treats his family, but Nwakibie had inherited his wealth and therefore does not need to use his household to rise above the poverty level. He does not have to push his family to work hard since he has the luxury of using sharecroppers, which is like the Western man's practice of indentured labor, in that his debtors pay back the principal with interest.

Finally, Achebe shows Okoye, who is a musician but is successful. Therefore, Unoka, Okonkwo's father, cannot rationalize his own improvidence and poverty on the ground of his vocation. Being an artist is not an excuse for slothfulness or failure. Achebe also seems to be saying that the culture's willingness to give a chance to anybody who is willing to help himself is a motivation for people to strive to get out of poverty, without counting the human cost of such a success. After all, in this culture, "Age was respected ... but achievement was revered. As the elders said, if a child washed his hands he could eat with kings" (6; ch. 1). Okonkwo is determined to wash his hands and to eat with kings. Okonkwo should not be castigated for the means he uses to achieve greatness. Okonkwo has to use all at his disposal to meet with the society's demand. He uses his strength, his wives', and his children's. Achebe also tells us that he is a success: "Okonkwo had clearly washed his hands and so he ate with kings and elders" (8; ch. 2). The society validates his methods. He is rewarded. To show him that he now counts as one of the people of importance in society, the clan gives Okonkwo the custody of a piece of property that belongs to it. This is the ill-fated lad, Ikemefuna. While chronicling Okonkwo's progress and his deficiencies, Achebe has managed to show the Umuofian philosophy behind his actions. These actions are not mindless. They have their own logic, embedded in the people's cosmology. After all, "if a man says yes in this society, his *chi* or personal god says yes too" (19; ch. 3).

Achebe uses marriage, another universal concept, to continue the amplification of his argument. Polygyny, which a Westerner would frown upon, even as he practices and sees nothing wrong in its consecutive variant, is shown here to have its merits as well as its demerits. Wives have duties as well as privileges. Although Okonkwo's wives work to increase his prosperity, they also enjoy the fruits of being part of a big household. His most senior wife, Nwoye's mother, takes care Ojiugo's, (the junior wife's) children. The most junior wife's daughter, Ezinma, runs errands for Nwoye's mother. The wives represent each other on social occasions like going to cook for a neighbor's wedding feast. Family relationships are shown to have both beauty and ugliness. Okonkwo, the focus of this novel, rules his household with an iron hand. His wives and his children fear him. But Achebe is careful to show that he is only stern, not cruel. He is ruled by the fear of being seen to resemble his weak and improvident father.

Fear is a universal human emotion and many people have done ugly things out of fear. Fear of the unknown affects the people of Umuofia. According to Achebe, the people had acute fear of darkness (9; ch. 2). But fear of the unknown affects almost anybody. When Okonkwo nearly shoots his wife, Ekwefi, it is because he has been taunted by his wife who has implied that he does not know how to use a gun or that he is too much of a coward to shoot her. Not knowing how to use a gun would have been considered a failure that would have diminished Okonkwo's esteem as a warrior. Not being man enough to shoot is a sign of weakness in his community, an admission that his power has its limits, and therefore, he is vulnerable, which no warrior would wish to admit. But he quickly goes to see that the woman is not hurt. He seems to be saying to her, *Do not toy with me. I am capable of doing it but have only chosen not to.* When the same woman and their daughter are threatened by the gods, however, Okonkwo goes to her rescue. When Chielo, the goddess of Agbala, takes Ezinma, their daughter, to the cave of the oracles and Ekwefi follows behind, Okonkwo makes several trips to the cave until he finds Ekwefi. He is unable to sleep. When Okonkwo is stern with Nwoye and Ikemefuna, he inwardly acknowledges that they are young (23; ch. 4). He only wants them to grow up to become men.

To further buttress his argument that the indigenous culture is as good as the colonizer's culture, Achebe examines another aspect of the people's life that has a universal application. This is the people's knowledge of agriculture. Once again, Achebe uses Okonkwo to illustrate his point. He demonstrates that the people have their system for gaining economic success, especially for those who have not inherited wealth from their fathers. Like any other economic activity, farming is an arduous and slow process fraught with uncertainties. The climber on the economic ladder, most often, becomes an apprentice or a sharecropper and builds his own fortune or barn from small earnings. The people's philosophy is that apprenticeship to the successful insures success: a man who pays respect to the great paves the way for his own greatness (16; ch. 3).

But the weather is one factor that has to be taken into consideration when one is paying that respect to the successful. The weather in Umuofia is as unpredictable as the weather everywhere. In all agrarian cultures, weather is the force that insures the success or failure of the crops. Hence, the reader watches, with amazement, Okonkwo's arduous task and heartbreaking struggle to save his yams from the unrelenting bad weather bent on obliterating his labor and stopping him from succeeding. Okonkwo's knowledge of agriculture is apparent when we see him preparing his seed yams and lecturing Nwoye and Ikemefuna on how to cut the yams for planting. The other farmers are also knowledgeable about agriculture and climatology as Achebe notes: "but every farmer knew that without sunshine the tubers would not grow" (17). Even though these farmers do not use the terminologies of western scientific discourse to explain their practices nor have knowledge of climatology and processes such as photosynthesis, they know that sunshine is crucial to crop production.

Achebe argues for the validity of the clan's mores, using the incident of the murder of an Umuofia woman who had gone to market at a neighboring village. Here, Achebe describes the town's means of communicating an emergency to its people and the town's ways of deliberating on issues that concern the whole town. The reader sees participatory democracy at work. The town crier summons the people to a meeting. This way everybody knows when important decisions are being made and has a chance to participate in the deliberations. But since most people's lives are wrapped around their clan's religion, the people must consult their oracle before any decision can be final. For instance, the people will not go to war unless their gods sanction it. And their gods are fair. They do not sanction any unjust war or a war of blame. In the case of this threatening war over the murder of a daughter of Umuofia, the oracle counseled against war without first of all giving the offending village the chance to make amends. The offending village is to choose between giving a maiden and a young man to the people of Umuofia and going to war. The village choses to give up a maiden and a young man, Ikemefuna. Umuofia is appeased and does not go to war. This incident is particularly important because it is this same oracle which later tells the people to kill Ikemefuna. If the reader accepts the decision of the gods as revealed by the oracle, in this case it counsels against (going to) war with the offending clan, the reader has to accept as valid the oracle's revelation/pronouncement that Ikemefuna must be sacrificed.

The meeting held by the people of Umuofia to deliberate on the incident of the murder of an Umuofia woman is one of the avenues which Achebe uses to expose the ugly as well as the good in Umuofia. If Achebe had projected only the good side of this culture through this meeting, his argument might have been suspect. But he seizes this opportunity to recognize one of the "imperfections"[13] in the culture: value placed on the number of heads that a man brings home with him from a war. Not only does the warrior bring home these heads, he actually drinks from the skulls. This act will make members of his primary audience cringe. Achebe heightens the offensive nature of this action by adopting a tone which seems to be celebrating and sanctioning this act, even making the warrior relish the fact that he drinks from a human skull. He is dispassionate enough to show this.

But after describing this revolting practice, Achebe presents a picture of the power of oratory. Fighting wars and drinking from human skulls are not the only preoccupation of this society. The people also enjoy good oratory and deliberation. Ogbuefi Ezeugo, the man who speaks to Umuofia during that deliberation on the murder of an Umuofia woman, is a consummate orator. He has a booming voice. He rouses his audience by his gestures, tone, and delivery as he tells his story, pointing out the victim of injustice who lost his wife. Here, Achebe seems to be arguing that this society uses the same rhetorical techniques that Westerners use. The crowd also behaves like a crowd in any Western civilization would behave. When outraged, the crowd shouts with anger and calls for blood.

This scene evokes the scene in *Julius Caesar* after Mark Antony's funeral oration at the Capitol.[14] The difference here is that, in spite of the people's anger and thirst for blood, the people follow the prescribed course of action when such a thing as the murder of an Umuofia woman happens: the offending clan must choose either war or make retribution of a virgin and a lad. Here, Achebe shows that although these people go to war and drink from the heads of war victims, their fights are not arbitrary or capricious or fought merely to assuage their lust for blood. They have a "normal course of action" (8; ch. 2). Umuofia is powerful and the neighbors know this and would not go to war against it without first seeking a peaceful settlement. Umuofia on its own part will give the neighbors opportunity to make amends before resorting to war because its gods will "never fight what the Ibo call *a fight of blame*" (9; ch. 2). The people respect their gods. This incident is noteworthy because later in the novel Achebe shows the white men's reaction when any white man is killed. The white men do not give the offending village a chance to make amends. The white men, like the Roman mob in *Julius Caesar*, give vent to their anger and lust for blood. They destroy the village and its people. He seems to say that they are equally revolting.

Another aspect of Umuofia culture that Achebe uses in his argument is the conduct of the judges in the Umuofia judicial system, who are seen to be well informed, fair, and just. The trial scene in the case of domestic violence has a ceremonious and orderly arrangement befitting the occasion. There is amicable settlement that takes human nature into consideration. Achebe shows the steps taken to maintain the anonymity of the judges, thereby ensuring probity and impartiality and avoiding corruption. This trial is important because it is compared to the trial that takes place in the white man's court. In this scene also, Achebe delineates the importance of the *egwugwu* as the upholder of the laws of the land, the awe it inspires, and the respect that it gets from the people as the spirit of the people's ancestors. *Egwugwu* is the masked representative of the ancestors. Even the highest man in Umuofia defers to the *egwugwu*. The *egwugwu* court is the highest court of appeal. By thus lining up these different facets of the people's lives, Achebe brings out the virtues of the people and their culture, thereby teaching his people that there is nothing to be ashamed of in a past like the one which he has shown in Part One of *Things Fall Apart*.

After exposing this past, Achebe takes Okonkwo to another village, Mbanta. This is a superb rhetorical strategy through which Achebe not only parades before the reader another society and its culture and philosophy in operation, but in so doing, he provides narrative time for the new invading culture to come and settle in Umuofia. In this way, the reader who left Umuofia with Okonkwo hears about the happenings in Umuofia at the same time Okonkwo hears about them. The reader, thus, will react at the same time Okonkwo is reacting. Also at Mbanta, the reader sees another elder like Ezeudu. Uchendu, Okonkwo's maternal uncle, is as wise as Ezeudu, who had counselled Okonkwo not to bear a hand in the killing of the boy, Ikemefuna, a child who had come to regard Okonkwo as his father. Uchendu chides Okonkwo for his uncontrollable grief. He points out this philosophy, which applies to Mbanta society as to any other society that might have existed then: "there is no one for whom it is well" (95; ch. 11). He buttresses his philosophy with the assertion of cultural relativism to the effect that "[t]he world has no end, and what is good among one people is an abomination with others" (99; ch. 11).

This idea runs through the whole novel and indicates that nobody has a right to condemn any other society's way of doing things. Umuofia people ridicule the idea of human beings being white and speaking through the nose or a child belonging to the mother's family instead of the father's family. Okonkwo believes that Mbanta is a womanly clan that has no place for real men like himself. Umuofia people ridicule the *ozo* title taken in other clans because the title is cheap in those villages where the *ozo* men do menial jobs. The people of Umuofia also criticize other villages' practice of giving severe punishments to people who violate the Week of Peace. Achebe spreads these kernels of evidence throughout the novel before the coming of the white man in order to argue that the white man's criticism of Umuofia culture and religion is not novel. Even villages that are neighbors with each other criticize differences they find in the practices of neighboring villages. The only novelty is the white man's ignorance and arrogation to himself of the power over other people and their ways.

Achebe argues that the white man destroyed Igbo culture out of ignorance of the people's way of life and the white man's inability to speak the people's language. He examines the effect of the white man's religion on the indigenous culture. The reader encounters the white man briefly at Mbanta and then fully at Umuofia. At Mbanta, just before Okonkwo leaves for Umuofia after serving his seven-year term of exile, the society is just beginning to experience change as a result of the intrusion of western religion. Evidence of an impending clash is already looming when one of the members of the new religion is reported to have killed and eaten the sacred python. The villagers ostracize the Christians but refuse to get in the way of the fight between the gods and their victims (158; ch. 18). Once again, a village in this part of the world has exhibited its normal way of doing things. The culprit reported to have killed the sacred python dies a mysterious death, which forestalls the clash that has been brewing. In Umuofia, much has happened before Okonkwo comes home. The white man has succeeded in causing rifts in the family and in the society. Nwoye, Okonkwo's son, has already left his family. The white man has cleared the evil forest and rescued twins without any calamity befalling him. Twins were thought to be cursed, and after birth, they were left to die in the evil forest. He has won converts among those considered worthless fellows by the society as well as among some worthy men.

Using intermediaries in an inadequate effort to surmount the language barrier, the white man has unwittingly brought bribery, lack of respect for the ways of the clan and for the elders, humiliation of the elders and the titled men, and even the hanging of a manslaughter convict. These things are possible because the court messengers and the white man's interpreters come from other villages that do not share Umuofia culture. The white man understands neither the culture nor the language, and the interpreters speak a dialect different from the Umuofian's. Earlier in the novel, Achebe has also shown that even among the people who speak the same language, customs differ. So the white man is no closer to understanding the people even with the help of interpreters. To make matters worse, the interpreters and the court messengers are corrupt, high-handed, arrogant, and have reason to hate Umuofia, the warrior clan. Umuofia is mightier than its neighbors.

So these foreigners, who are given an opportunity to get back at this warrior community, take every opportunity to insult and humiliate its people.

One might observe that there are also converts among the people of Umuofia. Even Nwoye, Okonkwo's son, is becoming prominent among the white man's group. Achebe anticipates this counterargument and takes care of it before it arises. The men who are converted from Umuofia are the *efulefus*, the "excrement" of the clan (143; ch. 16). Their conversion is an opportunity for them also to get back at Umuofia. In the case of Nwoye, Achebe has already shown the reader Nwoye's effeminate predisposition and preferences. He would rather sit in the kitchen with his mother and listen to folktales than work in the farm or listen to stories of valor. Nwoye also has an axe to grind with the culture that has killed his friend Ikemefuna and a father who has bullied him while trying to make him a man.

Achebe compares the white man's judicial system and sense of justice to the Umuofia system and ethics. In the trial scene depicted earlier in Part One of the novel, everybody knows everybody, and everybody knows what the other person is capable of doing or has done. The judgment is accepted by both parties. On the other hand, in the case against Anieto, strangers are sitting in judgment. The white man gives the piece of land in dispute to Nnama's family because the family has given money to the white man's messenger. Anieto is found guilty of murder and is hanged even though the charge against him is manslaughter. Okonkwo has earlier committed manslaughter, "female *ochu*," and has been sent into exile as has been the custom. In the same way, Anieto has prepared himself to flee the land for seven years, for his crime is also a female *ochu*, but the white man does not comprehend the facts of the case and of the autochthonous jurisprudence. Not only is Anieto hanged, but the elders in his family are also imprisoned and humiliated before being released.

Achebe also deplores the case of the Umuofia elders who are arrested for burning down a church. An overzealous church convert unmasks an *egwugwu* in public and the Umuofia people respond by burning down the church. To prepare the reader to react properly in favor of the elders, who sanction the act of burning down the church, Achebe has earlier shown the high esteem in which the *egwugwu* is held in the society. Therefore, the desecration of the *egwugwu* in unmasking him is sacrilege. Achebe has already exposed to the reader the people's way of expiating sacrilege. When Okonkwo commits a minor offense of disturbing the Week of Peace, he is given a minor punishment of taking sacrifices to the shrine of Ani, whom he has offended. When he commits manslaughter, he not only has to flee the society for seven years, but his house and property are also burned to cleanse the land of the pollution his crime has produced. This big offense attracts a big punishment. Desecrating an *egwugwu* is construed as the murder of the spirit of the ancestors. This is even greater than manslaughter or murder. So when the men of Umuofia burn the church, they are doing exactly what they would have done to one of their own who has committed the same offense.

To buttress this argument for the burning of the church building, Achebe has also shown the reader that the white man has carried out a worse punishment on a town in which a white man has been killed. The white man has embarked on the same kind of punishment that is prescribed in the Umuofia proverb that says that "if one finger brought oil, it soiled the others" (125; ch. 13). This is collective retribution. The white man wipes out Abame because some men in Abame killed a white man. The white men do not seek out the perpetrators of the crime. Rather, they have gone into a marketplace and have opened fire on all who are healthy enough to be in that market—men, women, and children. Here is a *tu quoque* argument. This is a species of the fallacious *argumentum ad hominem* which points a finger back at an opponent. It accuses an opponent of the same crime the arguer has been accused of.[15] The white men, despite their sense of superiority, can be seen to have done the same thing that the "inferior" natives do. But to wipe out a whole village because some villagers have killed one man is surely worse than burning a church building. In the eyes of the Umuofians, the church building is the house of the white man's God, and by the white man's faith, this God lives in that church. Therefore, burning the church is like desecrating the white man's God. By the same logic, the *egwugwu* houses the ancestral spirit of the town. To unmask the *egwugwu* is to desecrate the house of the people's gods. Every person in this culture has a personal god, *chi*, including the desecrated ancestral spirit.

Achebe's discussion of the importance of *chi* to an Igbo person, in his essay "Chi in Igbo Cosmology," makes clear the relationship of a person and his or her *chi* and why it was calamitous for the Christians to have desecrated an *egwugwu*. *Chi* is crucial to an Igbo person's existence, since it is the person's "other identity in spiritland—his spirit being complementing his terrestial human being." The ancestors who emerge as *egwugwu* at different occasions live in "spiritland where they recreate a life comparable to their earthly existence" parallel, similar, physical, and contiguous. As a result, there is "constant going and coming" between the ancestors and the living "in the endless traffic of life, death, and reincarnation."[16] However, in the usual Umuofia sense of justice and fairness, the Umuofia people do not touch the priest or his followers since these people did not touch the Umuofia people. Rather the Umuofia people go for the church, the seat of the white man's God and religion because in the eyes of Umuofia, the Christians did harm to the Umuofia religion. The Umuofia men, in the usual Umuofia magnanimity, extend to the priest an invitation to live among them and even allow him the option of practicing his own religion. This is in keeping with their philosophy of accommodation and harmonious coexistence articulated in their proverb: "Let the kite perch and let the eagle perch too. If one says no to the other, let his wing break" (14; ch. 2).

In delineating the ethics in and the system of the white man's administration, Achebe succeeds in sustaining the argument that human beings are basically the same everywhere. Earlier, in Part One, Achebe has exposed the complexity of the composition of the populace as well as the character of the people of Umuofia. In Part Three, he examines the priests from the white man's camp. Among the white men, there are even-tempered, understanding, and accommodating priests like Father Brown, as well as militant, bigoted, ignorant ones like Reverend James Smith. What is found among the white men is also found in Umuofia society. The two societies represent complex civilizations with complex peoples, each thinking that the other is strange. The audience inevitably ends by interrogating the white man's presumption to superiority which lies behind his arrogation to himself of the right and power to change the people of Umuofia.

Language is crucial to the drama in *Things Fall Apart*. One of Achebe's positions is that "No one can understand another whose language he does not speak (and 'language' here does not mean simply words, but a man's entire world-view)."[17] Achebe's insistence that contact with an alien culture has left the people of Umuofia with an adulterated language, which is no longer effective for communicating with either the natives or the foreigners in their midst, permeates the fabric of the novel, especially in Part Three, where the confusion in communication is at the root of the tragedy in the novel. Even when people speak the same language, there are chances of miscommunication arising out of ambiguity in the language. It is even harder to communicate, as Achebe has shown in this novel, when two people involved in the process of communication have a limited knowledge of each other's language and world view.

The situation is exacerbated when they are trying to communicate through an interpreter. Even though the people involved succeed in carrying out a conversation through an intermediary, they are once removed from each other and thus may be incapable of grasping the nuances of the language, which are, most often, lost in translation. For instance, in Mbanta, the interpreter translates "myself" as "my buttocks" because he speaks a different dialect of the Umuofia language. That kind of variation in dialects was a source of suspicion, ridicule, and rancor on both sides. One of the conversations between Okonkwo and Obierika brings to the fore the interrelatedness of language to one's worldview when Okonkwo questions the white man's knowledge and understanding of the Umuofia custom. In reply, Obierika asserts that the white man cannot know the Umuofia custom when he does not even possess the knowledge of their language (162; ch. 20). From this conversation, the reader sees that possession of the language is a prerequisite for and is fundamental to understanding a people's culture. The basic knowledge of a people is contained in the knowledge of their language is merely elemental. But it is the prerequisite for the knowledge at a higher level, the knowledge of a people's worldview as contained in their culture.

The result of the interference of the white man in the day-to-day activities of Umuofia in spite of his lack of knowledge of that society is that the people lose the ability to understand each other anymore. As Obierika succinctly puts it, in spite of this lack of elemental knowledge, the white man arrogates to himself the power to denigrate the Umuofia culture and even cause the converted Umuofia indigenes to join in denigrating the culture (162; ch. 20). Umuofia becomes not only a society in which Christian converts, who come from neighboring towns and speak the same language as the Umuofia people do, follow their white masters and denigrate Umuofia and its customs, but also a society in which its Christian members despise their own customs. Even though these Umuofia indigenes speak the same language and the same dialect of the language, their worldview is no longer the same, for as Obierika laments, "the white man has put a knife on the things that held us together and we have fallen apart" (162; ch. 20). Also since the people could only communicate with the white man through interpreters, the same converts who denigrate their customs and have limited knowledge of the Umuofia language, all parties in this conflict are speaking to one another but are not communicating. As a result, there is constant misunderstanding, misinformation, irritation, and sometimes anger in most of the speech situations involving all in the conflict.

Language is also essential to communication within the novel; it is essential to Achebe's style of communicating to the reading audience. Achebe's use of proverbs, choice of metaphors, and syntactic structures are conscious linguistic choices as well as rhetorical devices that help to disclose the role of language in the tragedy. These choices and devices are Achebe's attempt at achieving what Perelman and Olbrechts-Tyteca call *adherence of minds*[18] and what Burke calls achieving "identification" through "consubstantiation" with the audience.[19] In successful argumentation, Perelman and Olbrechts-Tyteca opine, the arguer's aim is usually to make contact with the minds he or she is seeking to persuade. To successfully make this contact, the arguer first forms "a community of minds" he or she needs to persuade and chooses adequate *topoi* and the vehicle for their successful transmission. The minimum requirement for ferrying these *topoi* successfully across the river of argumentation is the use of a common language.[20] Achebe faced a dilemma, for in his situation as a Nigerian, he has scores of languages that could adequately sustain a literature, but it was impossible for him to learn all these languages in order to reach his audience. Moreover, none of these languages enjoyed the currency in Nigeria that the English language did. At the same time, he resented the use of English language as the medium of his literary work because the language came with a baggage of atrocious arrogance and prejudice.[21] But as an astute orator he realized that he would be commiting the unpardonable error of throwing out the good because it came with the evil of English colonialism.

Achebe found inadequate the common language, English, that the Nigerian situation forced him to use. He has, therefore, adapted the English language to carry his message.[22] Since Achebe believed that his message was serious and should be earnestly [23] pursued, he fashioned an English which he describes as being "at once universal and able to carry his peculiar experience."[24] When Achebe is narrating, therefore, he uses a variety of the English language spoken by the educated Igbo and transliterates the thoughts of the characters from the indigenous language into the English language. Achebe's reason for adopting this linguistic strategy is that if one writes an African experience in conventional English, the form of the narration will be out of character.[25] Perelman and Olbretchs-Tyteca warn that the arguer should not settle for this minimum, the mere possession of the language of communication. The arguer has to "make contact."[26] The arguer needs to know the audience enough to be able to discern how to influence it, since "knowledge of an audience cannot be conceived independently of the knowledge of how to influence it."[27] Through his choice of metaphors that are indigenous to his audience, Achebe exhibits such deep knowledge of his audience and of the people he represents in *Things Fall Apart*.

ORATORY AND CULTURAL CHANGE

Achebe's use of oratory to advance the theme of transition in the novel is very effective. Through oratory, Achebe reveals to his reading audience the subtle transition of the society from a homogeneous to a heterogeneous one. He demonstrates, through speech, a modification of the people's language to accommodate the changes being experienced by the community at a particular historical juncture. An analysis of the two major pieces of oratory in the novel, one at the beginning and the other at the climax, clarifies the change that has occurred in the composition of the Umuofia audience because of the presence of the white man. That this change in the audience has affected oratory itself is evidenced in the language used, the ultimate terms evoked, and the commonplaces referenced by the orators in their speeches. The serious impact of cultural transition on oratory is revealed in the role of language used by the orators in the novel as well as that used by Achebe himself to communicate with the reader.

The impact of transition on oratory comes out vividly when one compares Part Three of *Things Fall Apart*, at the point where things have really fallen apart in Umuofia and there is a breakdown in communication among the people of Umuofia themselves, to Part One of the novel, where the community is still homogeneous and the people are still speaking the same tongue. The texts where the villagers assemble to discuss the two critical occurrences in their community expose Achebe's expert use of metaphors and proverbs to achieve "consubstantiation" as well as show the breakdown in communication that leads to the tragedy in *Things Fall Apart*. These two texts deal with the two oratorical occurrences in the novel, the killing of an Umuofia woman by a neighboring village and the sacrilege heaped on the Umuofia gods by the Christians up to the point where Okonkwo confronts the head messenger sent to disband this meeting. These excerpts show what happens to language when a society is in a state of flux. The two pieces of oratory differ in the language used by the orators in the novel, the ultimate terms invoked, and the *topoi* chosen to support the premises for persuasion.

The oratory and its delivery, in Part One, expose Achebe's view of the state of the clan before it came in contact with the alien culture. As Perelman and Olbrechts-Tyteca assert, the audience is the factor that makes oratory successful. Thus the composition of the audience affects the nature of the oratory presented to it.[28] The first oratorical occasion in the novel shows a homogenous and united clan. Things are predictable. People are sure of what they want and how they should perform and even how their neighbors will react. When a daughter of Umuofia is killed, the people know what to do. An orator normally speaks to the people on such occasions. Ogbuefi Ezeugo is the orator on this particular occasion. As the orator, he has to have his *ethos* intact as one of the grandees of Umuofia. And he does have his *ethos* intact. As I have already pointed out in the previous section, this is a society where achievement is revered (6; ch. 1).

In this society greatness is measured according to the titles taken. One of those titles that raise a fellow man above the rest is the *ozo* title. According to Robert Wren, "B. G. Stone, in an Intelligence Report (O.P.303) in the Nigerian National Archives at Enugu, identified the titles at Ogidi, in ascending order, as *Chi, Ifejioku, Ekwu, Ozo, Idemili, Omalo,* and *Erulu.*"[29] As Wren shows in his study of Ogidi, Achebe's town, *"ozo* was taken by a man as soon as his wealth and prestige made it clear that he was a voice to be attended to in communal deliberations. He belonged among the *ndichie.* The *ndichie* in Achebe's novels are the community; the town speaks collectively in their voice;"[30] the *ndichie* were the orators, spokesmen, and the common voice. Hence the *ozo* title is the beginning of prominence in the town as the *"ozo* title holder entered into the community of true men within his own clan. He was, in a sense, fulfilled. He had proven his dignity and worth, and his superiority over unfulfilled men. He was indeed for the first time truly a man."[31] Ogbuefi Ezeugo, being an *ozo* man, is also all these. He is an *Ogbuefi,* a name earned after one has taken the next title after the *Ozo* title, the *Idemili* title. The fact that he is an *Ogbuefi* raises him higher above many others, even above ordinary *ozo* men.

The name of this orator speaks volumes about men at this time in the society of Umuofia. *Ezeugo* in Igbo language means the king of the eagles or the eagle king. The proverb common among Ogidi people, Achebe's people, *ada afu ugo kwa daa,* which simply means that the eagle is not seen everyday, is a precise commentary on the precious rarity of the king of birds, the eagle. This proverb is normally used when one wants to compliment someone or something of note. The association of the orator's name with the eagle also exposes Achebe's grand vision of the Umuofia society at this time. It effectively evokes the image of the comet as associated with the happening in Rome during the time of Julius Caesar. The statement "When beggars die there are no comets seen"[32] evokes a similar image, highlighting the scarcity of the eagle which imbues an occasion with awe when the eagle graces human beings with its presence. For this orator to be referred to as the king of eagles is the grandest image of an orator an artist can paint. As Weaver rightly says, in classical times, the people carried themselves as if they were giants.[33] Surely, the image of a giant permeates not only the language but also its user in Part One of *Things Fall Apart.* Thus one can assert that worthy men are still present in the society; they talk to the people, and the people respond.

Umuofia before the coming of the white man is homogenous and so is the audience to which Ogbuefi Ezeugo speaks. This homogeneity of the audience means a homogeneity in experiences that come from beliefs and values. Definitely, there is what Mikhail Bahktin terms a "we-experience"[34] in the content of Ezeugo's oratory. Experience, according to Aristotle, is the whole universal that has come to rest in the soul.[35] The fact that the audience had the same experiences dictates that the audience's responses to events would be the same. Therefore, Ogbuefi Ezeugo, as the orator, is at liberty to take much for granted and to expect his audience to supply the right premise for his rhetorical enthymemes. The oratory taken from page 8 of the novel exposes all these about the audience and the orator. The composition and the response of the audience speak for the Umuofia of this period before the coming of the white man. It is taken for granted that every man answered the summons to the marketplace.

As Ogbuefi Ezeugo comes out to talk, the reading audience sees a dignified man, from a staid society. He has white hair and beard. His age adds to his *ethos*. He bellows his greeting, *Umuofia Kwenu*. He has a strong voice that befits a great orator. He adjusts his cloth, thus adding to the rhetorical effect of his speech. There is time for all these preparatory gestures before the real oratory; life is sedate because the emergency that threatens is one the clan knows it can contain. There is time enough for such dramatics as the one Ogbuefi Ezeugo exhibits (8; ch. 2). His dramatic gestures show mastery of delivery. The change of moods and expressions is rhetorical and elicits the appropriate *pathos*. Here Achebe is celebrating the past. The orator, Ogbuefi Ezeugo, is performing for the sake of performing. Although there is a serious reason for the oratory, he knows there is no serious threat that will adversely affect Umuofia. After all, Umuofia is feared by all its neighbors.

Ogbuefi Ezeugo, as an orator talking to a homogenous society, also takes much for granted. He is sure that the meaning of his gestures is accessible to all in the audience; therefore, the audience is capable of sharing in the suffering of a member. He does not show any sign that he fears that any other person would counsel against the normal course of action. The outcome of the meeting is predictable. Holding the meeting is a mere formality because in the end the clan will decide to follow the normal course of action. An ultimatum is immediately dispatched to Mbaino, asking them to choose between war on the one hand and, on the other, the offer of a young man and a virgin as compensation (8; ch. 2).

The linguistic choices Achebe has made in this excerpt also depict a stable society. The oratory is written in high-flown language. Everything is expressed in hyperbolic terms. There are maximum uses of what Weaver calls the "uncontested terms." These are such ideas as acknowledgement of the traditional penalty that the offending clan will give two people, a virgin and a lad, to appease the people of Umuofia. Nobody questions why Umuofia should demand two heads in place of one. Everybody knows that it is the normal course of action. As Weaver rightly observes, these uncontested terms seem to attract contest but do not do so in their own contexts. The orator is at liberty to use them when the premises they represent are accepted by all. When such is the case, the orator can count on the audience to respond uniformly to the same propositions.[36] The Umuofia of this period is such an audience. Ogbuefi Ezeugo, just as the orators in classical times, the times of

Aristotle, Cicero, and Quintilian of whom Weaver writes in his essay, "The Spaciousness of Old Rhetoric," uses the "uncontested" terms because he knows his audience and is sure of its composition. The orator normally uses uncontested terms in a homogeneous society because he knows that he can get away with it. He knows that his audience is uniformly informed and indoctrinated.

The words used in Ogbuefi Ezeugo's oratory have resonance. Weaver states that the orator in a homogenous society is able to use resonant words effectively because he sees continuity. He enjoys the privilege that allows him to assume that precedents are valid, that forms will persist, and that one may build today on what was created yesterday. Such orators do not need to explain certain claims because they would look ridiculous if they did. According to Weaver, the orator who pauses along the way to argue a point that no one challenges only demeans the occasion. Some things are fixed by universal, enlightened consensus; that is why the orators of old did not feel compelled to argue the significance of everything to which they attached importance. These things, fixed by universal enlightened consensus, are steps for getting at matters that are less settled.[37] Ogbuefi Ezeugo's oratory, like the oratory of old that Weaver analyzes, is not designed to make the audience think; it is designed "to remind people of what they have already thought." It does not aim at instruction but instead at inculcation. The audience is conditioned.

As I have explained earlier, cultural change affects thinking and, in the process, affects oratory. With the attack on the native culture, the people's mode of thinking changes. As Weaver rightly puts it, when the whole proposition of a culture is under attack, one is forced to think for oneself. What Bahktin calls the "I-experience"[38] takes precedence. By then, "interest has shifted from inference to reportage," and this affects oratory: "[t]he large resonant phrase is itself a kind of condensed proposition; as propositions begin to shrink with the general sagging of the substructure, the phrases must do the same."[39] Experience takes the place of logic. This is what happened to the oratory in the second excerpt taken from Part Three. The result is that the orator in the second excerpt pays more attention to style and empty political talk aimed at immediate effect, with very little regard for truth. He concentrates on what he thinks the people want to hear rather than on what the people believe. Thus he resorts to slogans and catchy words and argues from contraries, consequences, and circumstances. For instance, in the excerpt, he says that their gods are weeping. He calls out for war against the intruders when the custom demands that the people do not fight for their gods.

For one to appreciate the shift in the oratorical mode and the shift in the language from Part One to Part Three, one needs to follow the career of Okonkwo, the hero of the novel, from the Umuofia of old to the Umuofia to which he returned after his exile. I find it pertinent to outline the course of transition that affects this society and its hero. Before the point at which the second excerpt is taken, Umuofia has been a warrior clan feared by its neighbors. Okonkwo, the hero, is a man who becomes rich in spite of a background of abject poverty. His fame rests on solid personal achievement in this clan where, although greatness is cherished, achievement is revered. But Okonkwo has a deep-seated fear of being thought weak and being seen to resemble his father, who can not stand the sight of blood. His father is what any successful man in the culture aspires not to be, and Okonkwo is the epitome of success in this culture. Okonkwo kills a clansman, *albeit* inadvertently, and goes into exile for seven years. While he is away, a new culture, the white man's culture, comes into his clan and leads some people away from the ways of the clan because it comes with money culture. In discussing money as a sign of change and shift in economy, James Thompson rightly observes that

shift from moral or domestic to political economy involves a shift from inside to outside, from the moral to the financial, with an accompanying sense of secularization, from the management of the soul to the management of property. These changes also involve a shift from the micro to the macro, from management of the household or shop to management of the nation.[40]

Umuofia undergoes the same kind of change in its economy, politics, and religion. The society's agrarian economy gives way to the alien culture's money economy. Titles, which have been a measure of success, stand for nothing. The men considered to be the worthless fellows in the old culture acquire a new kind of wealth and become relevant over the grandees of the clan. Power shifts from the grandees to the new politically and economically strong *efulefu*. Respect for moral worth gives place to respect for wealth acquired in the new money economy. The concept of valor shifts, from being deft in cutting heads with a machete and proving one's prowess in intertribal wars, to having faceless backers who can supply one with guns and to being able to operate these guns, a skill that Okonkwo has never mastered as demonstrated by his two unsuccessful attempts.

The situation in the clan, brought about by the alien culture, weakens the fabric of this once united society. Obierika, an articulate man, tries to explain the situation in the clan, but Okonkwo is unable to understand the changes that have eroded every value that makes him one of the most respected and feared men of his time. While Okonkwo is still trying to understand how his values could have been thus eroded, the members of the new culture desecrate the clan's masquerade, thereby challenging the people's religion, the core of their very being. Okonkwo calls for action, and his people respond by burning down a church. The District Commissioner arrests the elders of Umuofia. The messengers working for the Commissioner mock and humiliate the elders. On returning home, the elders call for a meeting of the clan to decide the next action to be taken. The second excerpt starts at the moment when the people are going to this meeting and ends with the confrontation between Okonkwo and the head messenger who is sent to stop the meeting.

In the speech events in this excerpt, there are three interactions, each intensifying as the reader approaches the climax, which comes with the third interaction. The first interaction involves two equals who are also friends,

Okonkwo and Obierika. The second interaction involves Obierika, an unnamed group of villagers whom Okonkwo does not care to talk to, and Okonkwo himself. The third interaction, the most critical one, is between Okonkwo and the head messenger sent to disband the villagers. Sandwiched between the second and the third interactions is a catalytic, uncompleted piece of oratory that calls for war against the white man and his followers. Then, there is the author's narration that comes between these two different speech genres. The point where the author introduces the first speaker in the arena up to the point where Okonkwo and the head messenger confront each other is a good study of the extent of cultural transition this society has faced and the concomitant lack of communication that occurred which necessitate the tragedy witnessed in *Things Fall Apart.*

Achebe's use of language exposes the lack of communication that lies behind the tragedy in the novel. Achebe, as an accomplished orator, makes linguistic choices designed to persuade the reader on the extent of the change that has befallen this society. His choice of metaphors and proverbs helps to carry his message. In the scene where the author introduces Onyeka's role, the author describes Onyeka's action as he salutes the clan, thus creating mental pictures of the act of saluting. Onyeka raises his left hand and pushes the air with an open hand. Umuofia does not just answer; it roars its response. "Roar" here brings up the image of a lion. This is an ironic metaphor because Umuofia, at this time, is anything but a lion. The new culture has robbed it of its ferociousness. Then Achebe uses repetition to sustain the phatic communication taking place here: "he bellowed again, and again, and again, facing a new direction each time" (202; ch. 24). The phatic communication is effective because Achebe tells the reader that "[t]here was immediate silence as though cold water had been poured on a roaring flame" (202). The image of a lion "roaring" is still sustained, but Achebe introduces a contrasting metaphor that signals to the reader that all is not right; the silence that comes after the roaring is compared to the effect of cold water on a roaring flame. Earlier in this novel, Achebe has shown Okonkwo contemplating the action of one of his sons, Nwoye, who has converted to Christianity, and seeing himself as a roaring flame that has begotten cold impotent ash as a son (153; ch.17). This imagery also foreshadows the cold impotence the men of Umuofia show when it is time for action. Umuofia, the warrior clan, has undergone change. The white man is the cold water that has silenced Umuofia and turned it into cold impotent ash. This utterance and its associated imagery take the reader through the whole novel, comparing Umuofia as a ferocious lion in Part One and the silenced Umuofia in Part Three.

Also, the mention of the name of the village, "Umuofia" in the utterance, "The first man to speak to Umuofia...." shows the importance Achebe accords to the disintegrating community. Umuofia at this time needs to be spoken to, even rallied. The fact that Okonkwo, in this gathering, does not care to talk to the group of unnamed villagers who are chatting with Obierika shows the lack of oneness or "we-ness" that exists at this time. Okonkwo's experience at this point is no longer universal. He has been imprisoned and he has tasted, first hand, the messengers' insolence and humiliating actions. Even as Okonkwo is ignoring this group, he is busy searching for one of the elders, Egonwanne, who he is afraid will counsel against going to war. This also underscores the fact that the society is no longer speaking in one voice. Since "I-experience" has taken precedence over "we-experience," there is no longer trust among the people. Nobody is sure of other people's reactions. There is no longer a normal cause of action as the reader saw in the time of Ogbuefi Ezeugo. Earlier in Part One of the novel when the town is still homogenous, there are none of these signs of lack of oneness. It is assumed that the people would go to war had the offending village not complied with Umuofia's demands. Umuofians do not need to be rallied. Okonkwo's uncertainty on the cause of action the clan is going to take also exposes the disquietude in the air and the tremendous change the clan has undergone, especially if we compare this uncertainty to the certainty in Part One.

Achebe uses the metonymy, "Umuofia," in the beginning of this speech not only to give life to the village of Umuofia and to create empathy in the reader but also to call attention to the change the society is undergoing. In the first excerpt, the attention is on the speaker. The speech is glossed over and taken for granted. In this second excerpt, the attention is on the speech and on the society while the speaker is relegated to the background. The reader not only sees the town as animate but feels the full impact of the tragedy that has occurred because the colonizer has failed to see the town as animate. The section where the orator tells his audience about the sacrilege being heaped on their gods is full of *pathos,* due to Achebe's employment of metaphor and rhythm. He tells the audience that there is weeping from all the quarters they revere. The author could have made the speaker say that the gods and the dead fathers are angry or crying, but he chooses weeping. When someone is weeping, that person is doing more than crying. There is intense agony associated with weeping, and the personification here drives this intensity home because these gods are abstract, while the dead fathers are, of course, dead and whatever could make them weep must be really serious. Also, by calling these gods by their names, the orator has imbued them with a presence that makes them less abstract and makes them part of life, as they rightly are, in the clan.[41] But the orator is careful not to dwell too long on *pathos* as his means of persuasion.

Achebe also uses hyperbole to drive his views home. One apt instance is the confrontation between the head messenger and Okonkwo where the narrator says, "In that brief moment the world seemed to stand still, waiting" (204; ch. 24). The entire world does not stand still, as Achebe's well-chosen imagery leads us to believe. The world he is talking about here is the white man's world and the world of the clan. But the artistic excellence of this imagery looks beyond the village square, where these two people are and takes the reader further to the Western world with its colonizing mission and the African world that is being colonized; actually, the worlds encompass the two races, black and white.

Furthermore, the proverb involving the toad (203) means that there is no smoke without fire. But instead of using the imagery of smoke and fire which will radiate a Western worldview, Achebe resorts to imageries from the local fauna that will suit the character of the orator. The images contained in this proverb are things the Umuofia audience can relate to, hence Achebe's choice of imagery. Proverbs, "the palm oil with which words are eaten" (7; ch. 1) in Umuofia, are a great asset and a linguistic device which Achebe employs effectively in this excerpt. At the point where the orator is exposing the people's dilemma over what to do about their clansmen who have deserted the clan, the orator introduces another proverb to exonerate the action he is urging the clan to take. The reply Eneke the bird gave for refusing to perch on a tree shows astuteness and adaptation to change on the part of the bird (144; ch. 16). This proverb means that the world has changed, and they too have to change with it. The speaker follows this proverb with yet another that reemphasizes the expediency of the matter at hand and urges the clan to do take action immediately (144). This proverb, when completed, means that a stitch in time saves nine. All through this speech, the orator argues from consequences, pointing out what will happen if the clan does not take action. He also give contracdictory statements, one counselling astuteness and the other urging immediate action.

Achebe's attitude towards the occasion in question is clearly shown through his syntactic choices in the oratorical speech event. Achebe's choice of syntactic structure is another prominent feature of this excerpt. "The first man to speak to Umuofia that morning was Okika, ..." (202; ch. 24). This is written so that emphasis is given to the idea of speaking first not to Okika the speaker. By this, Achebe makes the speech more important than the speaker. He does this because speaking to Umuofia that morning is the main focus of his narration, not who spoke to Umuofia. After mentioning the speaker, there is a pause marked by a comma before Okika is identified as one of the six elders imprisoned by the district commissioner. This construction leaves Okika between two major focuses of the sentence: one shows Okika to have spoken first while the other shows him to have been imprisoned, thus diminishing Okika further as an important element in the narration since at this time in Umuofia, imprisonment is greatly abhorred. By this construction, Achebe shows Okika's sentiment to come out of personal experience or "I-experience" which does not necessarily depict the group experience at the time of this speech. The next sentence makes an attempt at establishing Okika's *ethos by* calling him a great man and an orator. This sentence juxtaposes Okika's credential with the less important position accorded him in the preceding utterance, thereby supplying the necessary information on why Okika should be the first man to speak out of the six men who were imprisoned. Achebe uses this sentence to restore a measure of importance that he has earlier robbed this man of in the previous sentence and also to give him enough stature to carry the burden of addressing Umuofia, a warrior clan. A great man in Umuofia is a big farmer, a warrior, a titled man. Okika is all these. Hence, the use of the adjective "great" to qualify him. Okika is also an orator.

However, Okika does not have the gigantic stature that Ogbuefi Ezeugo has. Even his name is both unimpressive and ambiguous. It could mean either procrastination or being greater than someone else, depending on how one tone marks the name when written or the way one articulates the vowels in the name in speech. He does not even have an *Ogbuefi* attached to his name. Achebe does not tell us if he even took the *ozo* title. He is just an elder. Actually, the uncertainty in the clan at this time seems to have spilled over into the name and the *ethos* of the orator entrusted with directing the clan on the road to take at this critical point of its political need. The situation at hand, the humiliation of the leaders of the clan by the white man and his messengers and the desertion of the clan by some renegades, is serious and demands serious measures. Therefore, an orator is needed to persuade the clansmen that something must be done to arrest the situation. Hence, Okika is chosen to be the first speaker. But at this point, Achebe introduces a problem by the contrasting sentence that exposes Okika's lack of a booming voice (202; ch. 24). This sentence exposes the imperfection of the clan which has been present from the beginning and at that moment, in particular, and which has always been the bane of the Umuofia society. Just like any other society, especially one under flux, it is not a perfect society. Required qualities do not reside in any one person or in any one society. There are always cracks through which the society may be defeated. This, in my opinion, is why Achebe makes the clause exposing what Okika lacks relate to the clause praising Okika's qualities   by coordination. He has given equal importance to Okika's good qualities and his flaws.

This lack of the appropriate instrument of delivery further diminishes Okika's *ethos* when Achebe introduces Onyeka, the man who has a booming voice. Achebe uses a compound sentence that has a longer pause, a semicolon bring this fact to the reader (202). This syntactic construction gives importance to the possession of such a voice; therefore, lack of it is a serious defect. The pause, signified by the semicolon, also makes it possible for the reader to keep the booming voice and its effect in mind before seeing its use. "He" in the second part of the compound is an anaphoric reference to Onyeka designed to reiterate the importance of his endowment with a booming voice. But that clause is in a passive form because his job is passive—just salute the clan and the real orator will speak. This evokes a modern image of someone ringing a bell to establish silence. Achebe further establishes here that the society is undergoing change. Features that normally make a great orator are now lacking in one person; therefore, the clan is forced to readjust in its procedure. This also foreshadows the clan's capability to adjust in the face of new values. In one of his essays, Achebe asserts that the Igbo society is one that embraces change. This potential for change endowed on the Igbo society eludes the hero, Okonkwo, as he fails to recognize its presence at the most critical time of the society's history. This adaptability in the face of change is also embodied in the "Eneke the bird" proverb quoted earlier. Achebe seems to want the reader to pause here and be fully aware of what is happening to this society, which even the hero is not aware of and which will lead to his tragedy because he will fail to understand the oratory and the need to readjust to events just as Umuofia has readjusted in his absence.

There is no decorum in Okika's movement when compared to Ogbuefi Ezeugo's movement to the podium. Okika "sprang" (203; ch. 24) to his feet while Ogbuefi Ezeugo "stood up in the midst of them" (10; ch. 2). The next two sentences are more actions than words. To achieve this, Achebe uses many coordinating conjunctions and semicolons to give equal importance to the action being enacted in this part of the narration. There are three coordinated clauses related to each other by addition, depicting the chronology of the action.

Bakhtin's theory can also be fruitfully used to explicate the effect Okika's use of language had on his audience. According to Bakhtin, language does not exist for its own sake, but can only be understood in dialogic terms. Utterances embody and reveal ideology through the way they are used in social situations, since signs derive from societal perceptions, ideologies, and cosmologies. Sharing common perceptions, ideologies and cosmologies allows the members of a group to understand an utterance with what it embodies. Thus inner speech underlies meaning in every utterance.[42] This meaning emerges and makes complete sense only in a social group. In Ogbuefi Ezeugo's oratory in Part One, inner speech makes possible the establishment of "consubstantiation" and, therefore, "identification" which, in turn, enables the orator to persuade the audience. Bakhtin further notes that discourse grows out of both the "I-experience" and the "we-experience."[43] Where a group has achieved cohesion and ideological clarity, a recourse to inner speech—which facilitates identification and "consubstantiation"— enables the orator to get directly to the soul of the group, even move it to collective action. The orator in the first speech is able to get to the soul of Umuofia because he shares a "we-experience" with the clan. Okika, on the other hand, lacks the capacity to get to the soul of Umuofia. The audience is not unanimous in its experience.

The content of Okika's speech and the language used depict this shift in the composition of the present audience. When Okika starts to speak, his first sentence establishes him as part of the clan by the use of the inclusive pronoun "we." The pronoun "we" also performs a second function. It disperses responsibility. However, much as the speaker indicates that he is part of the clan by the use of the inclusive pronoun "we," he is by the same token not accepting responsibility for convening the meeting. He lets the clansmen know that they are all there by their own volition and by their corporate belief in the threat they are facing. His only duty as the speaker is to reiterate to the audience what they already know. By doing this, the speaker puts the audience in a position in which they are bound to acquiesce with what he says, since they all know why they are there. It also makes the job of the speaker easier, since he does not need to narrate what has happened if the audience already knows it. However, this same sentence instills a feeling of "I" in the audience. It also includes the audience in the inherent blame that is in the act of gathering for the meeting. It makes the audience fellow culprits should the white man decide to retaliate on the act. The unstated premise thus asks the audience to take part of the blame for the gathering. Okika seems to be afraid of the consequences of the gathering and rightly so because, at this point, Umuofia is afraid of the white man's retaliation. Ezeugo does not have to exhibit this type of fear while rendering his speech because at his time, Umuofia does not fear retaliation; Umuofia is feared by his neighbors.

Thus when Okika gives the proverb about the toad he follows it up with an explanation of the proverb (203; ch. 24). It is unusual to openly relate the meaning of a proverb in a speech, but Achebe's choice of explaining this proverb reiterates the change that is occurring in the society. The speaker is no longer sure that the composition of the audience is wholly indigenous. It is possible that outsiders are in the audience. In this case, outsiders may be the outcasts in the society, the chaff of the society that are more interested in the white man's commerce, the people that are called *efulefu* in the Igbo language. In order to accommodate the uncertainty of the composition of the audience, the speaker is forced to give linguistic clues to the meaning of his proverb to avoid miscommunication. Also, the orator may have felt the need to explain himself because he is still afraid of being misrepresented or misinterpreted to the white man. The irony here is that in trying to communicate to the "nonmembers" and in order to protect himself, the speaker may have unwittingly miscommunicated to the members of the clan who will see his attempt as a sign of fear and even weakness, feel unprotected, and may decide to seek redress on their own or decide to run for cover, depending on individual disposition. Okonkwo, the hero, seeks redress while the rest of the clan members are inert. Thus, no matter what the intention of the orator in this speech is, the reader sees that the speech has turned the people of Umuofia into "a mute backcloth" (204). The experience they are facing has been turned into an individual experience, making it impossible for Okonkwo to invoke a "we-ness" which is necessary for facing the threatening invaders as a group. Even though Okika tries to ignite passion in his audience, he fails to realize what Aristotle asserts:

it is not ... every kind of pathos, which will give the orator so great an ascendancy over the minds of his hearers. All passions are not alike capable of producing this effect. Some are naturally inert and torpid; they deject the mind, and indispose it for enterprise. Of this kind are sorrow, fear, shame, humility.[44]

These emotions bedeck Okika's oratory.

The three sentences claiming that all their gods are weeping because of the sacrilege being heaped on them are designed to elicit emotional response from the audience (203). The speaker probably does that to make up for his softness and exhibition of fear suggested by the proverb-explanation strategy. In this case he may be trying to get back on the right side of the clansmen, but he may have overdone it. Instead of feeling outraged, the audience may be feeling sorrow, fear, shame, humility; these feelings are like a heavy weight on the spirit. They are not capable of leading to action. Understandably, the people of Umuofia do not respond to the call for action which Okonkwo's one-man act implies.

The orator pauses again. When he starts again, his utterance is short and crisp. "This is a great gathering." This sentence serves as a transition from the earlier part of the oratory to the admonishing part that will follow. This utterance, placed at this strategic position, is apt in the sense that an orator needs to concede a little before making a crucial point. Therefore, this is a concession from Okika. He knows fully well that the clan has lost its greatness and its clout, but he needs to boost the clan's ego. The irony may not be lost on the audience. The astute ones among them may begin to see that the clan is no longer great. Then the whip descends in the contrasting utterance, "But are we all here? I ask you:" (203). There are dramatic pauses and rhetorical questions in this utterance designed for a special effect on the audience. But these pauses are not like Ogbuefi Ezeugo's pauses which were merely used aesthetically. When the author makes the speaker say, "I ask you," the author is translating from his native language, Igbo.

When the author puts a colon after "I ask you," he is also following the Igbo speech pattern and rhythm. Normally in the Igbo oratorical situation, especially in the Idemili Local Government area of which Ogidi is the capital (both Achebe and I come from Ogidi), when a speaker asks this type of question, he pauses dramatically as if he is expecting a reply. No one ever replies. People may indicate approval or disapproval by nodding or by shaking their heads or by murmuring. This pause allows the impact of the point made to hit home before the speaker picks up where he has paused. Hence, the author indicates to the reader that "[a] deep murmur swept through the crowd." After the murmur, the orator utters another crisp, short sentence. The accusation then follows: "They are not." The tone is that of defeat. The audience knows why the others are not there. Some people in the audience may even be feeling that they ought not to be there. Okonkwo's earlier exhibition of the fear that Egonwanne will counter the argument against the presence of the white man in Umuofia is an indication of the dissent in the Umuofia audience.

The speaker then recounts the offense of the deserters and the dilemma the clan is facing about punishing the offenders. The next utterance is a call to take up arms against the deserters, the punishment notwithstanding. The italicizing of *now* in that call shows the emphasis placed on the word and also shows the emotional state of the speaker. He follows the proverb about Eneke with yet another proverb that calls for immediate action. But the orator does not have the chance to get to the end of his speech, as the ellipsis after the sentence indicates, when something happens. Therefore, the communication is not complete and, therefore, could be misunderstood. Also, the communication has not been tested for its effectiveness on the audience. Therefore, any action based on the substance of the speech may be disastrous. Achebe shows this potential of the speech first by not letting the speaker finish the speech; second, by not letting another speaker, the dissenting voice, like Egonwanne state his opinion; and third, by not letting the members of the audience show their reactions. Hence, miscommunication is inherent in this speech situation. At this point, the court messengers, the same offenders whom the speaker has urged the people to uproot from their midst, appear to disrupt the meeting. This incident takes the reader to another speech event, the confrontation between the head messenger and Okonkwo, the foremost man of the clan.

The author tells us that the moment Okonkwo sees who is causing the stir in the gathering, he "sprang to his feet," as Okika did earlier, but unlike Okika, he does not use words for his persuasion. This portion of the text is interesting because it exposes the differences between the two worlds confronting each other and shows the miscommunication that is at the core of the tragedy in *Things Fall Apart*. It also points back to the quotation from W. B. Yeats's poem, "The Second Coming," used to set off this novel because, at this point, the falcon cannot hear the falconer, and things have really fallen apart. Achebe uses three loaded sentences to indicate the happening in this scene the moment Okonkwo springs to his feet (204; ch. 24). There is a live-wire atmosphere created by these three sentences. Okonkwo did not just get up. He "sprang up." There is a threatening force behind this utterance. Okonkwo "confronted" the messenger. "Confronting" as a choice of word against other near synonyms is rather an extreme choice. It also indicates the lack of friendliness in the gesture. It indicates a serious business. The participial phrase "trembling with hate" indicates the state of mind of the hero, Okonkwo. It is not enough that he hates the messenger, but his hatred is visible; his whole body radiates it. Because the two worlds confronting each are not communicating in spite of speech, all these signs that an Umuofia man would have picked up as portending imminent danger are lost on the stranger or the clansman given a false sense of immortality by his association with the white man. The result is that the head messenger slights the angry warrior who has come back from exile to find that the world he left seven years before has completely changed.

On the part of Okonkwo, he has been away for too long to understand the power that he is confronting and that he cannot communicate with these people who have never seen him perform and therefore may not be in awe of him. He and the head messenger make their fatal mistakes, born out of their inability to communicate with and to each other. Although they are both engaged in a communication process, they are not speaking the same language in the sense that they are not operating from the same reference point since their worldviews are different. Achebe tells us, "In that brief moment the world seemed to stand still, waiting. There was utter silence" (204). There is a contrast between these two sentences, and this contrast arrests our interest and calls attention to the calamity that follows this confrontation.

The writer's juxtaposition of a long sentence with a short sentence enables us to feel the effect of this calamity. Also there is a pause before the word "waiting" and the pause calls attention to the word. On the one hand, the emphasis on "waiting" highlights the impotence of the warrior tribe in the face of this ominous interruption. Also, the audience hesitates because it does not know the full magnitude and import of a showdown that will ensue if the audience backs Okonkwo. It does not also know if it can contain a possible showdown with its adversary as the audience in the first speech is sure of its neighbor's response and as it is also sure of containing its neighbor's response to its demands of restitution. The audience has just listened to a piece of oratory that is fraught with mixed messages. Finally, the people of Umuofia who make up the greater percentage of this audience have been witnesses to what had happened to other clans that defied the white man whom the head messenger is representing. On the other hand, it highlights the hesitance of the other messengers regarding the right and wrong of what they are doing. Some of them may have just been converted; therefore, they may not fully understand the logic of the power they are representing. Moreover, there may still be remnants of the values their clans had inculcated in them, and these values may have prevented them from confronting this elder, Okonkwo.

However, the head messenger breaks the spell when he gives the order, "Let me pass!" In just these three words, the messenger has committed an abomination and violated many codes of conduct, going further to confirm the disparity between his worldview and that of the clan he is dealing with. The use of an exclamation mark indicates that he barked this order at this great man, Okonkwo. This is an abomination because younger people do not talk to elders in that way, let alone to an elder who is the most prominent man in a warrior society and whose stare alone was enough to make a whole clan tremble in the years gone by. Also, the man and the other elders had earlier been molested by court messengers because the court messengers were armed and this man was not. Moreover, an orator has just been interrupted in what seems to be a call for war against the new culture that is threatening to erode the Umuofia culture. Most important, the head messenger has caused this warrior to lose face, and if the man does not do something drastic, he would be ridiculed in the village. The prospect of being ridiculed is worse than death itself to this man who has a deep-seated fear of being thought weak (13; ch. 2). This was a man that cut down Ikemefuna, a child that called him father, and whom he loved as a son, just because he was afraid of being thought weak.

In this segment of the dialogue between the two, Achebe masterfully shows how catastrophic the failure of rhetoric can be, especially when there is a failure in communication because the people communicating do not speak the same language. Ivor A. Richards suggests that rhetoric should be the study of "misunderstanding and its remedies."[45] To Richards, words are an essential part of language, and words and their meanings serve the user in a peculiar way, and no direct relationship exists between a word and the object it symbolizes. Meaning mediates between the user's cognitive, affective, and volitional activities and the actual happenings they are concerned with. Meaning also mediates among individuals. Meaning binds people together because it represents the actual thing in the same way to the same group. All these imply that if an arguer intends to persuade a group successfully, the arguer has to have the same meaning for the same actuality as the group or, as Plato sees it, one should know the souls one intends to persuade.[46] It is only when the orator has the same frame of reference as his audience that the orator will, as Perelman and Olbrechts-Tyteca point out, be able to form a communion of minds with the group,[47]   and as Burke stipulates, achieve identification with that group.[48]   This is because words as signs are used to communicate thoughts. They are symbols which derive meaning because they belong to a context and serve his audience as a substitute for the part of the context that is absent. Okonkwo and the head messenger are not operating within the same context hence they do not share the same meaning.

Furthermore, one cannot assume that others have the same frame of reference for the same symbols if one wants to avoid misunderstanding since meaning exists in people, not in the symbols themselves; context gives meaning to words, and people have unique experiences, which may make them attach different meanings to different words.[49]   Richards' and Burke's ideas are very important in the oratorical events in this part of the novel. The two individuals confronting each other fail to persuade precisely because they fail to assume the same meaning and interpretation of events with the audience. The auditor in this case even has different meaning and different interpretation of the speaker's words. The speaker is no longer speaking the same language as the audience because time and locale have changed the meaning the words inhered prior to the period and the place, and the auditor is exposed to a different orientation and a different world view. Okonkwo's reply, "What do you want here?" seems to be a harmless "Wh-" question, but to a clan's man, it is loaded with threat. It is not even a question because Okonkwo was not expecting an answer. It is a serious order to the messenger to get out of the arena. A clan's man should have heard the bell the utterance was ringing and should have taken to his heels, but the head messenger is oblivious of the threat.

As I pointed out earlier, this situation indicates that although the two people are engaged in a speech situation, they are not really communicating. The two worlds they represent are too wide apart to allow for effective communication. Okonkwo's next action confirms this. While the messenger is answering what he takes to be a question, Okonkwo lets his hand speak for him. The utterances indicating the actions that follow are loaded with Achebe's attitude towards the whole tragedy. The drawing of the machete and the severing of the messenger's head happen very fast and Achebe shows the messenger's useless attempt at averting his fate. The short sentence used to indicate the messenger's futile action is artistically placed to buttress Achebe's view that once this messenger violates the codes in the clan, his fate is sealed. The well-balanced compound sentence that follows this short sentence buttresses Achebe's attitude to the whole tragedy. Being a compound sentence, the two parts of the sentence have equal weight, and they should because they bear the actions that seal the fate of the head messenger and the fate of Okonkwo, the hero of this novel, and by extension, the fate of this clan. The messenger's head lies useless beside the now useless "uniformed body."

Achebe calls attention to the lifeless body by the presence of the past-participial phrase, "uniformed body." The reader is conscious of this linguistic choice. The uniform has been used to terrorize the clan as Achebe shows earlier in the novel. It is the emblem of the power of the white man, but without the man's head, the uniform is useless. That is why, the moment the messenger is beheaded, the other messengers run. But, the "uniformed body" has a different implication for the clansmen. The moment the man is beheaded, the people break into tumult and start asking "why did he do it?" (205; ch. 24) instead of breaking into action such as beheading the rest of the messengers. Definitely, Okika has not been able to get to the soul of this audience, hence, there is no collective action.

The uniformed body has a more serious implication for Okonkwo. He too has crossed the boundary and is sure to face the white man's wrath, alone. He realizes, too late, that he too has failed to understand his own people, the call for war, and above all, he has failed to understand his people's deeplyrooted fear for the white man and his powers. With Okonkwo's epiphany on the state of events in Umuofia comes his suicide, the only option open to a warrior who has lost his soldiers.

This chapter has discussed the influence of audience on the art of persuasion in *Things Fall Apart*. Audience as the pivot around which arguments are woven is manifested greatly in Achebe's choice and the arrangement of materials in the novel. Also Achebe has used oratory effectively to portray how language shifts in the face of a changing society, to show how shift in the language is used to accommodate the audience, and to expose the fact that the contact of an alien culture with the indigenous culture causes the language of the indigenous culture to undergo flux, thus causing miscommunication and confusion in a once homogeneous and united society. He uses the orator effectively to show the movement from homogenous to a heterogenous society that has been infiltrated, and whose values have been compromised and adulterated. The audience of the oratorical pieces within the novel itself has also affected the ultimate terms invoked by the two orators, the language used, and the *topoi* chosen to support the premises for persuasion. The analysis of the two oratorical pieces in the novel has exposed the extent to which oratory changes to meet with the demands of a changing audience. The next chapter will examine the social responsibility that comes with oratory which demands that orators be competent in their art in order for them to successfully lead the society.

NOTES

1.   Achebe, "The Novelist as Teacher," *Morning Yet*, 71.

2.   Chaim Perelman and Lucie Olbrechts-Tyteca, *The New Rhetoric: A Treatise on Argumentation*, trans. John Wilkinson and Purcell Weaver (London: University of Notre Dame Press, 1969), 16.

3.   Ibid., 17.

4.   Ibid., 80-81.

5.   Ibid., 338.

6.   Ibid., 51.

7.   Plato, "Phaedrus," trans. Alexander Nehamas and Paul Woodruff, ed. J. M.

Cooper, *Plato:Complete Works* (Indianapolis: Hackett Publishing Company, 1997), 264c.

8.   Kevin Crossley-Holland, trans. "Beowulf" (Eighth Century? First printed in 1851). Brian Wilkie and James Hurt, eds. *Literature of the Western World,* vol 1 (New York: Macmillan, 1992), 1271-1342.

9.   Arisrotle, *Nicomachean Ethics*, Bk II. 1106b. 20, trans. Hippocrates G. Apostle and Lloyd P. Gearson, *Aristotle: Selected Works,* 3rd ed. (Grinnell, IA: The Peripatetic Press, 1991).

10.   Perelman and Olbrechts-Tyteca, *The New Rhetoric,* 117.

11.   Shakespeare, *Julius Caesar*, Act 3, sc. 2, 170-195. Quoted in Perelman and Olbrechts-Tyteca, *The New Rhetoric,* 117.

12.   Perelman and Olbrechts-Tyteca, *The New Rhetoric,* 411-412.

13.   Achebe, "Novelist as Teacher," *Morning Yet,* 72.

14.   Shakespeare, *Julius Ceasar* Act 3, sc.2, 165-250.

15.   Douglas Walton, *The Place of Emotion in an Argument* (University Park: Pennsylvania State University Press, 1992) 211-212.

16.   Achebe, "Chi in Igbo Cosmology," *Morning Yet,* 162.

17.   Achebe, "Where Angels Fear To Tread," *Morning Yet,* 79.

18.   Perelman and Olbrects-Tyteca, *The New Rhetoric,* 14.

19.   Kenneth Burke, *A Rhetoric of Motives* (Berkeley: University of California Press, 1969), 21.

20.   Perelman and Olbrects-Tyteca, *The New Rhetoric,* 15.

21.   Achebe, "The African Writer and the English Language," *Morning Yet,* 96.

23.   Ibid., 101.

24.   Achebe, "Colonialist Criticism," *Morning Yet,* 21.

25.   Achebe, "The African Writer and the English Language," *Morning Yet,* 100.

26.   Ibid., 101-102.

27.   Perelman and Olbrecths-Tyteca, *The New Rhetoric,* 15.

28.   Ibid., 23.

29.   Robert R. Wren, *Achebe's World: The Historical and Cultural Context of the Novels* (Washington, D.C.: Three Continents Press 1980) 87.

30.   Ibid., 85.

31.   Ibid.

32.   Shakespeare, *Julius Caesar*, Act 2 Sc. 2, 30-33.

33.   Richard Weaver, "The Spaciousness of Old Rhetoric," in *The Ethics of Rhetoric,* (Davis, CA: Hermogoras Press, 1985), 166.

34.   Mikhail Bakhtin, "Verbal Interaction" in *Marxism and the Philosophy of Language*, part II Ch 3, in Patricia Bizzell and Bruce Herzberg, eds., *The Rhetorical Tradition* (New York: St Martin's Press, 1990), 932.

35.   Aristotle, *Posterior Analytics* 11, 19, 100a, 7, *Aristotle: Selected Works.*

36.   Weaver, "Nature of Culture," in Sonja K. Foss, Karen A. Foss and Robert Trapp, *eds., Contemporary Perspectives on Rhetoric*, 2nd ed. (Prospect Heights, IL: Waveland Press, 1991), 62.

37.   Weaver, "The Spaciousness of Old Rhetoric," *Ethics of Rhetoric,* 172.

38.   Bakhtin, "Verbal Interaction" in *The Rhetorical Tradition,* 932.

39.   Weaver,"The Spaciousness of Old Rhetoric," *Ethics of Rhetoric,* 172.

40.   James Thompson, *Models of Value: Eighteenth-Century Political Economy and the Novel* (Durham, NC: Duke University Press, 1996), 42.

41. Achebe, "Chi in Igbo Cosmology," *Morning Yet*, 162-63.

42. Mikhail M. Bakhtin, "The Problem of Speech Genres," trans. Vern W. McGee, Caryl Emerson and Michael Holquist, eds., *M. M. Bakhtin: Speech Genres and Other Late Essays* (Austin: University of Texas Press, 1987), 84-87.

43. Bakhtin, "Verbal Interaction" in *The Rhetorical Tradition*, 932.

44. George Campbell. "The Nature and Foundation of Eloquence," in *The Rhetoric of Blair, Campbell, and Whately*, James L. Golden and Edward P. J. Corbett, eds. (Carbondale: Southern Illinois University Press, 1990), 148.

45. Ivor A. Richards, *The Philosophy of Rhetoric* (New York: Oxford University Press, 1936), 4.

46. Plato, "Phaedrus," in *The Rhetorical Tradition*, 138.

47. Perelman and Olbrechts-Tyteca, *The New Rhetoric*, 14.

48. Kenneth Burke, *Language as a Symbolic Action: Essays on Life, Literature, and Method* (Berkeley: University of California Press, 1966) 301.

49. Richards, *Philosophy of Rhetoric*, 11.

Chapter 3

Oratory and Social Responsibility: *Arrow of God*

ORATORY AND SOCIAL COHESION

Rhetoric has been seen as the bedrock of an organized society from the classical times to the present. It embraces the different arms of government in society, including the judicial, the political, and the ceremonial. Even though the art of rhetoric, from the time of Corax (5th Century B.C.), mostly concerned itself with judicial and political questions, it has also paid much attention to community values in epidictic rhetoric from the time of Gorgias (483 - 376 B.C.). Isocrates sees rhetoric as the foundation of human society, the means through which man expresses his wisdom and without which wisdom is inarticulate and inert. To Isocrates, rhetoric is the power by which we direct public affairs, by which we influence others in the course of our daily lives, and by which we reach decisions about our own moral conduct.[1] However, rhetoric has always had the social responsibility of guiding the audience in making the right decisions. After all, it became necessary only after there was a society and people to persuade.

Much as it brings about social cohesion, rhetoric has the power to cause disintegration and can have serious consequences when dismembered, with dialectics seeking to persuade alone and verbal dexterity performing the suasory function on its own. Rhetoric, according to Aristotle, uses *logos*, *ethos*, and *pathos* to persuade. The rhetor uses a combination of dialectically analyzed *logos* of the subject of persuasion arrived at through induction or deduction and appeals to both the ethical and the pathetical dimensions of the suasory situation in order to make the audience believe in the thesis presented to it. Hence Aristotle sees rhetoric as a counterpart of dialectics and recognizes that neither rhetoric nor dialectic can perform effectively in a suasory endeavor without the other.[2] Cicero stresses the need for rhetoric to go hand in hand with dialetics.[3] In the same vein, Quintilian defines an orator as "a good man skilled in speaking."[4] Richard Weaver, taking his cue from Aristotle, asserts that dialectic and rhetoric are distinguishable stages of argumentation, with dialectic defining the subject and rhetoric actualizing the possibilities raised by dialectical reasoning.[5] According to him, rhetoric is "truth plus its artful presentation."[6] He thus demonstrates in "The Cultural Role of Rhetoric" the fate of a rhetorician who has just dialectical skill but does not have power of speech to persuade.[7] In Weaver's "Language is Sermonic" and *Ideas Have Consequences* as well as in the works of such other eminent commentators on language as Michel Foucault (*The Order of Discourse*), Kenneth Burke (*A Grammar of Motives*), Ivor A. Richards (*The Philosophy of Rhetoric*), and Mikhail Bakhtin ("The Problem of Speech Genres"), language is never neutral and can, therefore, be manipulated to change the auditor's view. The rhetor, as a result, in Weaver's view, has the responsibility of discerning matters in their proper perspectives and of conveying the matters thus discerned in order to guide the audience in making the right choice.[8]

Chinua Achebe has demonstrated, through *Arrow of God*, the power of rhetoric in forging and influencing a society's choices. He has demonstrated the calamity that could overtake a society that does not have a rhetorician to guide it in its time of political need. Such a time is exemplified in the novel as the time that society is in imminent danger of cultural genocide unleashed by the agents of Western imperialism who have just settled in the indigenous society. The key people in the drama of *Arrow of God* are Ezeulu, the chief priest of Umuaro; Nwaka, Ezeulu's arch enemy; Captain Winterbottom, the British administrator in charge of affairs in the colonized society of Umuaro and its environs; Mr. Goodcountry, the representative of the Christian faith in Umuaro; and Moses Unachukwu, an Umuaro convert who constantly challenges Mr. Goodcountry's authority in matters concerning Umuaro customs.

Arrow of God demonstrates the ineffectiveness of logic devoid of rhetoric as a means of persuasion in social matters and the inability of rhetoric divorced from dialectic to lead a society to success when it is confronted by contingent matters that require the rhetor's masterly steering of the populace toward the right decisions. At each point in the novel, the reader sees that the protagonist, Ezeulu, is a wise man who knows how things ought to be in his society, is astute and fore-sighted enough to discern the impact which the invading culture is going to have, and tries to prepare himself and the society for it. However, in spite of his dialectical discovery of the truth, Ezeulu still fails to persuade his audience because he fails to evoke the proper *pathos* and because he lacks the appropriate *ethos.* Actually, at some point, he compromises his *ethos* so seriously that he loses his credibility. Although he clearly knows what the hierarchical order of values and the "ultimate term" for Umuaro have been before the white man comes and changes things, he fails to realize that the order of things and values has shifted.

Ezeulu's traditional prayer after the sighting of the new moon leaves the reader in no doubt as to what the hierarchy has been in Umuaro (6; ch. 1. All quotes in this chapter are from the 1989 Doubleday edition of *Arrow of God*). He constantly appeals to his audience never to lose sight of the order of things and values as he has shown them in this prayer. He is a good man, but he lacks the ability to speak well, a serious deficiency in an oral society in which oratorical skill is valorized. He goes mad because he cannot fathom why truth, which is supposed to prevail all the time, never does.

The premium Ezeulu puts on "hierarchical order" explains Ezeulu's disturbance during his prayer on account of the rift that has occurred in Umuaro. He does not know how to relate to the emerging new Umuaro that could not understand his torment. As Ezeulu expresses his dilemma, he is mandated, as the chief priest of Ulu, to tell the truth at all cost and to give accurate rendition of events as he heard them from his father, but his society, or a segment of it, expects him to compromise on the truth. Inability to joggle the mandates of his office and the expectations of his society, consequently, causes Ezeulu to lose the community that he is supposed to lead against the incursion from the West.

Ezeulu's oratorical failure is a good example of the Socratic rhetoric in Plato's "Apology," which illustrates the dilemma a philosopher faces who does not deign to use the ingredient of oratory to speak to fellow citizens.[9] His constant inability to achieve a level of "consubstantiality" ultimately leading to "identification"[10] with his audience can be discerned in his confrontations with all aspects of the speech situations in which he finds himself, especially in his confrontations with Nwaka who, although he possesses the power of speech, verbal dexterity, and the credibility to strike a chord in the audience, does not have the discerning ability to examine issues dialectically. Nwaka's ability to persuade the audience, on the other hand, is devoid of prudence and causes the clan to fail in every choice he persuades it to make. In the end, the church representative, Mr. Goodcountry, who has both the power of dialectics and the art to convey matters persuasively, wins, thus throwing the village into confusion, a state of panic succinctly expressed in one of the people's proverbs: "If the rat cannot flee fast enough, let him make way for the tortoise" (229; ch.19).

The unsuccessful struggle both Ezeulu and Winterbottom embarked on to preserve the soul of Umuaro is a classic example of the havoc rhetorical ineptitude can cause in a political situation. The profile of Winterbottom matches that of Ezeulu. Both are glorified heads of their communities, who have no real power. They are both chosen by a group of uneasy superiors. Although both are leaders interested in preserving their communities, they are ambitious and, inwardly, want to preserve their communities in their own ways, not as dictated by their superiors.

Both lack the tool for carrying through their designs for their communities. They lack rhetoric. They are able to discover the issues at stake through dialectics, but they lack the ability to choose the "persuasibles" from the "probables" in order to effectively make their audiences accept their thesis.

Ezeulu's struggle with his inner self runs through the novel. His counsel on the Okperi and Umuaro land dispute shows him as a man who has foreseen that the white man has come to stay; therefore, the people of Umuaro should be prepared to accommodate him. He has already set an example by sending his son to school to be his "eye there" (40; ch. 4). But Ezeulu lacks one crucial thing: the power to discern the pulse of the new Umuaro and the pulse of the Western values that are threatening to eclipse Umuaro values. Fuller powers of discernment would have enabled him to employ the proper *pathos* and build the proper *ethos* that would aid his logical reasoning. Thus, he knows but knows only in a vacuum, as he will demonstrate each time he is confronted with an oratorical situation.

The first time the reader meets Ezeulu, he has been searching for the new moon for days, but a cloud has hidden the moon. The cloud is analogous to the new values threatening to eclipse Umuaro values which impede the chief priest's ability to discern matters properly and accurately. The moon, when it comes out, is emaciated like a neglected child. Ezeulu's difficulty here and the emaciated nature of the moon foreshadow the shrinking values of Umuaro caused by the new and invasive values. They also foreshadow the battle Ezeulu would have in the future and the thinness of Ezeulu's argument, which will ensure that he loses all his oratorical battles. Even the moon will be part of his downfall because of his inability to see it in a foreign land (during his imprisonment at Okperi). This circumstance parallels his inability to think clearly in unfamiliar situations, which will lead to his downfall. In Ezeulu, the reader sees a man whose power is limited but who wishes to have and exercise absolute power. This accords with his limited power of speech and his inability to really recognize the change in the will of his people. Eventually, he fails to appeal to the ultimate terms in which his people believe. This inevitably breeds suspicion and leads to the people's desertion of him, their high priest.

Ezeulu's initial engagement in a battle of words takes place when he confronts Edogo, his oldest son, on the issue of carving an *alusi* (carved wooden symbolic representation of the gods). It is a minor incident but one that represents the larger problem facing Ezeulu. He has overheard gossip that his son is carving an *alusi,* and being the chief priest of the town, it is his duty to discourage citizens from indulging in such a dangerous task. Carving an *alusi* is taboo to ordinary citizens and anybody who ignores this prohibition may come to untold harm. Therefore, it is doubly offensive if a member of the chief priest's household indulges in the practice and breaks the law. Before this conversation takes place, the writer shows father and son sitting in Ezeulu's *obi* (the outermost house within the compound designated for entertaining his visitors and carrying out his priestly functions), with the son sitting in the dark and Ezeulu's face lit only by the fire from the sacrifice. Edogo, the son, can see his father's face clearly because the fire from the sacrifice has lit his face, but Ezeulu cannot see Edogo's face because he is sitting in the dark. This is symbolic of most of the issues Ezeulu will confront. The issues are beginning to be hidden from him because of the new order and the new values ousting the values he is elected to guide, and instead of searching these issues out clearly in order to discover the means of persuasion available to him, he confronts them with just the outmoded facts he has at hand.

Perelman and Olbrechts-Tyteca's view that facts and truths are established through a consensus is very important in establishing why Ezeulu is constantly unable to persuade in spite of possessing philosophical truth. According to Perelman and Olbretchs-Tyteca, facts and truth are matters of agreement between the arguer and the audience.[11] The idea of fact and truth plays a crucial part in the whole debate Ezeulu engages in. He constantly fails to see, as Perelman and Olbrechts-Tyteca put it, that a fact is a fact because everybody agrees that it is a fact. When any member of the group or audience doubts the proposition in question, it ceases to be a fact because "[a] fact loses its status as soon as it is no longer used as a possible starting point."[12]

The failed communication between Ezeulu and his son Edogo foreshadows Ezeulu's ineptitude and inability to reach this minor (one-man) audience. In the conversation between Edogo and Ezeulu, the reader is given a glimpse into the nature of speech relationships between parents and children, especially between fathers and sons. As Sunday Aigbe explains while discussing Nigerian socio-political problems, in the Igbo hierarchy the elders/parents come after the gods, the spirits and the ancestors before the young people, and the children follow, with the locus of authority distributed from top to bottom.[13] As Aigbe sees it, "[i]n order to have a harmonious cosmic order, there has to be a mutual communion; understanding, respect, and allegiance move from the bottom up to the top."[14] It follows naturally that there are conversational principles to follow and rules to obey. The son must show deference, and Edogo does so.

When Edogo comes into the *obi* in answer to his father's summons, Ezeulu ignores him for some time and attends to the sacred yam. By this, Ezeulu is showing that the deity comes first, but he is also sending conflicting signals. Ezeulu the father should have told Edogo why he called him, but Ezeulu the priest will attend to the deity first before attending to a human being. He is playing both roles simultaneously at this point. When he opens the conversation, he starts with a question "Did I ever tell you anything about carving a deity" (4; ch. 1)? Edogo does not reply, probably because he is confused as to who is talking to him, the chief priest or his father. Determining who is talking is important because that will determine how he answers. He is able to answer the second question, "Is Edogo not there?" (5; ch.1). He answers his father's question because "I am here" (5) is a safe reply that does not demand a different approach for answering whoever is asking, whether the priest or his father. It is a fact. Ezeulu repeats his question. In Ezeulu's tone, this time, the reader detects a mild admonition—the type of admonition a father gives who expects a son to reply to a question no matter how unpleasant the question may be. Edogo on his own part answers like a child: "You told me to avoid it" (5). Although Ezeulu's next question "What is this story I hear then—that you are carving an *alusi* for a man of Umuagu?" (5) conveys his displeasure, it is also not direct and as such gets a retort "Who told you?" (5).

Because Ezeulu does not ask a direct question, he does not get a direct answer from his son. There is *agon* here when there should have been none. As is to be expected, Nwafor, Ezeulu's innocent, youngest son, cannot make sense out of this dialogue. A non-Igbo reader may not be able to make sense out of it or understand the irritation and anger and frustration that affect Ezeulu and his son in this dialogue. But anyone who understands the father-child relationship and dynamics of conversation between parents and offspring in the Umuaro culture should be able to recognize what has happened. On this occasion, Ezeulu has determined Edogo should not carve an *alusi*, but he lacks the power of speech to convey his message without seeming to antagonize Edogo. He means well, but his message is not well taken. He is operating from a defunct value or a value that has since been adulterated by the coming of the white man. That value demands that Edogo should have answered his father's question directly and not try to match his wits with those of his father. In spite of the fact that the father errs first, Ezeulu expects that Edogo should have realized that Ezeulu is his father and that the custom demands absolute obedience from a son. Here, Edogo serves as a micrcosm of the society that is exposed to a new value and that is struggling to maintain the norms of the old value in spite of the constant assault of the new value on the old one. Later, the reader sees the same issue surfacing between Ezeulu and the society he seeks to lead. He constantly approaches his audience from norms based on a defunct value, a value that has been rendered impotent by the new dispensation.

Another issue at stake in this conversation is the conflicting roles Ezeulu is constantly seen to be playing. Ezeulu is the Chief Priest. As he is speaking to Edogo, he is speaking as both the Chief Priest and as a father who is concerned for the well-being of his son. As a chief priest, Ezeulu would have frowned at anybody carving an *alusi*. However, Ezeulu forgets that the white man has come and "turned things upside down" (41; ch. 4) and that the argument of absolute obedience is fast becoming obsolete given the new culture in town and the church that preaches "leave your yam and come to school" (43). Achebe points to the critical nature of this situation by placing Edogo in the dark, where Ezeulu is unable to see him. Ezeulu is not able to see him because he is not behaving like a true son even though the value system is almost defunct. Later, Ezeulu will demonstrate his inability to see other situations clearly, leading to his inability to choose the appropriate *topoi* for persuasion when faced with the Umuaro society.

One early speech shows off Ezeulu's dialectical skills to advantage. It arises when Obika, another of Ezeulu's sons, takes the law into his own hands. This is more like a forensic occasion and the handling of it demands expertise in forensics. Ezeulu is in his element; he is good at making a clinical evaluation of the issues, and he carries it out so creditably that his in-laws go home happy. In the case at hand, Ezeulu's son-in-law, Ibe, had severely beaten Ezeulu's daughter, Akueke. Obika then went to Ibe's village and not only beat him up but also tied him on his bed and carried him to Ezeulu's village. Obika's action is the height of humiliation both to his brother-in-law and to the brother-in-law's kinsmen. This type of situation, if not mediated properly, can cause a feud between the two families and could even spread to a fight between the two villages. A close examination of this forensic occasion shows how Ezeulu, the dialectician, succeeds when there is fact to deal with as compared with the time to come when there is no fact. First, his in-laws come in feigned humility to find out what has happened to their brother, Ezeulu's son-in-law.

The dynamics of this speech situation are similar to another in the novel where the speech goes awry and leads to a war. Both parties in these situations have to be careful and approach the matter delicately to avoid bloodshed. Both would not wish to be seen as pleading with the other for fear of losing face. But they would not wish to be seen to be disrespectful to each other either, or one side would feel affronted. But both parties know the customs. They play by the rules. In Igbo custom, the person who goes to take a wife from another family is in a subordinate position and must show deference to the in-laws even though he may not mean it and only pretends to be deferential. In the case of Obika's insulting action, the in-laws need time to allow each side's anger to subside so that nothing would be said that would later be regreted or rescinded. The in-laws, in this case, allow more than three market weeks to elapse before seeking answers. A market week is four days. When they come, they ask to be told what has happened. Although they know what had happened to their kinsman, it is customary for them to want Ezeulu's family to tell them. This is a covert way of conveying their displeasure. Also, it is a forensic occasion in which the case has to be stated so that everybody will be in full knowledge of the facts. Since the case is only being tried before in-laws, instead of narrating the facts in reply to the in-laws' question, Ezeulu treats the question as a rhetorical question. A nonnative or an incompetent person could have started to really answer the question as the court messenger did in *Things Fall Apart*, but instead of retelling the story and running the risk of incensing the in-laws, Ezeulu carefully placates them while not admitting to any serious misdemeanor on his son's part (12; ch.1).

Ezeulu is at home in this kind of rhetorical situation. He knows his source of inartistic proof and uses it to his advantage; he shows Akueke's injuries to his in-laws (12). If the reader remembers that the severe beating of Akueke was the reason for Obika's action against Akueke's husband, then the reader will appreciate Ezeulu's rhetorical move. He does not tell the story. He presents the proof of the story, the bearer of the story, and the evidence of the beating, and adds to the enormity of what the in-laws' eyes are seeing by saying "You should have seen her the day she came home" (12). His words are few, but they speak volumes. The implication of this is that the evidence of the beating is worse than whatever the in-laws are beholding at that time. If the reader remembers that the beating took place more than twelve days before the visit, then the reader, along with the in-laws, realize that the lady must have had a severe beating, must have endured the severest case of spousal abuse.

Ezeulu's next rhetorical move is to make an appeal to the collective ethics of the in-laws: "Is this how you marry women in your place?" (12). This is an effective use of the *ad hominem* tactic. He scores a rhetorical blow with this. The in-laws cannot say "yes." And to exonerate themselves from such an act of brutality, they will blame Ibe. Ezeulu clinches his argument when he says: "If it is your way then I say you will not marry my daughter like that" (12). No one can fault Ezeulu for his inductive reasoning. The forum demands that type of reasoning too. There is evidence in the case before them. His conclusions are cogent and reasonable. His in-laws cannot help but agree with him. So far he is at home. He has exhibited the use of *logos* and *ethos* in his persuasion.

However, Ezeulu's rhetoric stops at this level. He neglects the more social question of the humiliation of his son-in-law. There is no factual evidence to exonerate Obika from that act. Obika's action hinges on values and ethics and, therefore, could only be mitigated in terms of rhetoric evoking not only *logos* and *ethos* but also *pathos*. The in-laws move in on that omission, pointing out the slight in the action meted out to their brother—an action that questions their brother's manhood and the collective manhood of the entire kinsmen (12). Ezeulu should have raised the issue of manhood first when he had the floor. He should have asked why a man with a penis would go beating a woman. If he had, he would have taken the advantage away from his in-laws. But he did not, and he lost the advantage. The reference to penis is a good rhetorical move by the in-laws. It invokes the *pathos* they intend. The in-laws also follow the norm that one cannot deem oneself to be wiser than one's father-in-law. Their reasons for wanting answers is also reasonable. They do not want to be seen as cowards. They will need to explain why they do not do anything to avenge what has been done to their kinsman. A nonnative might take this piece of oratory to depict cowardice, but a wise native sees the danger it portends. It is a delicate situation that calls a man's manhood into question. Mishandling of this can lead to a disaster just as such a mishandling in the Okperi incident does. Hence, Achebe tells the reader that Ezeulu did rise to the occasion: "Ezeulu employed all his skill in speaking to pacify his in-laws. They went home happier than they came" (12).

DIALECTICS, SOPHISTRY, AND PERSUASION

Ezeulu's and Nwaka's oratories, while moving the theme of the novel along, demonstrate the interdependence of dialectics and rhetoric in a successful suasory enterprise. Ezeulu and Nwaka fail woefully as orators in their first speech because they do not fit definition/charaterization of the accomplished orator as is prescribed in Cicero's *De Oratore* and Quintilian's *Institutio Oratoria*. In Cicero's view, not only is eloquent wisdom the desirable ultimate possession for an orator, but also "nothing... has so potent an effect upon human emotions as well-ordered and embellished speech."[15] According to him, the perfect orator must possess "wisdom combined with eloquence." This is because oratory has the power to get "hold of assemblies of men, win their good will, direct their inclinations wherever the speaker wishes, or divert them from whatever he wishes." The duties of the orator, then, are to prove one's case (*probare*), to conciliate oneself with the audience (*conciliare*), and to excite the audience (*movere*).[16] In complete agreement with Cicero, Quintilian also believes that the orator must have a good moral character and that this moral character must be discerned from the speech.[17] Thus to Quintilian the perfect orator is a good man skilled in speaking.[18] Constantly in Achebe's novels, the reader encounters orators who move the plot forward. In such cases the orators are either effective or ineffective because they possess or lack the qualities of the good orator as prescribed by both Cicero and Quintilian. In *Arrow of God*, the orators' skills affect the society's fate tremenduously.

In the major scenes of oratorical combat, those between Ezeulu and Nwaka, Achebe is, in a sense, probing the relationship between dialectics and rhetoric. The struggle *(agon)* between Nwaka and Ezeulu can be likened to that between Mark Antony and Brutus in Shakespeare's *Julius Caesar*,[19] with Ezeulu, like Brutus the wise philosopher, insisting on the truth and hoping that it will be enough to persuade his fellow citizens and Nwaka, like Mark Antony, using his oratorical prowess to incite the people to war. In the deliberation involving the farmland contested by Umuaro and Okperi, Ezeulu has only facts to work with. In employing a dialectical argument he insists on telling what he alone perceives as the truth of the matter, and he thus conforms to the profile of the typical wise man. Ezeulu, inevitably, faces the same dilemma as a philosopher who does not know how to strike a chord in his fellow citizens. Clearly, dialectics alone is inadequate in the type of situation in which Ezeulu finds himself. It cannot move individuals on its own because it is not capable of obtaining commitment to a position or action although it may achieve mere cognition. Ezeulu needs the proper enthymemes that would enable him to enter into solidarity with the audience. According to Weaver, this type of enthymeme enables a rhetorician to enter into solidarity with the audience "by tacitly agreeing with one of its perceptions of reality."[20] Instead, Ezeulu trusts facts but neglects rhetoric. As a seasoned dialectician (as Weaver has demonstrated regarding all such dialecticians), Ezeulu knows, but knows in a vacuum, since he does not take into consideration the actual situation and reality of the speech occasion.[21] Because he aims at logical performance, he fails to consider the effect of his words on his community. His people, as a result, suspect him and accuse him of subversion.

In this first contest between the two, Ezeulu relies on facts he learned from his father. Ezeulu's father had told him that the farm land had been given to Umuaro by the Okperi people. The Okperi people had also given Umuaro their deities and had called them sons of *Udo* and *Ogwugwu*. Ezeulu's *logos* thus hinges on the testimony of his father, who happened to have married an Okperi woman and could, therefore, have been biased. Ezeulu himself was born of an Okperi woman and may easily have forgotten whether it was his father or his mother who had given him his facts. His village is the weakest of the six villages that make up Umuaro. Ulu itself, the god of which he is viceroy, is a dispensable god because the conditions that brought it to Umuaro and made it essential to the people of Umuaro no longer exist. Hence, although he is the chief priest of the highest god, Ezeulu's *ethos* rests on a shaky ground. In the actual speech performance, Ezeulu's delivery is flawed. For one thing, his communication is too brief, as though the mere presentation of bare facts were enough.

Just as in the scene between Edogo and Ezeulu, the ideas of fact and truth play a crucial part in the whole debate between Ezeulu and Nwaka. As usual, Ezeulu fails to consider that a fact is a fact only when everybody agrees that it is a fact. Once any member of the group or the audience doubts the proposition in question, it ceases to be a fact. As I pointed out earlier, Perelman and Olbrechts-Tyteca assert that "[a] fact loses its status as soon as it is no longer used as a possible starting point."[22] Because political deliberation deals with contingent matters, it cannot rely upon concrete facts alone. Its basis is opinion regarding probabilities. Therefore, a speaker needs to have the same understanding of what constitutes fact as the audience. An arguer who insists on facts that are not universally acknowledged runs the risk of alienating his audience. When everyone is not in agreement; moreover, the basis of the people=s morals and beliefs may be destroyed.[23] The issue before Ezeulu is squarely based on the culture and beliefs of the people. In several other instances in *Arrow of God*, Achebe has noted that according to Igbo custom, a father does not lie to his son. To swear by one's father is to claim the truth in Igbo society; "[T]o say *My father told me* is to swear the greatest oath" (93; ch. 9). When he seeks a confirmation of this philosophy from his wise and astute friend, Akuebue, he gets it, as is shown in their conversation (98). However, according to the same Igbo custom, one does not take sides against one's brother with a stranger whose origins one cannot ascertain. The complexity and the conflicting nature of these two philosophies impede Ezeulu's struggle and cause him to strive to stand always in the right, even at the risk of offending the clan. This situation evokes the typical conflict between the wise man and the city in which he lives. To Ezeulu, the refusal of his people to hear the truth, even from a stranger, is "an augury of the world's ruin" (7; ch.1). To the people of Umuaro, Ezeulu's testimony against the clan he has been elected to lead is the height of betrayal. Being a wise man, like Socrates, Ezeulu finds himself in a serious predicament and, as Larry Anhart observes, the predicament of such a person, as wise as Socrates, is that he

cannot fail to see the flaws in the moral standards of his community and in the piety upon which such standards rest. But if he goes too far in questioning the public orthodoxy, he runs the risk not only of arousing moral indignation but also of undermining the public sense of justice upon which any rhetorical defense of his life would depend. The success of Socratic rhetoric requires a prudent restraint upon the continual examination of common opinion that characterizes the Socratic life .[24]

The reason is clear, as Weaver articulates: "the dialectician is only half a wise man and hence less than a philosopher king, inasmuch as he leaves out the urgent reality of the actual, with which all rulers and judges know they have to deal."[25]

Ezeulu's refutation of Nwaka's argument is as ineffective as his opening speech and lacks decorum. His movement to the podium is not graceful; his salute is as brief as that of "an enraged Mask" (18; ch. 2). It has no dignity and does not show concern that the audience at this august, deliberative occasion consists of the dignitaries and grandees of the clan. Moreover, his first proverb is accusatory: "When an adult is in the house the she-goat is not left to suffer the pains of parturition on its tether" (18). Next, his invocation of the ancestors to authenticate and legitimize his saying is not a smart rhetorical strategy and actually weakens his argument, given that the ancestors in their own case had not constituted a homogenous society: Umuaro was formed from six different villages for contingent reasons that seem to have abated. Understandably, therefore, instead of reacting emotionally in his favor, the audience was made to feel threatened by Ezeulu's open confrontation and accusatory speech. For witnesses of the veracity of his claim, Ezeulu invokes Ulu, a god that seems to have outlived its usefulness and that has recently proved impotent in the face of the subversive mission of the white man. He sounds irreverent, especially in his second speech where he accuses the elders of cowardice. One can describe Ezeulu as a good man who does not know how to speak well.

On the other hand, Nwaka manifests the characteristics of the sophists and bases his argument purely on emotions. Philosophers and sophists are similar in some ways as Aristotle has shown in *The Rhetoric*. Both are experts—one in dialectical reasoning, the other in manipulation of speech to affect the populace. Aristotle's comparison of sophists to army generals finds great favor with Anhart who observes that "sophists were known to seek victory in argument above all else and to consider their opponents as enemies against whom they were to practice every sort of deception."[26]

Augumentation based on *pathos* plays tremendous role in Nwaka's success in persuasion. The place of *pathos* in an argument has been a seriuos pre-occupation of such rhetorical theorist as Douglas Walton. The fallacies *argumentum ad baculum, argumentum ad hominem, argumentum ad populum, argumentum ad misericordiam*, which Walton defines as the use of techniques that go against the legitimate goals of argument[27] are very useful in explaining the techniques Nwaka employs so successfully although to the detriment of the people's struggle. Although this misuse of technique, which could be intentional or unintentional, is not the best tool for effective persuasion, Walton insists that it has a place in informal argumentation when employed appropriately. Such an appeal to the emotion as *argumentum ad populum* is actually important in dialogic argumentation, especially in ethical and political deliberations where consideration of personal loyalties and commitment is part of a decision process, or in a situation where possession of all the facts does not influence the conclusion reached.

Furthermore, in a legal, political, or ethical discussion where the character or personal morality of the participants is the subject at hand, Walton believes that appeal to emotion may be a relevant and important part of the argument in order to achieve conviction and effective refutation of an allegation. Here the *ethos* of participants might be highly questionable, and the orators will use all in their power to establish their *ethos*. In treating the *ad hominem* fallacy, Walton shows how a personal attack against an opponent, in order to expose error and weakness in an opposing argument, can be relevant and important. In using a personal attack, the arguer is putting the opponent's *ethos* in question. *Ad hominem* can also be beneficial in evaluating the source of information, especially when it is difficult to get at the facts. It is actually necessary in legal situations. The reader sees Nwaka's effective use of *ad hominem* tactics in *Arrow of God*. If the decision to be reached in an argument requires a choice based on good moral character, the arguer may wish to show the general bad moral character of the opponent, especially in a political campaign.[28] Nwaka uses *ad hominem* fallacy to persuade the people to question Ezeulu's morals and motives.

Nwaka wins the first round of oratory against Ezeulu because he makes *ad populum* appeal the bedrock of his argument. Since *ad populum* is used to persuade a specific audience, as Walton tells us,[29] Nwaka makes the right choice in appealing to his audience, the people of Umuaro. In all *ad populum* appeals, what matters is that the audience accepts the speaker's premises enthusiastically, while concern for truth may be relegated to the background. In other words, the rhetor foregrounds the aspect of the matters under discussion that the audience will like to hear, while ignoring the truth in the situation at hand. In spite of this base trick, the *ad populum* appeal is not always a faulty appeal. It can be used legitimately. If one is arguing and using the premise the audience has already accepted, one does not need incontrovertible truth. As Walton notes, one can use presumptions, even conjectures, that cannot be established as fact.[30] That is precisely what Nwaka has done in weaving his argument around the premises his audience finds attractive, even though he has no hard facts to support his claims. He knows that Ezeulu has none either; therefore, both their arguments will be judged on the power of their oratory and the level of their popularity. Prosperous himself, Nwaka descends from a line of properous ancestors. He is one of the three men in Umuaro to have taken the highest title in Umuaro.[31] Nwaka has a strong standing in his community, and it would take a good orator to make a dent in his argument. The reader is told, "Nwaka carried the day" (15; ch .2).

The delivery of the speech is superb. In spite of his solid background, Nwaka does not take his audience for granted.   Achebe's detailed description of the speech delivery exposes the importance Achebe accords to the fact that Nwaka carries the day.   Nwaka's entrance and his communication are apt. He roars like a lion and does not just salute his audience. After his dramatic opening, he speaks "softly in the silence he has created with his salutation" (16). This is a classic move to condition the people's psyche and elicit their rapt attention and emotional support. As a seasoned orator, "owner of words" (144; ch. 13), he has all the gestures designed to win over the already divided audience. Achebe describes him as marching "forward and back as he spoke, the eagle feather in his red cap and bronze band on his ankle marked him out as one of the lords of the land—a man favoured by *Eru* the god of riches" (16; ch. 2). The picture created in the mind of the audience in the novel and the mind of the reader is that of a worthy man, if not a good man. Nwaka knows that his *ethos,* accentuated by his social-economic standing, is higher than Ezeulu's, and he capitalizes on it to his advantage. He has built his *ethos* on his personal wealth and, knowing that his audience respects success and wealth, he plays his good fortune to great effect. Marching forward and back calls attention to his regalia and to his person.

Nwaka's *exordium* is perfect. He starts with an apt proverb on which the thrust of his argument hinges: "Wisdom is like a goatskin bag; every man carries his own" (16).   This implies that one's character is indicated by one's mien, the way one carries one's goatskin bag. One can carry one's goatskin bag straight or askew, depending on one's disposition. By the same token, one can be myopic or clear-sighted in "carrying" one's wisdom. This is a clear argument from analogy, next to the highest in the hierarchy of places from which an arguer can choose *topoi.* Nobody will challenge this reasoning without seeming unreasonable. In using this analogy, Nwaka does not seek to destroy the people's belief in the veracity of one's father. But no one would maintain that a father cannot be mistaken. Hence, Nwaka's attack is directed at the very source of the knowledge which Ezeulu is claiming. By the logic of Nwaka's proverb, Ezeulu's father could have been wrong. His knowledge of the land could have been faulty. In which case, he could have unintentionally passed on faulty knowledge to his son, Ezeulu. After all, "[w]e all know that the lore of the land is beyond the knowledge of many fathers" (16). By using the collective and inclusive "we," Nwaka includes the audience in the select group of people who possess the knowledge that the lores of the land are beyond many fathers. Nwaka also attacks Ezeulu's strongest source of *ethos*, that of his position as representative of Ulu, the foremost deity in Umuaro. The matter of the land contested by Umuaro and Okperi predates Ulu, whose history is shorter than the history of the six villages. Therefore, Ezeulu is not competent to talk about "events which are older than Umuaro itself." Nwaka rightly asserts that the issue is beyond the knowledge of all in the arena since it dates back to a time before Umuaro itself was formed.

While parading his wealth, Nwaka proceeds to counter what Ezeulu's father had told Ezeulu, declaring, "My father told me a different story" (16). Since he has not destroyed the norm that upholds the legitimacy and credibility of fathers, Nwaka can still legitimately quote his father without inviting a *tu quoque* response. His refutation offers no other evidence, but it evokes the proper *pathos*. It does not establish a fact that Okperi did not give Umuaro people the land in question. Instead he touches on the audience's sentiment toward the white man by arguing that Okperi would not have dared ask for the land had the white man not settled in Okperi. Nwaka's argument shows that he is in tune with the pulse of his warrior town. By this argument, Nwaka makes a collective appeal against the things the new invader, the white man, has done to the old order of things. By assigning Okperi to the camp of the enemy, Nwaka has made Okperi a double enemy, insinuating that anyone who takes sides with Okperi is in collusion with the white man and assists in turning Umuaro "upside down." He, like Ezeulu, accuses his warrior clan of cowardice. However, unlike Ezeulu, Nwaka is subtle in making his accusation. He includes himself among the cowards by using the word "us." By so doing, he gives his audience room to react emotionally in his favor. He further rubs in his argument by suggesting that although members of the audience would not be the first known cowards, they should, at least, be able to admit their real reason for not going to war. Nwaka thus uses insinuation effectively in this argument by assigning the motives for the people's lukewarm attitude towards war with Okperi.

In the last segment of his speech, Nwaka uses both insinuation and consequence tactics to his advantage by predicting posterity's reaction to the decision. As a consequence of their action, they will eventually have to explain to their children why they left the disputed piece of land to Okperi.

By the reference to intermarriages in this speech, Nwaka has given the final and fatal blow to Ezeulu's inadequately presented truth. He suggests that because Ezeulu's mother is from Okperi, he may have reason to twist history and to counsel against war. With this one argument also, Nwaka has alienated Ezeulu from other worthy men in the gathering whose mothers or wives also come from Okperi. They will not want to side with Ezeulu lest they also be classified with the sentimental cowards who have lost the appetite for war. As Achebe tells the reader that audience responds with a long uproar of approbation, signifying Nwaka's success in destroying Ezeulu's speech (16).

The repetition of "let us" in Nwaka's speech is also effective, attributing blame to the collectivity which includes the speaker. According to Cicero, "the reiteration of the same word makes a deep impression upon the hearer and inflicts a major wound upon the opposition—as if a knife should repeatedly pierce the same part of the body."[32] Using the consequence tactic is also suitable to pragmatic thinkers' way of persuasion. It is the method adopted nowadays by journalists and politicians who want to present reality as threatening. Nwaka's "Let us" appeal is a good sensational closing, which successfully plays on the fears of the audience, especially since the audience believes that fathers must tell their children the truth. He thus exaggerates the consequence, the awful nature of the job of explaining to one's child that one had been a coward and had neglected to safeguard the child's birthright. In this particular situation, Nwaka exploits the people's fear of cowardice, thus showing his awareness of the discrepancy between men's private desires and their public morals. Nwaka shows that he knows "the souls" he has set out to persuade.

Ezeulu's second oratory fails as well because his second speech is as devoid of sensitivity to his audience as his first speech. In the second speech, he exhibits *pathos* and *logos* but lacks *ethos*. His actions before the second speech takes place have depicted him as one who does not have the goodwill of the clan in mind, his *ethos* having been seriously compromised by his actions. He has sent his son to join the white man, an action that is logical even though not expedient. He wants to learn the secret of the white man's success and use it to continue to lead the clan. However, he is too proud to take his clan into confidence. His son, as a result of this exposure to the white man's values, has violated the python which is sacred to the Idemili deity. In seeking to expiate this violation, Ezeulu chooses to carry out a private propitiation even though it would have been prudent to carry out a public one. That would have assured the villagers that he revered their deity. He reasons that his son's offense is private, therefore, should be dealt with privately (61; ch. 6). Thus he makes his space private in a society that views space as a communal property. He views his society's yearning to share his space as an intrusion, a negativity of his individuality, and a constriction rather than the enabler such an intrusion should be within its parameter. Copresence of others within that parameter should have enabled him to flower, to lead the others successfully against the West. Consequently, instead of showing that he is also suffering, like the people, from the calamity which the Westerners have wreaked on their culture, Ezeulu conceals his anguish from the people. Instead he riles at what he considers as an intrusion into his space because of his highly inflated but deluded ego which induces him to set himself above the society that elected him. His actions are, therefore, understandably construed as insensitivity and lack of respect for the society's deity. Like Socrates, he reveres his people's god but refuses to show his people that he does. Therefore, like Socrates, he is not seen to be one with the people; he is considered subversive.

Ezeulu also allows his contempt for Nwaka to becloud his reason as is seen clearly from his stand during his conversation with his best friend, Akubue, where Ezeulu reveals his awareness of the division and confusion his action has caused among the people and the political maneuvers in Nwaka's camp. However, political ineptitude leads him to exhibit nonchalance and arrogance of the man who believes in the rightousness of his cause. At Akubue's suggestion that jealousy motivates Nwaka, Ezeulu shows his indifference to Nwaka's tricks in these hubristic words: "The fly that perches on a mound of dung may strut around as it likes, it cannot move the mound" (130; ch.12). Ezeulu fails to realize that in matters of values and culture, right and wrong do not always play a great part and that no one man, however great, could win judgment against a clan. What matters is to be seen to be with the group, to be in tune with the larger body, the clan. But

Ezeulu's attitude is expressed nonchalantly and hubristically thus: "I have passed the stage of dancing to receive presents" (132), while reminding Akuebue of the progressiveness of the former Ezeulus. He sounds like Caesar when Caesar was being persuaded not to go to the Capitol. Ezeulu's utterance here is like Caesar's utterance: "The things that threaten me never looked but on my back. When they shall see the face of Caesar, they will vanish."[33]   Akubue, his friend, is forced to remind him that times have changed and that his action can not be compared to the action his father took since his father's action was not viewed by the society as an action taken to please a stranger.   Ezeulu's actions and attitude all work against Ezeulu and, therefore, against the clan at the most critical time of the clan's political life, the time their chief priest, Ezeulu, needs their intervention and support as he prepares to go to answer what the people all see as a threatening summons from a white man.

An analysis of Ezeulu's second speech divulges how in spite of adequate *pathos* and *logos*, an orator is still not able to persuade if one element, *ethos,* is lacking from his speech. In this second oration, Ezeulu is speaking to the clan on the issue of Captain Winterbottom's call. He includes in his speech everything one should do to persuade. His *exordium* and his phatic communication are appropriate. He maintains proper decorum, makes proper apologies, shows respect to the elders, and uses well-chosen and apt proverbs. He also concedes strength to the clan by another proverb which asked them to join him in deliberating on the matter (142; ch. 13). By inviting Umuaro to deliberate on the matter, he has shown that he respects the people and their trust in the elders. His snake and python proverb shows his awareness of the strength of the many as against the strength of one person. The clan as a whole would discern how to handle the matter better than he, one person. But the question is, isn't there a discrepancy between Ezeulu's prior actions and his words? His actions have shown him to believe he knows more than the clan and even more than the god he serves. Ezeulu's oratory is doomed even before he delivers it and Nwaka demonstrates this when he speaks. Nwaka repeatedly interrupts him, showing the contempt Nwaka feels for him and his speech. It also shows that Nwaka considers the summons a waste of the elders' time.   The audience's reaction to his speech reveals their general confusion as none gives a reply to his speech; instead, people talk among themselves (143). Ezeulu is unable to totally persuade because he has not identified fully with the audience.

Kenneth Burke's concepts of "identification" and "consubstantiation" aid in understanding the dynamics of the interplay of orators and audience in this situation. His idea of "identification" includes the unconscious factor in appeal. "Appeal," according to Burke, "is the essence of communication."[34] A rhetor has to achieve identification through consubstantiation in order to persuade an audience. Burke sees persuasion as identification of the orator and the audience instead of just persuasion of the audience by the orator. When the orator and the audience share the same values and interests, they establish consubstantiality.

Persuasion is necessary because the orator is dissociated from the audience by the fact that the orator believes to the contrary on an issue. The orator's purpose is to identify with the audience in order to move the audience to accept the orator's view.[35] The rhetor can use the structure or the style of the discourse to achieve consubstantiation because the structure can depict the rhetor's adjustment to fit the audience, and the style can also be the rhetor's conscious or unconscious effort to make the level of the discourse fit the level of the audience.[36] Ezeulu has used the appropriate style but he lacks the appropriate *ethos* which would have identified him with his audience and which would have allowed him to achieve consubstantiation.

Nwaka proceeds to destroy Ezeulu's speech. First, he concedes a little to Ezeulu. Ezeulu's speech is "good words," and he thanks Ezeulu for them. He asks for the approval of Umuaro for this observation and gets it when someone tells him "Speak on" (143). He also accepts Ezeulu's apology for not placing a pot of palm wine before the elders. That is immaterial. He also recognizes the respect and the high regard which Ezeulu has accorded the elders by seeking their opinion in the matter at hand. Nwaka thus exhibits goodwill towards the speaker in these trivial matters. Then he makes his oratorical thrust, feigning to be seeking clarity from Ezeulu, he makes it clear that Ezeulu has no case. Ezeulu has no reason to be afraid to answer a call from the white man whom the villagers have come to believe is Ezeulu's friend and whom Ezeulu seems to have chosen to please over his people (144).

Nwaka's argument is that Ezeulu has befriended the white man; therefore, Ezeulu should face the consequences of such friendship since "as soon as we shake hands with a leper he will want an embrace" (144). Nwaka's well-chosen pun on the people's concept of the white body which is equivalent to leprosy elicits the desired effect. There is laughter at Ezeulu's expense and Nwaka is given the praise name *"owner of words"* (144). His next statement totally destroys Ezeulu's argument for staying put in Umuaro because of his duties as the chief priest of Ulu (144-145). In his argument, Nwaka not only reminds the clan that Ezeulu has lost the status of immunity in being forced to leave the clan since Ezeulu had left the clan for Okperi of his own volition in an earlier occasion. He also reminds the people that the consequence of Ezeulu leaving Umuaro for Okperi on that occasion to testify was that Umuaro lost its land to Okperi on the strength of Ezeulu's testimony. There is no doubt that Nwaka is the "owner of words" as he has been called. But does that make him a good rhetorician? Has he spoken for the good of the clan? Is he a good man speaking well?

An examination of the issues confronting the clan shows that Nwaka has only spoken out of self-interest. Ezeulu had gone to Okperi before but not then under imminent threat or in danger of the unknown. Nwafo, a mere boy, knows that Ezeulu cannot sleep overnight away from Umuaro and observe the sky so that he can announce the coming of every new moon. The coming of the new moon is of the utmost importance to the economic life of the clan. By thus abandoning Ezeulu to face the white man alone, Nwaka has also thrown the fate of the clan to the white man. It is interesting to note that the same Nwaka, who faults Ezeulu for siding with the white man, also sends his son to school after the clan has disintegrated. Hence the reader is left to conclude that Nwaka's concern is based on self-interest and not on his concern for the good of the clan. The people as a whole recognize, too late, the truth and wisdom of Ezeulu's action after they had seen the effect of communicating with the white man in his own language (215; ch. 18).

The second set of people struggling to steer the affairs of the Umuaro society comprises Captain Winterbottom and the colonial administration. Their arguments also lack the ingredients of successful oratory. Winterbottom, the man directly in charge of the region, is also not an orator, and his ineptitude causes him to lose the society he is overseeing and even to send it to its ruin. Like Ezeulu, Winterbottom is a man immersed in dialectic. He too uses Socratic rhetoric although he means well as a politician. He has practical reasoning. His flaw is his inability to persuade his audience. This flaw also contributes to the disintegration of the society that he believes he is trying to protect and the indigenous culture that he is, in his opinion, trying to preserve. Achebe artistically shows Winterbottom's handicap through his name, his relationship with his peers and his superiors, and even his relationship with the native environment and the natives themselves.

The name Winterbottom is a metaphor for the man's character and his ineffectiveness. Winter is a cold period of the year in the Western temperate world, which has, in effect, intruded into the tropical climate of Africa. It evokes the picture of the lethargic state into which everything and everybody goes during this season. Bottom, that part of the body used for sitting down, houses the anus through which feces come out of the body. Bottom also has the connotation of stark stupidity in the Igbo language. If an Igbo person says to someone, "*I bu ike*," meaning you are bottom, that person means that the other is stupid, has no clue to anything at all. Mr Winterbottom's initials also bring out a serious statement. "T.K." has the connotation of someone who thinks he knows when in fact he does not. Hence "I. T. K." in pidgin English means "I too know." You earn this name when you behave as if you know it all when in fact you are ignorant. Therefore, to be the captain of "I.T.K.s" is the ultimate in delusion, arrogance, presumption, and ultimate ignorance. Hence, the description of Okperi, which Achebe gives at the beginning of Chapter Three when he introduces Captain T. K. Winterbottom, is that of a place seen through the eyes of an ignorant white man. Only a white man will see the coming of the first rain in the terms Achebe describes it. The native does not notice the ending of the dry season in such negative images as are contained in Winterbottom's perception (29; ch. 3). To the native, the arrival of the first rain is a welcome blessing which, in archetypal terms, insures solace, fertility, fecundity, fruitfulness, and life, not unbearable heat, burnt-out grass, brownish leaves, and furnace-like atmosphere as Winterbottom depicts.

Winterbottom sees himself as a hardened "coaster." This means that he is not an "unwary European" (29) anymore. In other words, he believes that he is acclimatized to the place and knows the people and their ways. But he is shown not to know. He is still adversely affected by the weather and the cultural practices in this country, which remain inscrutable to him. He merely knows the superficial, the factual, and, therefore, the inconsequential. He is yet to obtain knowledge of what Weaver calls the "metaphysical dream of the world," which is "an intuitive feeling about the immanent nature of reality," the level of philosophical opinion "the sanction to which both ideas and beliefs are ultimately referred for verification." [37] It is only when he attains that level of knowledge that he can rightly claim a knowledge of the people: he knows he has to take hot baths, not cold, no matter how hot he feels; he knows to imprison himself in a mosquito net. However, the drums disturb him at night. When his reactions to the drumbeats are compared to the reactions of the natives to the same drumbeat, the reader is exposed to the different effects the same stimuli can have on different people, depending on their levels of knowledge of the stimuli. To Winterbottom, the drumbeats cannot be for entertainment or for any other worthwhile reason. They have to be for an "unspeakable rite." They cannot be the heartbeat of the people or that of the African darkness (30). Hence Winterbottom does not see fit to search his own inner self for his reaction to the African drums. When he finally seeks the answers to the constant beating of the drum in his brain, he becomes terrified and fears that he is going crazy (30).

Winterbottom has a shaky *ethos* for his claim to knowledge of Nigeria. Although he has been in the country for fifteen years, that is hardly time enough for an outsider to really know a people. The climate and the food no longer depress him as they did fifteen years earlier, but "the climate still makes him irritable and limp" (30). He is also unable to relate to the people beyond the surface level, especially as master and servant, since he does not even allow the other Europeans under his care to relate. His expatriate training and his exposure to such literature about Africa as Joseph Conrad's *Heart of Darkness* have taught him that the natives are inhuman and have robbed him of the power to really know the people he is ruling, had he wanted to do so. If a relationship is allowed between the expatriates and the natives, it makes it possible to think that the natives are human, and, therefore, it goes against the white man's conception of the natives' alterity which has been ascribed to the creation of the black man and has created negative stereotypes of the black man. The white man's division of the human race consigns the black man to the lowest rung of the ladder of the evolutionary scheme. The proscription of contact and intimacy between his charges and the natives is one way of keeping the natives in their place; however, it has also robbed Winterbottom of that knowledge of the natives that he needs to function at the third level of knowledge of a people, the philosophical level. Hence his power of discernment of these people is deficient, and any persuasive endeavor carried out with this knowledge as the bedrock is bound to fail. In other words, Winterbottom, a European colonizer, lies to himself when he presumes to know the natives because he lacks the power to know. It is the repudiation of the colonizer's lie, this justification of imperialism which becomes the counterdiscursive and the political imperative of Achebe's project in such novels as *Arrow of God* and *Things Fall Apart*.[38]

To further buttress the ridiculousness of the white man in presuming to know the African and his environment totally, Achebe brings in the unpredictable nature of such a small thing as the coming of the first rain. First, it is late coming. Second it is disconcerting when it does come. Winterbottom, despite his claim to knowledge of Igboland in Nigeria, is so unprepared for this disconcerting and erratic change in the weather and the people that he does what he would not ordinarily have done: He exposes his eyes to the elements and envies the joy the native children derive from the first rainfall (31).

Winterbottom's inadequacy is not limited to his lack of real knowledge of the country that he believes he is striving very hard to protect from his superiors; he also lacks real knowledge of his own government's policy and politics. He believes strongly in the colonizing mission, but even though it is peacetime and other war veterans have discarded their titles, he still clutches at the title of "Captain." This action makes him an object of ridicule among his peers and reduces the merit of his argument for the preservation of the native culture. But he is the king's representative at the outpost. He rules on the facts that govern the setting for the representative. He takes the salute, and he lectures on the proper decorum. He knows how to act like the school prefect he is at the outpost. He bans anybody who refuses to abide by British decorum from coming to the club. He guards the club etiquette. He has a good knowledge of his duty as dictated by 'THE CALL" (33). However, he fails to see "THE CALL" as the embodiment of British rhetoric to justify its presence on another's soil.

A close examination of "THE CALL" and Winterbottom's perception of what it entails is enlightening in analyzing why Winterbottom fails to be effective. "THE CALL" practically tells the expatriate not to expect a life of hardship because, according to the writer, Nigerian earth is said to have "a deadly fertility" and the people are said to live under unsanitary conditions. Hence, "THE CALL" emphasizes the strenuous life of the expatriate and urges the expatriate to expect to deal with men as "others deal with material," to have the ability to "grasp great situations, coax events, shape destinies, and ride on the crest of the wave of time." The expatriate is a "law-maker, organizer, and engineer of the world." "THE CALL" is like a courage trumpet blown for the benefit of the soldier going to war. The writer imbues in the expatriate a sense of one undertaking a noble job. By listing other noblemen in history and the feats they performed and the fact that the British race had fought valiantly in the past, he is telling the expatriates that they are expected to perform the same valiant feats. One may ask how this call would affect a man like Winterbottom. Achebe shows that Winterbottom takes up the call literally. He sees it as a sacred call and almost dies in answering it. More especially, it has clouded his knowledge of both his people's mission and the knowledge of the native's worldview.

A comparison of Clark's reaction to "THE CALL" and Winterbottom's reaction yields valuable insight. Clark, the newly arrived (who was not part of the heyday of "THE CALL"), is therefore only remotely affected by its message. He finds Allen's ideas in "THE CALL" too dogmatic, even smug. Clark's opinion is that Allen denigrates the native culture totally.   Like the seasoned coaster he claims to be, Winterbottom's reaction to this adverse but true criticism of "THE CALL" is to call Clark a "progressive" in a derogatory manner. Winterbottom, having answered "THE CALL," believes that there is no humanity in the natives and does see them as "materials." This can be discerned in his remarks about his house boy whom he finds handsome but raw. He uses the Western standard to judge the "rawness" of the native. Yet in the same breath, he admits that the natives "understand seasons" (35).   Also, his inability to allow for the humanity of the natives is evident in his views concerning relationships between the natives and the expatriates. His attitude is a capsulization of the whole salience of the logic of imperialism, which exhibits "imperial arrogance," "bluff paternalism," "chauvinistic altruism,"[39] supported by superiority complex, which binarizes and inferiorizes all others and which made Europe consider it its manifest burden to take "civilization" to the benighted peoples of Africa and the world. However, the bearers of this burden, such expatriates as Winterbottom, are constrained, at all costs, to avoid contamination with the inferior "other," the natives. Otherwise, this other, who "occupies prehistoric chronotope" and who therefore shares no "coevalness"[40] with the agents of light (the expatriates), would get a poor opinion of them. Hence, any expatriate who recognizes the humanity of the natives by such actions as sleeping with them is not showing the proper decorum and must be ostracized from the club.   Yet even as Winterbottom remains in this state of detachment from, and avoids all intimacy with, the natives, he purports to be in a position to study, to understand, to know, and to control the natives, on behalf of whose culture he could actually convince his superiors to tread softly. In the same breath, Winterbottom would rather the British stamp out the native culture, even their humanity, just as the French did (35-36).   The approach Winterbottom prefers does not indicate a person who sees anything good in the Africa he claims to care about. Hence he smarts from being made to implement policies that he despises.

Winterbottom is also the epitome of logic in the face of the British administration's sophistry. Therefore, he, like Ezeulu, fails to protect the natives and fails to persuade his superiors. In fact, like Ezeulu, he is suspected of subversion.   The issue on which he wants to persuade his superiors is the appointment of paramount chiefs among the societies in *Arrow of God*. He disagrees with his superiors on very cogent grounds: the people's culture has no place for chiefs. He has tried to choose a chief, but the chief has turned out to be corrupt.   Instead of convincing his superiors, Winterbottom is suspected of stonewalling. His argument against the imposition of "indirect Rule" is cogent, but he lacks the skill and the *ethos* to convey his objection to it. When Watkins, his superior who is actually promoted over him, wrote a memorandum to him on his stonewalling, Winterbottom's response to it is akin to Ezeulu's response to his people. Like Ezeulu, he nonchalantly and arrogantly dismisses the concern of the people he is representing, the British government (55-56; ch. 5). Hence, he is too busy doing his work to try to adhere to the rules from headquarters. He holds his superiors and his government's policy in contempt just as Ezeulu holds his people in contempt because of their inability to face the truth.

Winterbottom's reaction to the British government's argument exposes his love for facts. To him, there are no facts in the government's claim because the Lieutenant-Governor has never "rescued a man buried alive up to his neck, with a piece of roast yam on his head to attract vultures" (57). Winterbottom has this fact and others to prove that indirect rule will be a disaster, but he has no hierarchical power to give him the clout he needs to support his view. He is almost at the bottom of the bureaucratic ladder, and he has also been seen as subversive because of his refusal to operate within the system. He does not have the rhetorical power to imbue his experience as a seasoned coaster with life and make it vivid in language full of *energeia* and *enargeia*.   As he has predicted, his attempt to impose chieftaincy on Ezeulu goes awry and destroys the native mind and atmosphere the government has intended to preserve. As a result of Winterbottom's actions, Ezeulu goes mad, and Umuaro society abandons its god and joins the Christians. Thus, Winterbottom, like Ezeulu, knows but knows in a vacuum. Like Ezeulu, he also accuses his people of cowardice. He knows that his superiors are mistaken in the course of action on which they are embarking, but his *ethos* has already been destroyed because he has alienated himself from the fold. Thus he withdraws from opposing "indirect rule" at the most critical period of the political life of Umuaro.

The British government in *Arrow of God*, does not succeed in its efforts to steer the affairs of the people because of its flawed rhetoric, flawed at least to the indigenes. The government's argument for their presence in Africa is aimed at the Western world. Hence it does not persuade the African of the good intentions of the British. This argument is embodied in the Lieutenant-Governor's memo to Winterbottom (55-56). The government wants an effective system of "indirect rule" based on native institutions. This proposal is laudable. Every right-thinking person would want an effective rule. The outside world would subscribe to effective rule. The natives are supposed to feel grateful. But what is not clear is the specifics of this effectiveness and the yardstick for measuring this effectiveness. It is not clear whose standards are to be used in measuring "effectiveness." The argument also assumes that what the natives already have is ineffective. The reader will find it difficult to agree with this claim after having seen the natives conduct their political as well as legal business in the earlier part of the novel. Also, after noting the shallow knowledge of the natives exhibited by Winterbottom, the reader will be uneasy about the argument.

Furthermore, the new rule is to be indirect. The natives are supposed to have a say, through "native institutions" (56). These catchy phrases are drawn from the ultimate terms that obtain in the Western world and will, therefore, persuade the Western audience. The rationalization of the British presence on the African soil is couched in phrases that show that the government's intention in Africa is good. Hence the lieutenant-governor is in tune with his culture and is operating within it. He shows how different, well meaning, and better the British colonial policy is — other imperial nations govern the natives themselves, and the British government is against that—it wants to govern the natives through the natives. The question may arise as to why the British government would want to govern an African country at all. The lieutenant-Governor preempts this question and answers it in his "while" clause: "while we endeavor to purge the native system of its abuses" (56). The lieutenantt. governor does not say what the abuses are, but if there were abuses, purging them would be logical. The lieutenant-governor chooses *topoi* that will appeal to and persuade the Western world and attest to the ethical nature of the mission.

The government shows its goodwill to the African people by preaching sensitivity to their humanity. It uses a pathetic appeal that seems to praise what is within while bringing something from without to destroy it. However, as Achebe has demonstrated in *Arrow of God* as well as in an earlier novel, *Things Fall Apart*, and as Yeats has demonstrated in his poem, "The Second Coming," which demonstrates the predicament of British colonialism in Ireland, the cataclysmic encounter between Europe and Africa/Ireland inevitably results in the destruction by Brtitish colonialism of the vital elements of the colonized regions. To expect the two cultures to be subsumed harmoniously in one cultural order is to ignore the inherent tragic displacement of the one by the other with unassimilable fragments of both nestling uncomfortably together. Thus catchy phrases like "soundly rooted stock," "the hearts and minds," and "thoughts of the people" are designed to occlude the real issues. As in Nwaka's speech, the issues here have not been discovered dialectically; rather, they have been obscured. The appeal is just to emotion.

The next claim of the memo is that indirect rule will enable the British government to more easily establish native governance, "moulding it and establishing it into lines consonant with modern ideas and higher standards, and yet all the time enlisting the real force of the spirit of the people, instead of killing all that out and trying to start afresh" (56). One thing that comes out clearly is that indirect rule makes life easier for the British government. The rule does not really serve the interests of the natives. Achebe shows that the British government is not really interested in the well-being of the natives but that it uses these catchy phrases to obscure its real intention of exploiting them. Achebe shows that although the British Government claims that it does not want to kill the spirit of the people or "destroy the African atmosphere, the African mind, the whole foundation of his race" (56-57), that is precisely what it has done through such agents as Winterbottom, Clark, and the road engineer who flogs Ezeulu's son, thereby, temporarily exposing Ezeulu's impotence in the face of the white man's power.

While the outside world sanctions the British government's argument as well-meaning, the natives watch as their culture disintegrates due to the intervention of the British government and its attempt to create a king where there had been none and for a people who have no concept of what it is to be a king.

When the British government's argument is examined in the light of Achebe's portrayal of the whites, the reader finds the argument full of holes. Winterbottom claims to know his natives, but Achebe shows him to be ignorant. If Winterbottom is ignorant and is taken by surprise even by the rain, how can he sustain his claim to knowledge of the natives? If Winterbottom, who is on site, does not have a real knowledge of the people and their world, how can his superiors who get information through him have a knowledge of the natives for whom they are proposing a form of government? These are the questions Achebe is raising in *Arrow of God.*

Achebe shows that church oratory was efficacious. St. Augustine's teaching on *ethos* and style in *On Christian Doctrine* provides surprising insight in explicating why Church oratory was efficacious in *Arrow of God.* For St. Augustine, moral probity is mandatory to the preacher's persuasive effectiveness. St. Augustine puts moral probity above eloquence and stipulates that the sermon must be cogent and solidly based on the authority and the natural eloquence of the Holy Scriptures.[41] He recommends the use of the art of rhetoric from Cicero in the propagation of the Scriptures so that the preachers can move their congregations with their preaching. He encourages preachers to keep in mind the three duties of the orator—teaching, delighting, and moving—and to remember that the teaching function dominates the persuasive function.[42] As a result, he encourages the cultivation of the simple style because it is suited to didactic purposes.[43] Achebe favors the simple style in his novels since the primary mission of his novels is to educate. This explains why the Christian evangelist in *Arrow of God* mirrors so closely St. Augustine's teaching in his preaching. Achebe shows in this novel how the principles of St. Augustine, which were incorporated in the tenets of the medieval *Ars predicandi,* help these preachers in their evangelizing mission and enable them to disrupt the societies they address.

Christian oratory in *Arrow of God* divulges how rhetoric is able to triumph over dialectic and sophistry. Mr. John Goodcountry embodies church rhetoric; hence, he persuades the people of Umuaro effectively and offers them a direction to take in the time of their greatest political need for guidance. Achebe uses the role of Mr. Goodcountry to demonstrate the duty of rhetoric informed by matter and manner to achieve success in persuasion. Church rhetoric as prescribed by St. Augustine in *De Doctrina Christiana* is rooted both in the classical rhetorical practices and in divine power. St Augustine's prescription that the rhetorical techniques of the ancient Romans and Greeks be used to propagate the word of God is efficacious in *Arrow of God.* The aim of church rhetoric was to teach, please, and move or convert people to Christianity. In order to accomplish its aim, church rhetoric shunned display alone, inflation, and thirst for applause which both

Nwaka and the British administration embraced in their suasory endeavors. As St. Augustine asserts in *De Doctrina Christiana* where he is prescribing the mode of church rhetoric: "I think I have accomplished something not when I hear them applauding, but when I see them weep."[44] The preacher, while propagating the truth, must combine wisdom with eloquence in order to instruct, win, and move, since "the eloquence of the church, when it seeks to have something done, must not only explain to instruct and please to hold, but also move to win."[45] Ezeulu and Winterbottom, while propagating the truth, lack this skill. Achebe imbues Goodcountry with this skill.

Goodcountry's profile is typical of the missionary. Achebe, the orator, imbues him with all the biblical images and authority which the church claims as the source of its *ethos*. In the Bible, John was the name of one of the sons of Zebedee and an Apostle of Jesus Christ. Jesus Christ actually promised to make him and his brother, James, fishers of men.[46] What this means is that they were given the power to convert people to the Christian faith. Although Mr. Goodcountry is not a white man, he speaks the white man's language fluently. He can support his claim with the knowledge of history. His people from the Niger Delta had killed the sacred iguana and destroyed its shrine but nothing had happened to them as the heathens claimed it would. He had a kinsman who suffered martyrdom. Therefore, he can make the ultimate sacrifice to defend this new religion he is bringing to the people of Umuaro. His instruction is that the Christians should kill the sacred python. He is sure that nothing would happen to them. He tries to show the Christians that the sacred python is an ordinary snake and that killing the snake will have no consequence since the god that the python represents is a false god.

One might wonder why Achebe lays so much emphasis on the killing of the sacred python. But the sacred python represents the people's belief in their religion, which is the symbol of one of their gods. If a new religion is going to win converts from among the practitioners of the indigenous religion, it is pertinent that that new religion render the indigenous religion impotent. One way of doing that is to arrest the people's fear of their god by inciting one of their own to kill the representative of the god. Making John Goodcountry, a foreigner, kill the python will not have the same impact as making a native of Umuaro do it. Achebe endows Goodcountry with the astuteness of an accomplished rhetorician. As an astute rhetorician, when confronted with this task of rendering the native god powerless, he uses not only a native, but a native with a high status: the son of the chief priest of the highest Umuaro god!

Moses Unachukwu, the Christian convert, whom Achebe uses to defend the indigenous religion to Mr. Goodcountry and to his fellow converts, lacks eloquence although he possesses wisdom. As a result, his persuasive endeavors are ineffective. His constant attempts to counter Mr. Goodcountry are doomed from the beginning because of Mr. Goodcountry's rhetorical power, which is so filled with wisdom and eloquence that the people are persuaded in the end. Moses

Unachukwu is half-educated and, therefore, not as knowledgeable and as confident as Mr. Goodcountry. He even does not have the title, "Mister," attached to his name as Mr. Goodcountry does. He is plain Moses Unachukwu. Even the choice of his name, Moses, is a skilled rhetorical move on the part of Achebe. In the Bible, even though Moses saved the Israelites from pharoah, he was not allowed to see the promised land because of a transgression he committed against God. Moses was also a child of Israeli parents during a period the Israelites were under slavery and severe bondage, at the worse time of Israeli history. Because he was adopted by the princes of Egypt, he bestrides the two worlds, the Israeli and the Egytian worlds. As a result, heis portrayed to have double allegiance and thereby lacking the absolute trust of neither.   The Israelites constantly went against him in the Bible. Moses Unachukwu suffers the same fate and, therefore, is ill-equipped to defend the indigenous faith. His surname Unachukwu is also a serious rhetorical statement. The name connotes a negative attitude towards God. Translated, the name could mean one who is mouthing obscenities towards God—in a crude palance, one who is "barracking" God. It could also mean one who, by conduct, does not honor God and, therefore, has attracted God's displeasure towards himself. The name, therefore, is diminshing. The play on both his given name and his surname portrays Moses Unachukwu as an inadequate person to lead the people, and he fails in that enterprise.

As the proponent for the preservation of the sacred python, Moses Unachukwu is made to appear inadequate to his two audiences in the church, the Umuaro converts and the rest of the Umuaro congregation, in several ways. He is from Umuaro and from the same village as the priest of Idemili, the owner of the python.   Therefore, his fellow converts may view him as having a vested interest in the matter. Because he is a member in good standing in Umuaro, he is also suspect among the Umuaro indigenes converted to Christianity since he belongs to the system the converts are seeking to leave behind them, a system that had either made them less than humans or made them the chaff of society.[47] Hence, although he is held in high esteem in the church because of his exposure to the white man and the Christian religion, he also lacks *ethos*. When he argues, he mixes his *topoi* selected from the Bible and from the lores of the native culture. Therefore, because his position is not clear, he is unable to persuade the people. For instance, in his argument in defense of the python, he narrates the story of how the python came to be sacred and insists that, although God had put a curse on the head of the python, neither the Bible nor the catechism asks converts to kill the python. Unachukwu's speech momentarily causes a division in the audience. His narration of the lore about the python draws smiles from some of the converts, who recall the story that still reminds them of their roots and their affinity with the tradition. However, Unachukwu's story is deeply rooted in the tradition that the converts are now forsaking, the tradition that is rapidly being rendered obsolete by the forces of Western cultural imperialism.

In contrast, Achebe carves a solid structure for the propagator of Christian oratory, Mr. Goodcountry. All through Unachukwu's argument, Goodcountry listens patiently but contemptuously. He sits like a rock. Achebe paints a picture of a man who is sure of the source of his authority. In Christian rhetoric, as George Kennedy rightly observes, "authority is analogous to *ethos* in classical rhetoric, but at a different metaphysical level."[48] When Unachukwu has finished speaking, Mr. Goodcountry refutes his argument with the single statement: "A story such as you have just told us is not fit to be heard in the house of God" (49; ch. 4). He avoids getting into an argument about Unachukwu's biblical allusions but focuses the attention of his audience on the vulnerable spot of Unachukwu's argument, the use of the lores of a defunct religion, the religion of Umuaro, to argue on behalf of the python.

The missing premise of the enthymeme contained in this statement makes those who believe in Unachukwu's story pagans who cannot belong in the house of God. With this one statement, Mr. Goodcountry has given an ultimatum: If you believe in Unachukwu's story, you do not belong in the church, the house of God. His utterance proclaims truth which the church holds irrefutable. The preacher does not need to prove this truth. The authority behind this truth is confirmed by miracles. God's miracle, therefore, rather than logical argument, serves as the mode of persuasion. According to Kennedy, the truth being invoked on occasions like the one Mr. Goodcountry found himself in "is the simple enunciation of God's truth, uncontaminated by adornment, flattery, or sophistic argumentation; it differs from philosophical rhetoric in that this truth is known from revelation or established by signs sent from God, not discovered by dialectic through man's efforts."[49] As a result, persuasion which uses this truth comes from authority, not logical argument. Hence, members who heard Mr. Goodcountry are forced to dissociate themselves from anybody who tells a story that is not fit to be told in the house of God. Although there is no support from outside the scripture offered in Mr. Goodcountry's refutation, just as there is no concrete fact but myth in Moses Unachukwu's argument, Mr. Goodcountry is invoking divine authority and superiority.

Mr. Goodcountry's second rhetorical move, that of using a native to refute a native, is also effective. Oduche is a good choice. He is the son of the chief priest of the highest deity. He is young, immature, and therefore full of zeal. Achebe shows how ripe Oduche is for exploitation when he shows him to have acted on impulse. In situations like the one Oduche finds himself, the immature person who is still learning the art of public speaking is always the instrument to be used, and Goodcountry exploits Oduche's ignorance, innocence, and precocity. Although Oduche's utterance uses a Christian myth to refute a traditional myth, in his defense of scriptures, both Oduche's and Unachukwu's claims are operating from myth. None has proven that one is truer than the other. However, their disagreement serves the divide-and-conquer purpose of the church because Mr. Goodcountry latches onto it. With the simple question: "Do you hear that Moses?" Mr. Goodcountry succeeds in diminishing Moses. Moses may have wanted to counter Oduche's argument, but Mr. Goodcountry, being a strong rhetorician, does not give him another chance to argue. Instead, adopting a superior pose, he starts upraiding and denigrating him. He elevates Oduche, a child, over Unachukwu, a respected adult, thus in that deft move, he elevates his church, a new dispensation, over native teaching, the old dispensation. His portrayal of native teaching as "heathen filth" entails that the members of the church would not want to identify with it even though Goodcountry had not proved logically that it was filth. Goodcountry further diminishes Unachukwu by painting the picture of Oduche as a babe, who is full of knowledge as against Unachukwu, an adult, who lacks the knowledge expected of him. He cites the Bible, the teaching of which has already been raised above the lore of Umuaro religion, to support his recognition of Oduche's wisdom: "Is it not as Our Lord himself said that the first shall become the last and the last shall become the first" (49)? This statement also promises to elevate anyone who challenges the respect and envied Moses.

One sees characteristic features of Christian rhetoric embodied in Goodcountry's speech. According to Kennedy, these features are a "strong element of authority, character of the speaker, the evidence he can present in his speech, the extent to which he can arouse feelings of emotion, including hope of future reward or fear of punishment."[50] Mr. Goodcountry sought to underlie the permanence of this new dispensation, which is bound to drive out the old, with yet another biblical assertion: "The world will pass away but not one single word of Our Lord will be set aside... . When the time comes for your baptism," Mr. Goodcountry promises Oduche, "you will be called Peter; on this rock will I build my church" (49). These are rewards for being a good Christian. Goodcountry aims at appealing to the emotions of the people, and he succeeds; he is applauded. Goodcountry also succeeds in arousing Moses into exhibiting undignified characteristics and resorting to threat. Threat as a means of persuasion fails if the one threatening does not have the means of enforcing the threat. Moreover, the fact that Moses Unachukwu displays anger in the face of Goodcountry's cool demeanor further promotes Goodcountry and diminishes his opponent, Mr Unachukwu's image. Mr. Unachukwu ends up appearing childish and ignorant. When the people then lose their chief priest to madness, the most logical and natural thing to do is to run to Mr. Goodcountry's church for protection from their gods' wrath.

All in all, Achebe has tapped into the classical rhetoricians' views of the relationship of rhetoric with dialectics to persuade his audience on how the African indigenous religion came to lose to Christianity. Plato condemns rhetoric precisely because of rhetoric's potential to be misused. Aristotle also recognizes that rhetoric, like all good things, could be used to do good as well as bad. Richard Weaver's explication of the relationship between rhetoric and dialectics, like Aristotle's, goes further to explain the success or failure of some of the oratorical situations in the novels.

Weaver, taking off from Aristotle's views, discerns that dialectic and rhetoric are distinguishable stages of argumentation, with dialectic defining the subject and rhetoric actualizing the possibilities raised by dialectical reasoning.[51] As Weaver rightly observes, this will enable rhetoric to arrive at the truth before persuading, since discovering the truth is as important as conveying the truth. Hence, he perceives rhetoric as "truth plus its artful presentation."[52] Weaver's argument hinges on his opinion that rhetoric is cognate with language. Utterance is language, and since utterance is never neutral, language is also never neutral.[53] Rhetoric is a conscious act and has consequences for the world,[54] since "[E]very use of language, written or oral, exhibits an attitude, and an attitude implies an act" Even factual and logical statements have rhetorical implications. There is always an intention behind every statement. This intention is rhetorical because utterances are attempts to make others see the world in a particular way and to accept the values implicit in that point of view.[55] This is precisely what Achebe has aimed at achieving, as he has repeatedly articulated in his essays and views on African literature and its mission.

As Weaver argued, there is a link between values and rhetoric. Because rhetoric has the power to orient the audience towards a worldview, it has the power to influence people's values. As a result, it has the duty to identify and evaluate its controlling ideas (that is, ideas it wants to support or propagate), based on the ethics of the discourse.[56] In this opinion, Weaver agrees with Kenneth Burke's comment that "rhetoric is a rhetoric of motive," as speech comes from the will to alter or support something.[57] Weaver insists that ethics are woven into the fabric of an argument, and argument from definition is the most ethical form because it takes its premise from what is already there, "the being."[58] Since dialectic leads to knowledge of essences and principles, rhetoric needs it in order to gain *ethos*. In this way, ethical rhetoric can "perfect men by showing them better versions of themselves, links in that chain extending up toward the ideal which only the intellect can apprehend and only the soul have affection for."[59] Here, Weaver echoes Plato, who believes that although rhetoric should be condemned for its sophistry, it is capable of perfecting a man when it is based on dialectic, which aims at the truth.[60]

Weaver considers rhetoric as the most humanistic of all the disciplines, not only because rhetoric addresses itself to the whole human beingl—the ethical, the rational, and the pathetical—but also because it takes time, place, and people into consideration.[61] He asserts that "[r]hetoric is advisory; it has the office of advising men with reference to an independent order of goods and with reference to their particular situation as it relates to these."[62] In *Ideas Have Consequences*, he distinguishes three levels of knowledge and asserts that knowledge at the universal level of first principles embodies value judgment, which is based on a vision of reality.[63] According to Weaver, order of values is the ultimate sanction of rhetoric because values are important in making man live a life of direction and purpose. And since rhetoric deals with choices involving values, the rhetorician is a preacher and can use his power to steer society towards making noble or base decisions. Weaver echoes Aristotle's assertion in *Rhetoric* that the deeds that come out of virtue are noble and so are their signs. According to Weaver, therefore, it is important that the direction the rhetorician shows the society is the right and virtuous one and that the rhetor is the master of his art.[64]

This is the same charge Cicero gives to the orator when he says that oratory must be "combined with integrity and supreme wisdom," for if "we bestow fluency of speech on persons devoid of those virtues, we shall not have made orators of them but shall have put weapons into the hands of madmen."[65] As Brian Vickers explains it, "[a] man can confer the greatest of benefits by a right use of these and inflict the greatest of injuries by using them wrongly"[66] Achebe's recognition of the power of ethics and values in the art of persuasion is manifested in the choices of the "persuasibles" made by the orators in *Arrow of God* and the results of these choices. By this the reader sees rhetoric as a tool in the service of the orator. Relevantly, however, one needs to ask if any of the people seeking to direct the people of Umuaro at a critical conjuncture in their cultural-political history used the tool of rhetoric to the benefit of the people of Umuaro.   Achebe does not answer this question. He leaves the reading audience to draw its own conclusions.

NOTES

1.   Isocrates, *Antidosis*, trans. George Norlin, ed. G.P Goold (Cambridge, MA: Harvard University Press, 1982), 18-21.

2.   Aristotle, *Rhetoric,* I I. i.

3.   Cicero, *De Oratore,* Bk 1: 50.

4.   Quintilian, *Institutio Oratoria* XII. intro 3-1. i.

5.   Weaver, *Ethics of Rhetoric,* 27.

6.   Ibid., 15.

7.   Weaver, "The Cultural Role of Rhetoric" in *Visions of Order: The Crisis of Our Time* (Baton Rouge: Louisiana State University Press, 1964), 65. Quintilian also asserts that the one reason Socrates lost his case before the audience of eminent Athenians was his choice of a speech he deemed becoming to his person over the excellent, expedient, and effective speech prepared by Lysias. *Institutio Oratoria* Book XI I 8.

8.   Weaver, *Ethics of Rhetoric* 17-18.

9.   Weaver, "The Cultural Role of Rhetoric," 71.

10.   Burke, *A Rhetoric of Motives,* 20-21.

11.   Perelman and Olbrechts-Tyteca, *The New Rhetoric* 68.

12.   Ibid.; see also Weaver, *Ethics of Rhetoric,* 52-53.

13.   Sunday A. Aigbe, *Theory of Social Involvement: A Case Study of the Anthropology of Religion, State, and Society* (Lanham, MD: University Press of America, 1993), 113-114.

14.   Ibid., 115.

15. Cicero, *De Oratore* II. trans. E. W. Sutton, ed. T.E. Page (Cambridge, MA: Harvard University Press, 1976), I. vii. 30.

16. Cicero, *De Optimo*. trans.E.W. Sutton, ed. T.E. Page (Cambridge, MA: Harvard University Press, 1976), 1. 3. Quintilian also advocates this in *Institutio Oratorium* Bk XII. ii. 11.

17. Quintilian, *Institutio Oratoria*, Bk XII. I. I.1.

18. Ibid., intro., 3-1. i.

19. Shakespeare, *Julius Caesar*.

20. Weaver, "The Cultural Role of Rhetoric," in *Professing The New Rhetoric*, 82.

21. Ibid., 83.

22. Perelman and Olbrechts-Tyteca, *The New Rhetoric* 68; see also Weaver, *Ethics of Rhetoric*, 52-53.

23. For discussion on the use of fact in argumentation, see Perelman and Olbrechts-Tyteca, *The New Rhetoric*, 67-68 and Weaver, *The Ethics of Rhetoric*, 53-54.

24. Larry Anhart, *Aristotle on Political Reasoning: A Commentary on the "Rhetoric"* (De Kalb: Northern Illinois University Press, 1981), 154.

25. Weaver, "The Cultural Role of Rhetoric," in *Professing the New Rhetoric* 83.

26. Anhart, *Aristotle on Political Reasoning* 149.

27. Douglas Walton, *The Place of Emotion in Argument* (University Park: Pennsylvania State University Press, 1992), 67.

28. Ibid., 67.

29. Ibid., 69.

30. Ibid., 70-71.

31. For a discussion of titles and their ranking in Ogidi, Achebe's town, see Wren, *Achebe's World*, 86-87.

32. Annonymous, *Ad Herennium* 4: 28-38.

33. Shakespeare, *Julius Ceasar*.

34. Burke, *A Rhetoric of Motives*, 20.

35. Ibid., 22-23.

36. Ibid., 45-46.

37. Weaver, *Ideas Have Consequences* (Chicago: University of Chicago Press, 1948), 18.

38. Achebe, *Hopes*, 44. Achebe's "Novelist as a Teacher" discusses his mission to teach that his culture is as good as any other culture and that his people should divest themselves of results of years of denigration. See this essay also in *Morning Yet*.

39. Kate Turkington, *Chinua Achebe. "Things Fall Apart"* (London: Edward Arnold, 1977), 49.

40. Johannes Fabian, *Time and the Other: How Anthropology Makes Its Object* (New York: Columbia University Press, 1983), 31, 40, and 41. According to Fabian, the denial of coevalness is the distancing of the other which emanates from a culture deeming itself superior in time and place. In the case of the colonizers, it is the distancing of the colonized because the colonizers place the colonized in time and place other than their own, therefore, deeming the colonized inferior in time and place. This necessitates the isolation of the colonized.

41. St. Augustine, *De Doctrina Christiana*, Bk IV. 30, in Bizzell and Herzberg, eds. *The Rhetorical Tradition*, 399.

42. Ibid., 49-55.

43. Ibid., 45.

44. Ibid., 24.

45. Ibid., 13.

46. *The Catholic Living Bible* (Wheaton: IL: Tyndale House , 1971), Mark 1, verses 15-16.

47. Compare the calibre of people converted to Christianity in *Things Fall Apart*.

48. George A. Kennedy, *Classical Rhetoric and Its Christian and Secular Tradition from Ancient to Modern Times* (Chapel Hill: University of North Carolina Press, 1980), 121.

49. Ibid., 122.

50. Ibid., 122.

51. Weaver, "Dialectic and Rhetoric at Dayton, Tennessee," *Ethics of Rhetoric*, 27.

52. Weaver, "The Phaedrus and the Nature of Rhetoric," *Ethics of Rhetoric*, 15.

53. Weaver, "Language Is Sermonic," in *The Rhetoric of Western Thought*, 316. Lecture delivered at the University of Oklahoma, 1963. See also Richard L. Johanneson and Ralph T. Eubanks, "Richard M. Weaver on The Nature of Rhetoric: An Interpretation." Edward P. J. Corbett, James L. Golden, and Goodwin F. Berquist, eds., *Essays on the Rhetoric of the Western World* (Dubuque, IA: Kendall/Hunt, 1990).

54. Ibid., 315.

55. Ibid., 317-318.

56. Ibid., 317.

57. Ibid., 315.

58. Ibid., 310.

59. Weaver, "Phaedrus and the Nature of Rhetoric," *Ethics of Rhetoric*, 25.

60. Plato, "Phaedrus," in Bizzell and Herzberg, *The Rhetorical Tradition* 141.

61. Weaver, "The Cultural Role of Rhetoric," in *Visions of Order,* 71.

62. Weaver, "Language Is Sermonic," in *The Rhetoric of Western Thought,* 307.

63. Weaver, *Ideas Have Consequences* 18; Weaver, *Ethics of Rhetoric* 30-31.

64. Weaver, "Language Is Sermonic," in *The Rhetoric of Western Thought,* 316.

65. Cicero, *De Oratore* III. xiv. 55-56.

66. Brian Vikers, *Classical Rhetoric in English Poetry* (Carbondale: Southern Illinois University Press, 1989), 21.

Chapter 4

Locale and Argumentation:
No Longer at Ease

ORATORY AND THE DYNAMIC SPACE

No Longer at Ease is the story of a young, brilliant, British-trained Nigerian, who came into the Nigerian Civil Service determined to operate above the level of bribery but who succumbed to it as a result of the many social forces of the time and place in which he found himself. Achebe uses the unfolding of the action and the many speeches in the novel to expound the issue: to refute and debunk the white man's all-knowing theory and argument on the issue and to build his own case on the forces at play that inevitably push a young Nigerian man to undo himself through a single act of bribery.

The story is also reminiscent of the theme of T.S. Eliot's poem, "Journey of the Magi," in which one of the Magi reflects on the experience of the journey to the Christ child. He despairs of understanding its meaning, finding nothing changed at home, and being unable to fit into the old dispensation. Achebe prefaces the novel with the last four lines of this poem to show that the Nigeria Obi Okonkwo returns to contrasts drastically with his vision of the place. Obi Okonkwo starts by resisting the urge to join the decadent rest, but eventually succumbs to the corruption existing in the transitional state. Achebe's vehicle for conveying this anarchy is an innately good, young, educated African man who, in the course of the novel, becomes corrupted because corruption has now become the norm in the new society.

Many critics have viewed this novel as less accomplished than Achebe's other novels. One of their criticisms is that its plot is episodic while its characters are underdeveloped.[1] However, it is my opinion that Achebe, the educationist and orator, has achieved precisely what he set out to achieve in this novel. *No Longer at Ease* is a profound novel when seen as an analysis of the predicament of the young elite in the newly formed Nigeria and as an argument on the wrong-headedness of stereotyping of the African as innately corrupt. It takes up the issue of corruption where *Things Fall Apart* left off and continues to advance the argument that the coming of the white man to Africa was detrimental to African culture if not totally destructive of the good values in that culture.

Locale has tremendous impact in advancing these arguments in *No Longer at Ease*. Locale has an impact on the language, on the *topoi* used, and on the *ethos*, *logos*, and *pathos* addressed or evoked for effective argumentation. Perelman and Olbrechts-Tyteca contend that the speaker should conceive "the anticipated audience as close as possible to reality."[2] This means that the arguer must have an adequate "picture of the audience." That being the case, the orator has to, among other things, take the locale of the argument into consideration. The argument that persuades a particular audience in one locale may not persuade the same audience in a different location. Bakhtin also contends that language is dialogic and is interpreted in context. The role of locale in the arguments used by both the orators in the novel and by Achebe himself, as the orator who has argued his case in the novel, manifests greatly in the interrelationships of words in particular contexts.[3] As effective orators, both Achebe and the orators in the novel need to locate their audience in its social setting. Locating the audience entails locating it in time and space. The audience's psychological make-up can change in time and space. The orators in the village and the orators in the city show great awareness of the space and the time of their oratory. Achebe also uses this power of oratory to respect the time and the space in order to elaborate the theme of the novel.

The theme of the novel centers around the issue of corruption. The judge makes a crucial statement in the forensic oratory that occurs at the beginning of the novel: "I cannot comprehend how a young man of your education and brilliant promise could have done this" (2, ch.1 all quotes in this chapter are from the 1960 Heinemann edition of *No Longer at Ease*). Mr. Green, one of the witnesses and the young man's boss, has an explanation: "The African is corrupt through and through" (3; ch 1.), but that is not acceptable to Achebe. He, therefore, devotes the entire novel to the background of the case, what brought on the trial, demonstrating why such a person as Obi Okonkwo, the hero of the novel, could take a bribe. He is intent upon refuting Mr. Green's assertion that the African is corrupt through and through. In undertaking this argument and the refutation, Achebe puts to great use the effects of locale on argumentation in order to advance the thesis that the nation (the "unnation" and the demands of the clan conflict with the white man's intrusion and the new imported technology. These are behind the kind of tragedy Achebe views as the real tragedy, the type that never ends, like the eating of wormwood, the type that lasts *"uwa-ta-uwa*, world without end" (36; ch. 5). In other words, the tragedy in *No Longer at Ease* is the kind that lasts forever because the new element is unassimilable. Simon Gikandi rightly discerns the entire novel as a refutation of Mr. Green's remark about the nature of the African man and the effect of the African climate on the African psyche.[4]

Each of the oratorical pieces in the novel is a major advancement of the theme as well as a reply to Judge Galloway's question. In this regard, locale of the oratorical pieces advance, refute, or defend the arguments. There are two major locales, each with subsidiaries. The first locale is Lagos, a city that is a microcosmic representation of the new nation-state with its affluent and slum cultures and its conglomeration of different tribes, all struggling to have a share in the political control of the country whose independence is imminent. The second is the Umuofia locale as a village with a confused understanding of the dichotomy between, and the shading into each other of, the indigenous culture and the Western culture. In the Lagos locale, one could discern three major subsidiary locales. The first is the world of the colonialists represented by the court and the club. The second is the Umuofia Progressive Union meeting ground. The third is located wherever Obi happens to be at the material time, whether with Joseph or Christopher or Clara or his bribe-giving clients. These different locales give Achebe the opportunity to argue his chosen subject, which is corruption in the new country and which, as can be seen, is as complex as these different locales. As Simon Gikandi has interpreted the situation, "the new nation of Nigeria is a locus of paradoxes, a crossroads of different forces and ideological claims," which "the narrator" is not authorized to organize "into a coherent whole." Instead, he is at liberty "to evoke the reality of places and things, since this still remains an important mandate of the nove."[5]

Achebe the orator has utilized the locales effectively to refute the myopic view of bribery by the colonial master. He has expanded the issue to incorporate the role of the colonizer in bringing about the atmosphere of corruption and to incorporate the effect of the confusion that emanates from an anarchic situation in which the falcon in, *Things Fall Apart* stops hearing the falconer. The Igbo people have a saying that if anyone wants to know the source of murder, the person must go to the ironsmith. By highlighting the corrupting role of the colonizer, Achebe has done precisely that: he has pointed out the source/root of corruption.

Oratory in the Lagos metropolitan Locale starts with the first instance of oratory, set in the court, a Western institution whose deficiencies have been part of the subject of *Things Fall Apart*, the novel preceding *No Longer at Ease*.[6] On this forensic occasion, Achebe summarizes the judge's speech instead of giving it a full treatment. However, he gives such a detailed description of the judge and the actions that go on in the court before and during the hearing that he evokes the proper courtroom atmosphere and makes poignant comments on the issue he is defending. In this opening scene, Achebe's ironic treatment of the issue leads the reader to recognize that the issue of bribery is confusing, almost unfathomable to the natives and probably also to the intellectuals. The spectators who come to hear the case had to bribe doctors (other educated men), probably young ones, in order to be free (on sick leave) to come to court to watch an educated man being tried for bribery. This is an adequately delineated social context in which the confusion of bribery is enacted.

This social context is a complex interaction among the African past, the colonial encounter, and the emergent hybrid culture. The context gives great insight into the response of the individual to corruption. According to Bakhtin, arguments should be seen as dialogic in order to be adequately interpreted. Dialogism entails taking into consideration the social context out of which the argument grew.[7] In this case, taking into consideration the past and the present of both this new country and its character yields greater insight into Achebe's argument. Kenneth Burke's suggestion that social context informs argumentation and its techniques is also contained in Wayne Booth's claim that "terrain determines tactics."[8] The court locale serves as a forum for raising the crucial issue to be refuted. In the judge's question, the issues center on the words "young man," "education," and "doing that." The reader is left to furnish the rest of the enthymeme: it is proper for an old man to take a bribe, and it is proper for an uneducated man to take a bribe, but it is incomprehensible for a young educated man to indulge in bribe-taking. One also assumes that bribery in itself is not a crime. The crime is taking a bribe when one's training should have predisposed one not to take it. The idea of Western training has been to curb one's inherent corruption as a member of the African race.

Achebe uses the court to show that even Western values cannot be viewed simplistically as the western-trained judge does. The description of the judge in the court carries a message that cloaks his oratory. The name of the judge, Galloway, evokes the image of prison. The judge is the way to prison. He is not just a judge; an encounter with him is synonymous with a prison sentence. The trial is probably a formality because the judge may be incapable of answering or discerning why a young educated man would resort to bribery, and, like Mr. Green, he probably believes that the African is innately corrupt. In that case, extenuating circumstances are not relevant to Obi's trial and will not be used to mitigate his prison sentence. Achebe is extending the work of the court system in *Things Fall Apart* here. In *Things Fall Apart*, he has shown that the court system is equally corrupt and that the judges reached their decisions in ignorance. The judge's actions in *No Longer at Ease* are also those of one who does not feel obligated to respect the people in his court. The court is his kingdom, his territory, his jurisdiction, in which he ignorantly carries out the business of the day as he wishes, and he expects absolute obedience. When the reader first encounters the judge, he is looking at the defense lawyer so fixedly that his gaze is compared to that of a collector on an insect that he has made inert with formalin. The inescapable fate of the judge's victim shown in the image of the insect and the formalin is the overriding metaphor for the young educated man in Nigeria, as Achebe sees it. Hence, as the judge is busy asking why Obi accepted bribes, Achebe is also busy using the judge's actions to answer his question. The young educated Nigerian is incapable of escaping from his fate in the "nation" or "unnation" in which old values become confused and ideologies are blurred. If a defense lawyer is powerless before the judge, what would be the fate of the defendant? The defense lawyer's reason for coming to court late is also ironic. His car had broken down. If a defense lawyer is not capable of owning a car that will guarrantee an efficient and timely performance of his duty, the nation that has created that condition needs to be reexamined. Part of the reason Obi Okonkwo takes bribes is that he feels too embarrassed to lose his means of mobility, his car. As Obi Okonkwo discerns, it is like a betrayal for one to answer that his car is not functioning when one is asked how one's car is doing. It is tantamount to the masquerade replying to another masquerade that he does not understand the language of the masks (90; ch. 10). The judge confirms Obi's conclusions on the issue. The judge is obviously not impressed by the "excuses about the problem of locomotion" (1; ch. 1). He probably is ignorant of what havoc a lack of locomotion can wreak on a "young man of your education and brilliant promise," or he does not want to acknowledge the acute importance of a car in the nation he represents as he sits in judgment. Either way, he is not fit to judge the young man before him. Achebe does not give his speech in full because, as far as its relevance to the advancement of the novel is concerned, it has done its duty. It has set the stage for different reactions to Obi Okonkwo's ignominious downfall.

The next locale is the country club, which exhibits the same social, class, and racial divisions found in the European Ikoyi suburb. This is where Mr. Green gives his famous but simplistic exposé on the endemic nature of corruption on the African soil, the part the climate and diseases played in imbuing Africans with such a social ill, and the inability of the African to rid himself of that malady, no matter the amount of Western education wasted on him (3; ch. 1). Achebe uses the pungency of his power of description to partly refute Mr. Green. First the club is dominated, if not entirely occupied, by Europeans. The club is in Nigeria and the only black people in the club are servants, who are just like part of the furniture. In fact, the furniture might have had more recognition than these African servants. Mr. Green's decalaration"—They are all corrupt ... . I am all for equality and all that. I for one would hate to live in South Africa. But equality won't alter the facts" (3)—is part of the falsehood which Achebe needs to refute. And through the British Council man, he joins in asking Mr. Green, "What facts?" The issue of fact will also be the focus of the controversy. What are the facts? Mr. Green's working relationship with Obi, actually with all his Nigerian subordinates, refutes Mr. Green's claim of believing in equality. He even contributes to Obi's alienation.

Another locale is Lagos mainland at the house of the president of the Umuofia Progressive Union (UPU), where the members of the Union always have their meetings. Three different meetings held in this locale expose the effect locale has on argument and advances the plot towards its climax while answering the question posed at the beginning of the novel and refuting Mr. Green's assertion in the process. The first meeting in the real time of the story was called to welcome Obi from his sojourn abroad. The next was one of their normal meetings, although Obi came to it in his new car and made a speech requesting an extension of his debt period. The last is the scene that opens the novel where the group tries to decide how to save Obi from going to prison. In this locale, as in the court locale, the issue of bribery is very complex.

Obi's homecoming is another *topos* for Achebe's argument. First Obi comes back to Nigeria without the normal pomp and pageantry. He comes home unannounced, thereby robbing his kinsmen of the opportunity to display their prize and bask in their achievement of having trained someone overseas. This is a serious breach, which both robs Obi of the proper *ethos* and sets him up for failure because he is gradually losing the awe that his position in the civil service, his exposure overseas, and his acquisition of Western education should have given him. His status is further diminished during the ceremony to welcome him. He appears in his shirtsleeves and speaks the English language that is filled with "is" and "was" while his kinsmen expect him to use highfalutin words (29; ch. 4). His kinsmen are unimpressed by his speech. He has robbed himself of another opportunity for placing himself on the pedestal where his people expect him to stay. He has tarnished his image further.

All these incompatibilities militate against Obi when he makes his speech and needs his people to respect his privacy. Obi's speech goes further to buttress Achebe's implicit argument that British education is inadequate for preparing a future Nigerian leader. Compared to Obi's speech, that of the secretary of the Umuofia Progressive Union is more the type expected from an educated Nigerian. Someone even suggests that he be sent overseas himself. This speech occasion goes further to support Achebe's refutation of Mr. Green's assertion. First, the turnout at Obi's reception is ceremonial, as "[e]verybody was properly dressed in *agbada* or European suit." (28). The word "properly" is indicative of the expectations of those gathered, who consider proper dressing as all-important. However, Westerners, whose way of life Obi has been sent to learn and whose mode of perception Obi is emulating at this function, would look down on this ceremonial gathering and would not wear formal clothes to attend it. To buttress the formality of the occasion, there was a written "Welcome Address" which the secretary of the Union formally read to the assembly. This fact goes further to show how out of fashion are the returnee's shirtsleeves. The *logos* of the address as well as the language used to convey it is so formal that it even borders on the ridiculous. But the people take the occasion seriously. Therefore, the returnee is supposed to take the occasion seriously.

Achebe uses the Welcome Address itself to show the people's confusion and misunderstanding of the Western language and ethics which they are adopting. First, that the speech is written before being delivered to the audience as opposed to an extemporaneous oral delivery puts a distance between the mode of speech before Obi left for Britain and the mode of speech after he came home. The *exordium* of the speech is tailored more to the mode of the speech of the European Middle Ages than to a modern Nigerian "nation." Hence, the reader sees a people practicing an imported, outmoded culture and upholding a speech ethics that is foreign to their way of life. The *exordium* sounds ridiculous, highfalutin, and riddled with cliches. However, in spite of its pretentiousness, and blatant misuse of some of the words, the speech sends across the intended message clearly: Obi has returned from the United Kingdom where he went "in quest of the Golden Fleece," and his people are going to benefit from his achievement and "join the comity of other towns in their march towards political irredentism, social equality and economic emancipation." It is also interesting to see that the officers and the members of the Union "show humility and gratitude" while appreciating Obi's "unprecedented academic brilliance" (28).

The reader is thus shown that Obi has been imbued with the same awe with which his predecessors, the white man, had been imbued. He is expected to replace the white man. He is clearly inadequately prepared to fill this role, but the people would rather have him with his failings and inadequacy than have a stranger run their affairs. Unfortunately, Western education has been used to insure the perpetuity of Western values and ethics while the white man has insured the permanence of the confusion of the newly emerging rulers and the people they are being trained to rule. The newly emerging intellectual and the white man's protégé, his uneducated understudy, speak different brands of the English language, the language of governance. This is one of the divide-and-rule tactics that has been so masterfully deployed by the colonialists. Hence, neither the indigenous language, the highfalutin words, or the simple words on their own are appropriate for conveying the people's feelings and wants. The speaker who hopes to persuade this postcolonial society has to be properly versed in the language and the mannerism of the defunct regime of the colonialists and learn how to juggle the highfalutin language, the indigenous language and its proverbs, the simple English filled with "is" and "was," and at times the pigdin English. Only when the elite are able to do this will they have their fingers on the pulse of this conglomeration called Nigeria. The reader is then left to wonder if the people have actually got a nation or if they are merely representing the people they are seeking to oust and are just pawns in the game of chess that their colonizers are playing with the fate of their nation. This confusion is explored in full in Achebe's *A Man of the People*, which is the subject of Chapter 5 of this book.

The speech also exposes another confusion: that of the duty of the elite to the community that trained him. Obi's education financed by UPU is supposed to bring honor to his town, Umofia. It was made clear to him at the time of his departure that his people did not expect him to bring back human heads as had been the practice in the time of Obi's grandfather, Okonkwo, in *Things Fall Apart*. The welcome address confirms that he has indeed brought back to his people the kind of honor they expected from him. But bringing such an honor entails further responsibilities. The expectations of the Union as contained in its secretary's speech expose the conflict of interests now confronting Obi. The irony contained in the the use of the word "comity" to describe the groups in the nation is one way Achebe tries to articulate the confusion of the times and the situation that would lead a young man of Obi's caliber to accept bribes.   There is no friendliness, no politeness, no courtesy, and definitely no manifestation of the qualities of good breeding apparent or real in the conflicts among the different ethnic groups or even within the same ethnic groups that are lumped together in the conglomerated polity called Nigeria. The fact that the "subnations" are pursuing political irredentism is an apt irony which exposes the misnomer contained in the ascription of the nation as a *comitas* and forecloses the possibility of unity in a nation facing domination by an outside unwanted government.   The Union is not actually joining Umuofia to the body politic but is trying to get that which they will call their own since "ours is ours, but mine is mine" and it is prudent for the clan to "possess that of which it can say: This is mine." Obi is the Union's investment and, like every investment, he is expected to yield dividends. Obi, like his grandfather, is placed squarely in the middle of this struggle to get Umuofia's share of the national cake since having him in the vanguard of the march for the nation's progress is irrefragably important to the Union as can be seen when the Union expects him to indulge in nepotism. After all, Obi is the Union's property; he belongs to the Union. Achebe's argument is that the conflict of interest contained in this speech can cause the downfall of a young man of Obi's educational level.

That Obi does not take the occasion for this Welcome Address seriously is one argument Achebe is using against the type of education that robs the elites of the sensitivity required to function among their people. Although Obi is self-willed, judging from his escapades in primary school, he was sensitive enough, before leaving for Britain, to feel sorry for Hitler, whom he thought was getting all that bad publicity. However, the same Obi (or should one say) the Obi that comes back from Britain has lost all sensitivity and has turned his self-will to selfishness. He is unable to dress properly for the occasion because of the heat. He is also unable to indulge the people who have taxed themselves mercilessly to send him overseas for further studies, people, who in spite of his ill-advised decision to study English rather than the law they had sent him to study,   have the grace to accommodate his irresponsibility and have taxed themselves further to provide this ceremonial occasion in his honor.

The chairman's question,"Have they given you a job yet?" during Obi's welcome ceremony indicates the crux of the matter and the root of the idea about bribery. Achebe shows the reader why the chairman would refer to the government as "they" and points the reader also to the effect of this perception of the government on the people's attitude and ethics. To Obi's disclosure that he would be attending an interview, the chairman suggested that, if Obi were an underdog, Obi would have had to bribe the interviewers, but since the interviewers were going to be white men, Obi would not need such an advance assurance of success in interviewing. However, the reader is told right away that the chairman is deluded in his thinking that educated people do not need to bribe their way to a job. As someone is quick to correct the Union president, white men are also corrupt, "[t]hey eat more than black men nowadays" (30).

The second meeting of the Umuofia Progessive Union is an occasion for Achebe's argument on the reason bribery occurs in Nigeria. This meeting unlike the one held at Umuofia, has a formal agenda, a concept that has come with Western culture. Western culture insists on codification, and the people are ready to codify in order to accommodate their needs as Umuofia indigenes living in Lagos, a metropolitan city. Because this locale is in Lagos, language plays a very important role in the perception of speeches made to the audience. The Union members have their native language, Igbo, and they also have the colonial language, English, which has become the official language of the country as well as the language of interethnic communication. It is easier to lie or indulge in unethical practice or use uncouth language as long as one does not speak it in one's indigenous language. Just as the people see a civil service job as an alien duty useful for self-aggrandizement as long as one avoids being caught, so they see the use of the Western language as an alien language that can be used to codify anything no matter how unethical. The people do not seem to be aware that what they do in the alien language has any bearing on who they are or how they are perceived. Hence, when they advance money to a member for the purposes of bribing his way into a job, the minutes of the meeting read that the loan is for "the explicit purpose of seeking re-engagement" (72; ch. 8). The people's idea that they come to Lagos for money and not for work also explains why they see government work as "alien" work. All these necessarily make a young educated man, who wants to do the right thing, feel ridiculous and, therefore, unable to hold steadfastly onto the values learned from his education. He is alienated from the center of being of his people, and this alienation will be manifest not only in his speech but also in his actions.

Obi's second speech before the Union is another incident that reveals confusion, which the confused and confusing locale has helped to bring about. Lagos is the country's capital, and Obi is trained to serve the country in this locale. However, he is hearing a different song that demands a different allegiance: allegiance to the Union, to the clan; an allegiance that enjoins each member to "look out for openings in his department and put in a word for Joshua" (72), an allegiance which spells out his duty to the Union (72). The confusion that emanates from the Union president's speech forces Obi to choose the particular argumentation technique and *topoi* to appeal with, as well as the *ethos* and the *pathos* that will best suit his locale. His *exordium* is aimed at eliciting the goodwill of the Umuofia Union as well as ensuring his oneness with the group. Being seen as one of the group means endorsing all that it stands for, whether or not Obi expresses this solidarity explicitly. In fact, he goes to a great length to be on their right side as is evident in the whole speech. But it does not take long before he starts feeling threatened by their invasion of his privacy. The altercations in the meeting over an alleged mishandling of Obi's welcome party are another indication of the nature of the audience in this locale, which affects the way Obi presents his speech. Although the accusation of mismanagement of funds leveled against the elders "caused a lively exchange of hard words," Obi knows that the words lack "bitterness; especially since they were English words taken straight from today's newspaper" (73).

Again, the portrayal of the English language as a carrier of signs not meant to be taken seriously is part of what affects Obi's choice of oratorical approach. Obi's speech, the reader is told, is started in the Igbo language spiced with good Igbo proverbs. Although his *exordium* is designed to put his kinsmen in the right frame of mind to receive his request, Obi turns to the *topos* of Christian values: "did not the Psalmist say that it was good for brethren to meet together in harmony" (73), and adds an apt proverb: "Our fathers also have a saying about the danger of living apart. They say it is the curse of the snake. If all snakes lived together in one place, who would approach them? But they live every one unto himself and so fall easy prey to man" (73). This proverb evokes one of the elders' earlier charges that they must act as kinsmen towards any kinsman in trouble because being endowed with human beings has precedence over possession of money.

In his speech, Obi acknowledges the wisdom in this earlier speaker's injuction and weaves his speech around the theme of the wisdom of close affinity among kinsmen. Obi buttresses the value of having kinsmen with another proverb which speaks to the much-appreciated welcome the Union has given him: "If a man returns from a long journey and no one says *nno* to him he feels like one who has not arrived" (74; ch. 8). His audience is highly impressed even when his speech becomes a mixture of English and Igbo. But the reader notices that his speech starts tending towards English as he approaches the real object of his speech, which is to ask for an extension of the grace period before starting the repayment of the loan given him for his study abroad. The author tells us that his audience admired English. Because Obi is going to make a request he knows may not be viewed favorably by some people and because he also has the unpleasant task of begging for an extension, the most appropriate medium for the audience in this locale, which has earlier shown its admiration for the English language, is the language of the master, English. It is the language that reminds them of that for which they tasked themselves when they sent Obi to England. Obi chooses English, which he knows is the most appropriate language to use if he hopes to persuade this audience. Not surprisingly, his request is granted.

However, in the spirit of community, which entails common destiny, joy, and sorrows, the president has to say something on a matter Obi considers private. The president frowns at the fact that Obi is seeing an outcast and may even be thinking of marrying her. In *Things Fall Apart*, Achebe has discussed the concept of the outcast system in Umuofia society. Outcasts are taboo. They are not allowed to associate with the freeborn. Any person who marries an outcast condemns members of his entire lineage to becoming outcasts. In Umuofia, when one finger touches oil, it smears the rest. Although Obi as an individual is entitled to a space in his society, as an Umuofia man, his appropriation of that space is determined by the society's definition of that space. However, Once again, as in *Arrow of God*, the reader is made to see that this seeming intrusion into an individual's space does not mean the negation of individuality since the Igbo person is very independent and individualistic.

The intrusion into space is not a constriction; it is an enabler within the parameters of the intrusion. Co-presence of others within that parameter enables the individual to flower. That is why in *Things Fall Apart*, Achebe tells us that people are measured according to their worth; therefore, the intrusion is not meant to limit. Thus in *No Longer at Ease*, the president of the Union is within his right to intrude into Obi's space and admonish Obi on his actions and his associations. But Obi Okonkwo bridles at this because he has been exposed for too long to Western culture. Therefore, the moment the president broaches the issue of his association with an outcaste, an *osu*, the music changes. Obi no longer cares to persuade. He resorts to the English language and its values and ethics. It is easier to be angry in a foreign language. Obi's angry words, "This is preposterous! I could take you to court for that ..." (75; Ch. 8), show how easy it is to conceal one's anger with high-sounding English words, the meaning of which is lost to the audience anyway. It is easier to say nasty things in a foreign language without revealing the enormity ordinarily associated with the nasty word in that language and without necessarily being burdened by the values encapsulated in one's mother tongue. Hence, Obi and his kinsmen make up as the reader is told later on. Anger against a brother is felt in the flesh, not in the bone. The words in the English language have no meaning and cannot hurt; they are, therefore, easily forgivable and forgettable. The words whose import Obi really want his kinsmen to take seriously are spoken in the Igbo language: "'And if this is what you meet about,' he said in Ibo, 'you may cut off my two legs if you ever find them here again'" (75; ch. 8).

The third important session of the Union takes place after Obi's conviction and sentencing. It demonstrates vividly the effect of locale on argumentation. The meeting that takes place after the trial opens with the traditional prayer over the kola nut. The narrator tells us that the president of the Union said a short prayer and presented three kola nuts "to the meeting. The oldest man present broke one of them, saying another kind of prayer while he did it" (7; ch. 1). Among the Igbo people, the kola nut is of great significance for it symbolizes life, a sense of communality, and common destiny. No gathering can do without the kola nut since no aspect of any ceremony can take off without the ritualized breaking of the kola nut. The breaking of the kola nut precedes every other item in the program (5-6). Whoever breaks the kola nut voices the most pressing need or the most excruciating pain or fear of the society and prays for its progress or aversion as the case may be. This prayer focuses on the pain of seeing their hope go to prison. The crux of the prayer is that the Umuofia people are not seeking to hurt anybody; they, therefore, do not expect anybody to seek to hurt them. The reader is left to wonder who is hurting the Umuofia people. No one has caused their son to take a bribe. The Umuofia people are frightened by the prospect of losing their foothold in the civil service. They fail to accept responsibility for what is happening to Obi. The author uses this prayer to show the ridiculousness of indicting the young man who has taken a bribe and to poke fun at the Union because by the time he tells us what had led Obi Okonkwo to succumb to bribery, the Union has been shown to have been partly the cause of the downfall of the man they taxed themselves so mercilessly to educate.

In another part of the prayer, Achebe reveals that these people are strangers in Lagos who are only interested in the good things they can get there, with the hope that they will not be affected by the bad. Achebe is saying that this is impossible since the Umuofia people in Lagos have become part of the landscape. In this regard, they influence and are influenced by the landscape. There is no way they can avoid the good, the bad, and the ugly of that landscape. They are not being realistic if they believe that they can live in that landscape without being affected by it. This explains, in part, Obi's conflict with them over his intention to marry Clara, the outcast. The landscape has influenced Obi. The landscape preaches that all are equal before God. Hence Obi does not see why the Union should meddle in his affairs. In order to stop their meddlesomeness, he opts to pay off his debt to the Union rather than accept the grace period extended to him. By doing this, Obi overexerts his pocket, caves in under his financial load, and accepts bribes.

The third point made by the prayer is a reiteration of the innuendo in the first point. Umuofia has only one person in the Civil Service but its enemies are threatening to remove that one person. Again, the focus is on the outcome of the bribery, not on the act itself. Here also, Achebe shows how the people are mixing the European concept of prayer with the Umuofia way of praying. Although most of the sentences in the prayer are taken from Umuofia proverbs, the response is European response, "Amen." Even the invocation of the ancestors' intervention draws the "Amen" response. Thus the locale of Lagos has a great influence, both good and bad, even as the people wish that this influence be limited only to the good. The prayer refers to Obi as "an only palm fruit," exposing the burden that is heaped on him both by his family and by the Union, a burden that is part of the ordeal that leads to his downfall. First, in a patriarchal society, Obi is the first son after a series of girls. His full name, Obiajulu, chosen by his father, means "the mind at last is at rest" (6; ch. 1). The name expressed the father's sentiment at having a boy, but the name has an ironic significance given Obi's predicament. In a warlike society that had been robbed of the power to defeat its neighbors, Obi has been chosen to lead a different kind of war for which he has been inadequately prepared.

Obi's role in the novel evokes his grandfather's role in *Things Fall Apart*. Obi's grandfather, Okonkwo Unoka, was chosen at an early age to be the emissary of war. He was qualified for that role. He rose from abject poverty to be one of the lords of the clan. He was the greatest wrestler of his time. He had great prowess in warfare. He performed creditably in leading the mission to Mbanta, and the reward was that he was given the lad Ikemefuna to keep in custody for the clan. Nobody had warned him that the clan might want to kill the lad after he had grown attached to the boy, who called him father. The clan, like its *Agbala*, kills one when life is sweetest to one. And it turned out that Okonkwo was put in a position in which he had to kill the boy who called him father. From the moment he killed the boy, his fate turned for the worse and continued downhill until his suicide. In the grandson's case, Obi passes his Standard Six certificate examination at the top of the class at an early age. He wins a scholarship for secondary school. He passes his Cambridge Certificate examination with distinction. Like his grandfather, he is the village celebrity. As a result, the clansmen in Lagos tax themselves and send him to Britain to study. But he has to repay the money they have given him. He is forced into debt to the clan at the same time that he is struggling to discharge his reponsibilities in his father's house. He is a self-willed person, but he is chained to the obligations both to his family and to the Union. Between these two obligations and his self-will, he is bound to disappoint one or the other or even fail in both. He fails in both.

The meeting following the trial reveals the rift among the people caused by the fact that they are no longer homogeneous. One set of arguments would have Obi Okonkwo suffer the consequences of his action. The reason for this line of argument is that by his choice of girlfriend he has disrespected his kinsmen, who had paid a huge sum of money for his training in Britain. He also earns a big salary, and the kinsmen do not know what he does with so much money. The fellow who has urged that Obi Okonkwo be left to his fate has also indicated that he had known for some time that Obi's case was hopeless and had argued that money should not be spent on a lost cause, for "[h]e that fights for a ne'er-do-well has nothing to show for it except a head covered in earth and grime" (5). The second set of arguments, while conceding the truth in the first set of arguments, counsels prudence, in keeping with the people's philosophy that one has to save a sibling in trouble, not blame that sibling and that anger against a sibling is only skin deep. That is why the Union paid for the services of a lawyer on Obi's behalf. But the case is lost. Therefore, the Union has to deliberate on the next line of action.

This first exchange shows the division among the kinsmen who had hitherto operated on the principle of communalism and solidarity. The people are no longer of the same opinion since some of the values inherent in the Lagos locale, which is far away from Umuofia, has replaced those values which the people had brought with them. No matter how much they would want to hold onto the values which had formed them, the author shows, through their arguments, choice of *topoi*, and choice of *ethos* that the locale has influenced their values and the commonplaces for argument. The more progressive ones tend towards individualism, which is now reflected in their values, arguments, and *enthymematic* reasoning. They have lost the values embedded in the symbol of the kola nut in the Igbo culture. In the prayer that preceded the meeting, the prayer conductor affirms the life-giving force of the kola nut.

This idea of a clan and its common destiny has been declining, hence this quest for individual destiny as exemplified by the kola nut. Like Obi, these young men in Lagos are also portrayed as choosing individualism over communalism. Achebe seems to be saying that the result of Western education is the loss of group cohesion and solidarity. However, this tendency to abandon the group comes with a penalty:

that of standing alone and losing one's emotional center or value center. When this center is lost, the individual disintegrates, becomes dissipated. The individual succumbs to outside forces, which could have been surmounted had the individual remained within the fold. But being in the fold has its sacrifices: the most important being the loss of one's privacy. In the communal setting, every action is public knowledge, and the indvidual is both strengthened and weakened by the group. Obi Okonkwo dispenses with communalism—its benefits and its restrictions—hence he becomes vulnerable to the outside forces of bribery.

The president of the Umuofia Progressive Union, the proponent in the second set of arguments, represents the voice of Umuofia outside Umuofia. He is, therefore, closer to the indigenous culture of Umuofia. Although possessing Umuofia values, his values and his mode of persuasion have also shifted to accommodate the influence of the Lagos locale. For him, it is shameful for a senior civil servant to be sent to prison on account of twenty pounds. The issue for him is not the shamefulness of taking bribes but the taint that will be heaped on the Union and by extension on Umuofia if their son goes to prison. Although he is "against people reaping where they have not sown" (5), he believes that people should eat a fat and juicy toad if they ever choose to eat one. Another member on this side of argument lays the blame on the method of receiving the bribe and not on the act itself. As far as he is concerned, Obi is the rat that went swimming with his friend the lizard and died from cold because his hairy body kept him wet while the lizard survived because his scales kept him dry. However, the overall desire is to preserve Obi since that entails preserving the corporate body of Umuofia.

Thus Achebe uses the prayer oratory at the outset of the meeting locale to expose further why "a young man of such an education" would take a bribe. The fact that the Union does not see its role in the tragedy is tragic in itself. The Union seeks the reason and the solution outside of itself instead of locating the blame within it and its well-intentioned but burdensome scholarship. Therefore, Achebe shows the reader that in all the arguments among the Union members, no one says categorically that the act of taking bribes itself is wrong. Thus Achebe makes the reader see that the Union is as confused and implicated in the corruption as Obi Okonkwo.

ORATORY AND TIME CHANGE

The oratory in the Umuofia locale before Obi goes to England exposes further the people's expectation that is the driving force behind Obi's view of his role as well as his internal conflict and alienation from his center of being, the clan and his family. There is the man-of-two-worlds motif in all his encounters with his people, whether they are praying for his safety or advising him on his conduct. Reverend Samuel Ikedi's first speech, which is not reported in full, sees the occasion as fulfilling Biblical prophecy. The people of Umuofia have been sitting in darkness, and Obi's departure to England for further studies is an act of bringing the light to his people. Even before he leaves, he has been given the burden of bringing light to his dark village. This light has the power to rescue his people from "the region and shadow of death" (7). Seeing Obi's departure as the fulfillment of this prophecy is rather grave, considering the nature of the young man who, as a boy, had seen it fit to write a letter to Hitler at a time when it was an abomination to show any pro-Hitler feelings. Actually, it was a time when Obi and other students were made to gather palm kernels which were to be sold to support Europe's war efforts against Hitler.

The reverend's second speech puts an even greater burden on Obi than the first speech does. In spite of the impoverished state of the citizens, Obi's father goes all out to provide a feast greater than a wedding feast. This speaks to the topsy-turvydom of the times. Isaac Okonkwo is emulating his father, Okonkwo Unoka, whose generosity is common knowledge in *Things Fall Apart*. However, he is misguided because where his father had the wherewithal, the Christian religion does not pay Isaac Okonkwo well enough to afford the type of feast he has provided. Hence, he is imposing an old value in a new situation. The reverend's speech brings out the values of the new age clearly through his reference to invitation cards as the gateway to a wedding feast. Times have passed when people engaged in the kind of extravagance and ostentation that Isaac Okonkwo has. The reverend's story in effect takes away from the praise because it suggests it is not prudent on the part of Isaac Okonkwo to give such a sumptuous feast. The reverend is aware of the history of Umuofia as well as aware of the changing times, having come from the township. He charges Obi to go after knowledge since these times no longer require him to go to wars and bring home human heads as was required of his grandfather, Okonkwo Unoka.

However, the reverend later contradicts himself: Obi must not dare to marry a white woman because "[a] man who does that is lost to his people. He is like rain wasted in the forest" (9). The new religion teaches that all people are equal before the eyes of the Lord, but the reverend is preaching the ethnocentric difference between marrying a wife from among one's kin and marrying a foreigner. In his scheme of things, marrying a foreigner will be tantamount to being lost to his people. Obi is also charged to keep enjoyment in abeyance while pursuing knowledge, else he becomes "like the young antelope who danced herself lame when the main dance was yet to come" (9). The image of the young antelope foreshadows Obi's fate. Obi ends his civil service career prematurely by going to prison. The real dance in the new nation-state has not yet started, but Obi is no longer in the dance.

The image of the feast persists in the reverend's speech. If the people had not answered Isaac Okonkwo's call, he would have been "like the King in the Holy Book who called a wedding feast" (10). This allusion to the Bible also evokes the image of the changing times and the inherent confusion brought about by the change. In the Bible, the king does not have to give invitation cards to a select few, but in spite of that, the feast is not well-attended.[9] In this case, even though the feast is well attended, the times demand that Okonkwo should have chosen his guests and not made it open to all and sundry. Nevertheless, the reverend sees it fit to thank the attendees, more out of politeness than out of real need. After all, the reader has been told that the attendees could not believe that in some townships they would have had to wait to be invited to a kinsman's feast before attending.

The prayer at this send-off party, like the Umuofia Progressive Union's prayer in Lagos, points to the confusion of the times, which in the case of Umuofia indigenes at home leads to the misguided perception of the nature of Christianity and makes fanatics of some of the new Christians. Mary, who leads the group in prayer at Obi's send off, is a friend of Obi's mother; it is, therefore, probable that Obi must have seen her quite a lot. Also Obi, like every other member of the clan, must have been aware of the fanaticism which makes her come to church every day and come so early that she has to finish her sleep in the church. This fanaticism is another burden on Obi Okonkwo when his parents, who exhibit it, turn around and ignore Christianity's precept of equality in their opposition to their son's intended marriage to Clara. In Mary's prayer, the reader is again made to appreciate the confusion and the meshing of the two worlds, the Christian and the indigenous, in Umuofia. These two worlds have different values and hierarchies, and the two are constantly in conflict. This intermingling is behind the confusion of values in the novel that leads to confusion of expectations and actions, and to compromises in Obi's actions.

The language of the prayer in the Umuofia locale is more confusing than the language of the prayer in Lagos, although both prayers are said by Umuofia people. The Christian religion still has a firm grip on the people in the village because they still naively believe in its doctrine. Views about religion are shown to change with an individual's level of exposure. At the Lagos level, there is still religion, but religion modified. For "a been-to," which Obi has become as a result of his studies in Britain, religion has lost its grip and potency and has become a thing to be manipulated for winning arguments when it suits the arguer to use it. Mary's prayer exhibits this primitive view of religious belief which sends a young man to England but where he will experience religious disillusionment.

Mary's prayer divulges the values inculcated in this son who is going to bring light to the dark village. God is the beginning and the end. As Mary sees it, God holds the yam and holds the knife, and no one can eat unless God cuts that person a piece. This concept of almighty God directing every event is widespread and is behind every Christian's motive for seeking self preservation through the Christian religion. It tells the believer that he is nothing without God. This is the concept of God Obi carries with him. This concept of God is propagated by Europeans. Obi, naturally, will expect to see the Europeans uphold this concept of God in England. If the Christian religion came to him from the white man, by logic, the white man is supposed to be guided by its tenets more than the black man who had received it from the white man. But it turns out that Obi sees that his fellow men have become like the visitor that is crying more than the bereaved. The result is that Obi abandons religion or just pays lip service to it in order to retain his father's approval. Also, according to Mary's prayer, human beings are ants before God. They are like little children who do not even know how to bathè their whole bodies. This image of helplessness before God is carried by the true believers. The image also adds to the confusion of the role of the protagonist who goes "to the place where learning finally came to an end" (16; ch. 2).

This idea that learning finally came to an end in Britain is another concept that Achebe is going to refute. If learning began and ended in England, Obi would not find himself learning how to cope with the new nation-state when he came home. The idea that learning is an on-going thing contravenes in the reader's mind and underscores this irony of learning coming to an end in Britain. No wonder, by the time Mary finishes her prayer, people have to rub their eyes to get used to the light again. The prayer and the length of time it takes temporarily rob people of their vision. Achebe is showing how naivete can rob one of one's vision, necessitating one's action to repair the vision. Symbolically, Obi is about to take the action that will repair his vision of religion and Christianity. He is going to England. By the time he comes back, he will have encountered situations that will give him another vision of Christianity, and he will also have been away so long that he has to rub his eyes to regain the vision of his society and be able to fit into it because of the disparity between the Nigeria he comes home to and the image of the one he carried with him during his absence. This is so, especially as his knowledge of Lagos is secondhand from soldiers who came home on leave.   The image of Lagos for him before he went to Britain was the image of a place without darkness, where electric lights shone, where there were cars, and where people did not need to walk. This is the image of Lagos that induced Obi to write a lofty poem to Nigeria. The Nigeria he had in mind while writing that poem offered sweetness and ecstacy, jocundity, and music (14; ch. 2).

The process of rubbing his eyes to regain this vision is what the novel is really all about. Obi needs to rub his eyes and clear his eyes in order to recognize the Nigeria he has returned to, the Nigeria that contains "the less formidable of Lagos slum areas" standing "side by side with cars, electric lights and brightly dressed girls" (13); a Lagos that has two living areas, one for the Europeans and one for the Nigerians; a Lagos where people run down dogs and leave them in the drain to rot and smell; a Lagos where little boys sit on the roadside and sell *akara* and a nightsoilman is a common sight (14). The people all need to rub their eyes after a period of temporary blindness in order to have a clear vision, and only with a clear vision will the people begin to see the decadence that is juxtaposed with lofty idealism in the society and be able to understand why a young educated Nigerian would resort to accepting bribes. In this case, Mary's song at the end of the gathering points to the assistance they all need in order to grapple with the vision before them when they get used to the daylight. "Leave me not behind Jesus, wait for me" (11) becomes an apt and eloquent plea for divine protection in this situation.

After Obi's return, an argument that takes place on bribery exposes not only the inadequacy of the education the young Nigerian elite have received in Britain but also the effect of the passage of time on old values. This education is useless before the problems that face the new nation-state, Nigeria. Two people give the reader the Nigerian intellectuals' perspective on bribery. However, none has a handle on the issue since none can adequately invoke history to help him in deciphering "where the rain started beating their people," necessitating the present impasse. Christopher, who undertakes a factual and scientific analysis of bribery, and Obi, who takes the artist's view, counter for the reader the ruling elites' side of the argument as opposed to Mr. Green's statement that the African is innately corrupt. With the argument of these two people, Achebe again deals with the issues of fact versus opinion, intellect versus emotion, science versus art, and the scientist versus the artist, in articulating the problems confronting the new nation. The new nation-state, like the repulsive word "OSCULATE," which is eloquent in its multicolor, is filled with people from different ethnic backgrounds, struggling to shine into prominence, but ill-matched to jell into a coherent unit. In such a situation, Achebe seems to propose that scientific or dialectical reasoning must be married with emotion and ethical reasoning in order to create a whole and healthy system. Hence Achebe pits an economist against a poet, and they both fail woefully to discern the real causes of bribery in the country as well as how to arrest that malady and rescue the life and the health of the new nation-state. It will require the two—the economist and the poet—working together to achieve a holistic vision of a healthy nation.

Christopher always refuses to be persuaded by Obi's argument because, according to Christopher, Obi's argument is not based on factual or scientific analysis (17; ch. 2). In Obi's opinion, there is corruption in the civil service because of the presence of the old and experienced men at the top who have had to bribe other people in order to rise to the top. According to Obi, these men do not have the intellectual foundation required to uphold high ethical standards. Because these men have bribed in order to rise to the top, they do not see bribery as an unethical and immoral practice. Their ethics are grounded in and validated by the saying "that if you pay homage to the man on top, others will pay homage to you when it is your turn to be on top" (18). On the other hand, the young men straight out of the university will not have the need to take bribes because they have not had to bribe anybody to get to the top; therefore, they can afford to be virtuous. They will find bribery repulsive. Even if any of them, like the land officer who had been sent to jail recently, indulges in bribery, he will be an exception, an anomaly rather than the norm (17).

Obi as one of the educated elites and a poet is not prepared for the country he is coming back to rescue from the colonialists. Hence, Obi is speechless before his first exposure to bribery. The customs official that came to clear him as he returned to his country suggests that he would pay less duty for his belongings if only he would forgo the official government receipt. The idea is so repugnant that Obi threatens to hand him over to the police. However, Obi is yet to learn that even policemen are not aboveboard since they also take bribes. The issue, as Achebe keeps telling us, is not in the giving or the taking but in knowing how to take bribes. The customs official knows how to do it. The policemen know how to do it. Everyone but the sensitive artist does. Therefore, whenever the sensitive artist, like the rat, jumps into the water of bribery with the lizard, the experienced man, the lizard will come out dry-bodied while the rat will die of cold because its hair will not let it dry. The "baggage" of his Western education proves useless before the reality of life in a country where everybody, every ethic, and every value has been compromised and polluted by Amodern" values, ethics, and people.

While Christopher serves as the proponent of the scientific-style argument, both he and Obi actually exhibit the Socratic method of evaluating an issue through the Socratic dialogue, the only difference being that Obi and Christopher do not possess the depth of probing that the Socratic characters possess. Nor do they have the intellectual level of these characters. As the narrator tells us, "they theorized about bribery in Nigeria's public life. .... Whichever line Obi took, Christopher had to take the opposite" (17; ch. 2). Thus the reader can see that their arguments are more of a mental exercise than a genuine attempt to probe an issue of national importance. Moreover, they do not have the perseverance necessary to exhaust their chosen subject to the extent necessary to arrive at a solution or a definition of the issue at hand. Analyzing the old generation's propensity for bribery, Obi uses the paying of homage proverb which the old men have misapplied to suit their time and place.

Even though proverbs do not occur prominently in *No Longer at Ease*, they are used in significant ways when they do appear. Proverbs are occasionally twisted to suit the locale, just as language is modified to suit the occasion. Thus, such Umuofia proverbs as the one referred to above have undergone a transference of meaning, enabling their use in support of the argument on bribery. Because both Obi and the old men he is quoting have been removed from the source of this proverb by both time and place, they do not fully comprehend its real meaning. They thus transpose the proverb from its classical locale to the new locale, and in the process, it loses its meaning. This proverb was once used during the time of Obi's grandfather's encounter with the great farmer Nwakibie who had to lend yams to Okonkwo. In their reciprocal exchange, Okonkwo had given to Nwakibie what belonged to Okonkwo and expected Nwakibie to give back to him what belonged to Nwakibie and not what belonged to the clan or even somebody else. Thus the use of this proverb in the new locale is a misapplication. Obi's use of this proverb in this situation is symptomatic of his own confusion even as he argues against bribery. His ideology is neither fully nor clearly focused, and its roots are shaky. His father, Isaac Okonkwo, as an early convert to Westernization and Christianity, had not stayed long enough in the indigenous system to learn enough to pass unto his children.

Christopher does not also have a proper understanding of the issues surrounding bribery. In answer to Christopher's query on the opinion of young men on the issue of bribery, Obi gives an elaborate answer in which he claims that educated young men can afford to be virtuous. Their virtue does not come out of being better than others but out of their unque position of not being required to bribe their ways into jobs. Instead of probing the ethical issues raised by Obi's statement, Christopher merely said "'Very well put' and turned his attention to his food" (18). Instead of presenting a strong argument on the issue of bribery, Christopher only succeeds in poking holes in Obi's argument by supplying facts contrary to Obi's position. First his reaction, "[y]ou don't believe in experience?" (17) questions Obi's disdain for experienced men and puts Obi in a position where he must modify his claim about inexperienced men: "I didn't say *straight* from the university, but even that will be better than filling our top posts with old men who have no intellectual foundations to support their experience" (17). Also, when he points out the fact that a young educated land officer, "*straight* from the university" had taken a bribe, Obi defends the action by saying that the man is an exception. Christopher does not advance any argument why bribery is rampant in the nation or how bribery can be stopped. Achebe has, therefore, used these two people's arguments to move the plot of the novel further. He has also used Christopher's shallow probing to manipulate Obi into condemning his own action in advance since Obi ends up taking a bribe and going to prison.

By Achebe's argument, many social forces are responsible for Obi's predicament. Especially, the Union is culpable for the way Obi turns out. Obi has been given a Western education in preparation for a responsible position in the emerging "nation" where he is expected to work for the success of that new nation. But ironically the Union, which had paid for this education, expects Obi to participate in the divisive activities that will insure the downfall of the nation. He is also expected to carry a financial burden which he is incapable of carrying. The old order he left had changed by the time of his return. His education is inadequate for dealing with issues confronting him in the new order. Obi, the man in the midst of all these conflicting expectations and situations, will either fail one group or both or himself or all three. Achebe argues that it will be difficult for Obi to satisfy all three expectations and remain sane. In *Arrow of God* and in Ayi Kwei Armah's *Fragments*,[10] the protagonists, Ezeulu and Baako, pulled by similar antagonistic forces, go mad. Achebe seems to be saying that madness is too simple a solution. Hence, he makes Obi succumb. Achebe sends Obi to prison, the most dreaded of all horrors by any Nigerian, the biggest taint any Nigerian, especially an Igbo man, can bring to himself, to his family, to his clan, and even to his town. That is why the Umuofia Progressive Union is ready to do anything, pay any amount, to make sure that that type of shame is averted from their group. Thus Obi's type of tragic fall becomes the type Achebe advocates through Obi in his job interview (37; ch. 5). As Achebe articulates this type of tragic situation in one of his novels, *Arrow of God*, when "a dog tries to answer two calls, his jaw will break."[11] This is precisely the fate of Obi Okonkwo: a fate that is akin to, if not worse than, the fate suffered by his grandfather, Okonkwo Unoka, whom he is said to resemble, "Okonkwo *kpom-kwem, exact*, perfect" (49) and who also, in spite of his having risen to the height of celebrity, had committed suicide in order to avoid going to the white man's prison. These are the vital issues with which the novel deals, the questions and interests that the rhetoric of this novel has had to deal with, clarify, and strive to resolve. Achebe uses the effect of locale on argumentation to explore these issues.

NOTES

1.   For critical discussions on the novel, see Appendix II of this book.
2.   Perelman and Olbrechts-Tyteca, *The New Rhetoric,* 20.
3.   Mikhail Bahktin, *Problem of Dostoevsky's Poetics,* trans. & ed. Carl Emerson (Minneapolis: University of Minnesota Press, 1984), 183.
4.   Gikandi, *Reading Chinua Achebe,* 63.
5.   Ibid., 85.
6.   Actually, critics are in agreement that *No Longer at Ease* is a sequel to *Things Fall Apart.* Achebe himself makes constant allusions to events in *Things Fall Apart* in some of the oratorical situations in *No Longer At Ease.*
7.   Bakhtin, "The Problem of Speech Genres," 65-66.
8.   Burke, *A Rhetoric of Motives,* 42.
9.   *The Catholic Living Bible,* Matthew 22, verses. 1-11.
10.   Ayi Kwei Armah, *Fragments* (London: Heinemann, 1974).
11.   Achebe, *Arrow of God,* 230; Ch 19.

Chapter 5

The Rhetoric of Governance:
A *Man of the People*

ORATORY, POWER, AND A NEW NATION

In *A Man of the People* Achebe shifts from his primary purpose of showing his people where the rain began to beat them to showing how long exposure to the rainfall has had tremendous consequences that eventually rob the society of its independence. He also shifts from a valorization of his culture in relation to Western culture, which had intruded and sought to destroy it, to a demonstration of the politicization of society in which, in Robert Wren's words, "the political platform has become 'the new shrine,' and 'the chief celebrant' is unprincipled, corrupt, powerful and vengeful."[1]

This novel focuses on Nigeria's inability to develop as a result of the long exposure to the torturing rainfall of an alien system imposed during colonization. Claude Ake, a renowned social scientist, makes a critical observation on Africa's continuing underdevelopment when he says:

In the context of colonial rule, politics was a power struggle unmediated by legitimacy norms: it never raised the issue of good government, only the issue of locus of power. This is the tradition of politics which our leaders took to independence; they have not only retained it, but they have also reinforced it. Because they were insecure when they inherited power, they cling tenaciously to the idea of the rulers' exclusive claim to power.[2]

Sunday Aigbe also articulates Nigerian politics and power in the First Republic succinctly when he states, "[p]ower is not only intoxicating, it has the potential to create an insatiable propensity to ask for more of it in the individual or group of individuals who have tasted it."[3] The issue that Ake deals with in his essay, Achebe has addressed in novel form. Like Ake, Achebe attempts to answer the question, "Why Is Africa Not Developing?"

Achebe's argument in *A Man of the People* is that the type of independence or self-governance given to Africa is a nonindependence or a nonself-governance when examined in the light of the attitude of the colonizers towards the now ex-colonized elite, the type of people who inherited this power, and the nature of the country at its independence. As Achebe explains it in an essay, as a creative writer "in independent Nigeria," he "found himself with a new, terrifying problem on his hand. He found that the independence his country was supposed to have won was totally without content. The old white master was still in power. He had got himself a bunch of black stooges to do his dirty work for a commission."[4] Thus, Achebe's *A Man of the People* eloquently operates as a textual platform for his study of the white man's contempt and distrust of the educated Nigerian, which was inherited by the new group of leaders, the stooges of the white man; the intoxicating nature of power; the insecurity of the new leaders; and the absence of *a people* in the newly formed nation-state.   The interplay of these factors culminated in making Nigerian independence a sham, which inevitably has led to the disarray that makes it possible for the army to intervene and inaugurate the protracted and hardly interrupted regime of authoritarianism in Nigeria.

The events after independence were enough to push the people into apathy, and Achebe has very good reasons for being angered by these events. Irony is one argumentation technique Achebe, the orator, uses effectively in *A Man of the People* to express this anger. To match the content of his new vision with the form of expression, Achebe changes his strategy and adopts the ironic mode as a technique for arguing out his thesis. An Igbo proverb aptly describes this strategic rhetorical change thus: "when the dance rhythm changes, the dance steps change as well." Or as Ezeulu in *Arrow of God* describes the propensity for change, "[t]he world is like a mask dancing. If you want to see it well you do not stand in one place" (46; ch. 4). The ironic structure of this novel hinges on the notion of the members of the governing group as beloved politicians, each of whom has a claim to the title "a man of the people." This novel accomplishes this by showing that the politicians are indeed loved, but by a very ignorant, naive and apathetic population who do not yet constitute "a people." The reader inevitably asks: who are "the people" announced in the title of the novel?   Achebe masterfully deploys Perelman's and Olbrechts-Tyteca's concept of incompatibility to debunk Chief Nanga's claim to popularity. In showing Chief Nanga as popular and unpopular at the same time, he succeeds in asserting and negating his qualities, thereby rendering them unstable and eliciting condemnation rather than praise for him. His use of irony works well to advance his thesis. In Wayne Booth's words:

Some of the finest effects of modern literature have been achieved by authors who have learned how to shift their assertions of irony from local to universal and back again, being more or less overt all the while, seldom calling for reconstructions of covert irony but at the same time demanding of the reader an intensity of attention comparable to that required for reading covert irony.[5]

Achebe's irony transcends the particular society he is portraying and speaks of any society that has the misfortune of not having achieved nationhood. It also speaks of any group of people who owe allegiance to that society where the idea of nationhood is an aberration—people, who do not recognize their destiny as being tied to the destiny of their polity. This type of society will be susceptible to and will dictate the kind of persuasion technique the governing leaders adopt, for, as Perelman and Olbrechts-Tyteca have said, the audience is the determinant of the type of argument put before it.[6]

Although the irony here is overt— that is with Odili, the major character, used to deconstruct Chief Nanga but ending up deconstructing himself as well—the deep structure of the irony used is subtle and is contained in the fact that the people are upholding the man they perceive as their representative, but who is actually exploiting. Achebe tries to explain the situation by suggesting that after being in the rain with their leaders for a long time, the leaders have gone into the house to seek shelter from the rain and have persuaded the people to desist from arguing else they "subvert and bring down the whole house" (37; ch. 3. The quotes in this chapter are from 1989 Achor edition of *A Man of the People*). The situation exposed in the ruler's argument is very much like that in George Orwell's *Animal Farm* where the animals, having been exposed to the hardships of Farmer Jones's days, are willing to go through any hardship as long as Farmer Jones does not come back to be their master. Thus, one argument that the exploiting leaders use to silence the people is that it is preferable that a people be governed, even if exploited, by their own people. The vision articulated in the novel is like that which Robert Lee discerned in *Animal Farm*, where this type of mass delusion results in the difficulty of distinguishing the pigs from the humans. In Malcolm Muggeridge's view of the event in *Animal Farm*, Orwell argues that "the loftiest schemes to reform the world end by imposing more ruthlessly oppressive systems than any they replaced."[7] Thus as Lee's analysis corroborates, the event in *Animal Farm* is similarly enacted all over the world in most political situations where one group of oppressors replaces another whom the people had deemed odious. As in all such situations, "[t]he emergent African states, having successfully got rid of Farmer Jones, now have to reckon with Napoleon and his dogs."[8] And since the worst fear of the people is the return to power of their former rulers, the people will remain in the vicious cyclical situation unless there is divine intervention. This, precisely, is what the people have done in *A Man of the People*. This situation results in cynicism and apathy among the people.

To debunk the argument that the politicians are really the people's representatives, Achebe explores the criminality, graft, and political murder perpetrated by the governing group as well as the political naivete of the people, demonstrated by all their inept political decisions. In seeking to persuade the people and cover up their actions, the leaders bias the people against the intelligentsia, the experts, who ought to be acting in their interests. Although the intelligentsia have the moral responsibility to inform the people of the truth, they are denied one weapon for carrying out their duty: the voice which their opponents have. The big irony here centers around the people's inability to discern that their leader is a consummate performer. This inability to discern explains their enthusiastic reception of him. Achebe uses the occasion of Chief Nanga's visit to his electorate, through a masterful employment of irony, to expose the people's blindness. While the people, among whom are the Hunters' League, are dancing and the hunters are shooting their guns in ecstacy and anticipation of the visit, Achebe, the ironist, uses the narrator to tell us that "[m]ost of the hunters reserved their precious powder to greet the Minister's arrival—the price of gunpowder like everything else having doubled again and again in the four years since this government took control" (2; ch. 1). Ironically, the hunters respond to inflation but are not critical of the source and cause of that inflation since they are wasting that same scarce gunpowder to welcome one of those who have caused the scarcity. Achebe is clear about what he thinks of the populace who accord this dupe a rousing welcome; it is a "silly" and "ignorant" populace (2; ch.1).

Achebe shows the governing group as consummate actors and crafty sophists through his typification of Chief Nanga. Chief Nanga appears to his people as the approachable politician who is in politics to make sure that his people get their own share of the national bounty. He has to appear approachable in order to gain the people's trust and not alienate them. He needs to show goodwill because that is the only way he can insure that the people remain deceived as to his real character and his corrupt practices. His rhetoric of governance works. Chief Nanga, the model politician, is the political descendant of Nwaka in *Arrow of God*. He has acquired affluence, but he is not a model orator in the sense Cicero, Quintilian, and the other eminent rhetoricians have described an orator: the good man speaking well. However, his oratory has shifted from Nwaka's dependence on popular opinion without knowledge to that of manipulation and control of knowledge. He succeeds especially in manipulating through blocking or stopping communication and through deliberate shifting of meaning in language. Where Nwaka can be excused on the grounds of ignorance, Chief Nanga cannot be exonorated from the worse crime of manipulation and control of knowledge because he is educated and is a teacher, a position considered to be noble and even sacred, whose mission is to enlighten the people, guide posterity, and shape the future of a nation. As an Igbo proverb has it, the water has been muddied from the source. Chief Nanga, as a teacher, is a source of knowledge and, therefore, has the responsibility to lead the nation in the right direction. Because he had been Odili's teacher, his crime becomes doubly inexcusable in the eyes of his pupil.

Another ironic technique that moves Achebe's argument is the use of the characters to deconstruct each other as well as deconstruct themselves. Achebe employs autophagia to great effect. Autophagy can occur when, for instance, there is incompatibility of claims between an act and the principle it is opposing. Autophagy in this case results from "*self-inclusion.*"⁹ When Achebe uses Odili to excoriate the corrupt politicians, there is incompatibility in the fact that Odili argues against the validity of Chief Nanga's reasoning and actions but ends up committing the same crime of which he accuses Chief Nanga. He only goes into politics because he wants personal gratification. He embezzles his party's money and converts its property to personal use. He actually uses the money to pay for his wife's bride price.

Chief Nanga, the politician, also ends up deconstructing himself as he plays to his enraptured audience while being deconstructed by the same audience that holds him in awe. Chief Nanga constantly goes after what he and the prime minister condemn the experts for while the audience bestows on him the values he condemns in the experts. At a reception where Chief Nanga gives a speech that invites his people to partake of the national cake and not leave it to the highland people alone, the audience praises him and calls him "Owner of book!" (12; ch. 1). This praise name reminds the reader of the praise-name given to Nwaka "Owner of words,"¹⁰ only this time the medium has changed from spoken words to printed words, from orality to technologization of the word. The age has progressed from an admiration of spoken words to admiration of book knowledge. The narrator tells us that, as this admirer of Chief Nanga gives him the appellation of "Owner of book," he assigns "in those three brief words the ownership of the white man's language to the Honourable Minister, who turned round and beamed on the speaker" (12; ch.). The great irony here is that the educated experts have been condemned precisely because of their "book" education, which is equated to collusion with the white man. The villager that bestows Chief Nanga with such an honorific title may have forgotten or may not even have understood the implication of the praise-name he has chosen for the minister. The minister himself, who now basks in his new honorific, has ironically forgotten that the ministerial position which he now occupies became vacant when his predecessors, accused of the knowledge of the white man's language, lost their jobs. This situation evokes the scene where Brutus tries to tell the Roman mob that Caesar was ambitious and a commoner clamors that Brutus be made Caesar. The people in both instances do not really understand the game of politics, hence their unwitting role as pawns in the chess game being played by political adversaries. The greatest irony in the condemnation of the educated is shown in Chief Nanga's secret yearning for a higher degree, which makes him associate his initials M.A. with a Masters degree and which makes him happily and eagerly accept an honorary Ph.D. degree from an unknown college in the United States.

Another irony rests on the distrust the colonial administration felt toward the newly educated, which emanates from the educated acquiring the same knowledge that hitherto had been the exclusive right of the colonizer. The lack of dialogue between the British administration and the growing educated elite in *No Longer at Ease*, ironically, is also a rhetorical strategy adopted by the Nigerian governing group to disparage the intelligentsia and keep the people from discovering the truth.   According to Michael Crowder, there was "lack of dialogue between the British administration and the growing educated elite," and many of the British officials "were quite blunt in their contempt for the educated African"[11] as is exemplified by Alan Burns' (a former chief secretary of Nigeria) conception of the Nigerian experts: "the worst effect of education in Nigeria has been the manufacture of bad imitation of Europeans instead [of] good Africans."[12]   In *A Man of the People*, the same contempt and distrust of the educated elite surfaces in the governing but undereducated elites who have received the baton from their colonial masters whom they still hold in awe.   In *No Longer at Ease* as well, the reader notices this attitude of the governing group towards the growing educated men in the Honorable Sam Okoli's conversation with Obi Okonkwo. In that conversation, Okoli reveals that he favors a white man "who went to Oxford and," by implication a superior institution, and who, in spite of his education, "say sir" to him, over a Nigerian graduate whom he considers to have gone to an indigenous, therefore, inferior university, and in spite of the inferiority of his source of education, has a head that is "swollen like a soldier ant."[13]

The biggest irony centers around the idea of Nigerians as a people because the country has not homogenized into one entity. It is this absence of "nation" that the leaders exploit in preaching their message. One strong argument Achebe makes about the empty independence that was granted Nigeria is that it is difficult for the conglomerate Nigeria to survive as one entity because of tribal or sectional allegiances which have turned "the Nigerians, 'nationalism' into regionalist versions of anti-colonialism, with the British role ... that of referee."[14] In the words of John Ostheimer, on the eve of the birth of the first republic, "[c]olonial rule failed to mold all Nigerians into one economic and constitutional system. Therefore, no basis for a dominant set of *political attitudes and ethics* was created."[15] This idea, incipient in Achebe's preceding novel, *No Longer at Ease*, when the nation was still at its conception stage, blossoms into the general attitude of "mine is mine and ours is ours" where allegiance is more to "mine" than to "ours." In *A Man of The People,* where the villagers will refuse to speak against one of their own who steals from the country's coffers, this attitude leads to the total abandoning of "ours." After all, a corrupt politician like Chief Nanga is only getting the villagers' share from the national bounty.

Behind this attitude towards "nation" is the nature of the forming of that nation. According to Aigbe, when Flora Shaw (later the wife of Lord Lugard, the governor of Nigeria just before independence), coined the name, "Nigeria," for the British colony, the seed of disintegration and divergent aims and aspirations and inability to form a unit was sown right away. Although Shaw recognized that the conglomeration she was thus naming comprised "pagan and Mohamedan states," she believed that it might be permissible to coin a shorter name for these people who had never been described as an entity.[16]   As a result of this enterprise, according to Akin Mabogunje, "[t]wo hundred and eighty ethnic groups occupying 923,768 km and speaking close to three hundred languages became known as Nigerians."[17]   It is this impossibility of forming a nation out of the Nigerian disparities and discontinuities that Wren aptly characterizes when he says:

A useful way to imagine Nigeria is as a unified Europe, with Scandinavians, Germans, Dutch and Poles to the north; Spaniards, French, Italians, Slavs and Greeks to the south; and distinct groups like Basques, Bretons, Finns, Hungarians, and Albanians amongst them. Those familiar with Europe can easily recognize that Milanese Italians differ from Scicilian; Bavarians contrast with PrussiansCand so on. It is difficult to imagine the nations of Europe submerging their nationalistic fervor to a unitary system, yet it was expected in 1960 that somehow a British-based parliamentary system would work among the three arbitrary regions of Nigeria. It is an example of hope and faith triumphant over reason.[18]

Of course, hope and faith have no power over reason in the face of the anomalous conglomeration called Nigeria whose people have for centuries been disparate and remained unintegrated and for whom no amount of amalgamation can make into one people.

Therefore, the people, who could not grapple with the political burden created for them by colonialist political disingenuousness, add cynicism to their ignorance. As Odili tells the reader, the fact that the politician uses his position to enrich himself is not contemptible to the villagers who would not expect that "a sensible man would spit out the juicy morsel that good fortune placed in his mouth" (2-3). The people develop this attitude towards the "national" wealth because they do not feel that they have any claim to be a nation. In a free-for-all Nigerian situation, the national wealth then belongs to no one in particular. The grabbing tendency exhibited by the politicians and the silent acquiescence and cynicism exhibited by the people stem from the fact that the colonizer had unjustly made himself the owner of the country's wealth. Achebe shows that had the sense of individualistic ownership existed among the peoples, they would have taken charge of their affairs on the departure of the colonial ex-proprietor.

The case of the shopkeeper and the blind customer exemplifies the type of collective action of which the people are capable. When Josiah, the shopkeeper, tries to use the blindman's stick to make a charm that will insure that the shoppers do not question the prices of his commodities, the villagers have a sense of ownership in Josiah's intended act in that he wants to make them blind shoppers. They realize that the shopkeeper has taken enough to make "the owner" of the wealth being looted notice, and they ostracize him. In the case of the nation, since the polity has no owners, it is difficult for any "missing part" to be noticed since only an owner has the power and the interest to keep count of his or her possessions.

ORATORY AND POWER MANIPULATION

Oratorical technique, the tool for acquiring power, takes a more sophisticated dimension in *A Man of the People* from the way it is in *Arrow of God*. Although Nwaka in *Arrow of God* manipulates power through his sophistry, he does not have the type of technology the new politicians in *A Man of the People* have, nor does he have the same type of audience. The handling of the slump in the international coffee trade shows another means by which the governing group manipulates the governed through the use of oratory. Because the prime minister is afraid of losing the election, he opts to print more money to pay coffee planters instead of telling the people the truth. The expert minister of finance, who has a Ph.D. in public finance, has a plan for dealing with the situation, but he lost his job because his plan does not support the prime minister's political agenda; rather it has the interest of the masses as its focus. He should be a man of the people, but the people do not recognize him because he does not speak their language, nor does he know where the people's pulse is located. Aristotle urges that a rhetorician must have political wisdom or "good sense," virtue, and goodwill.[19] The minister of finance appears to possess virtue and goodwill but lacks practical wisdom, and therefore is politically inept. Like Ezeulu in *Arrow of God*, he knows but is unable to communicate his knowledge properly without seeming to be subverting the system. Therefore, he is unable to achieve, in Kenneth Burke's terms, "identification" through "consubstantiation"[20] with his audience. Like a dialectician who knows in a vacuum,[21] he is unable to take cognizance of his prime minister's fears, and the prime minister, with the support of the masses, does away with him. He ends up seeming to be subverting the very system he aims to protect.

The prime minister, who speaks the people's language and knows where to find their pulse, uses his radio address to accuse the expert of conspiring with foreign saboteurs, thus making him into a traitor who aims to destroy the "new nation." This ploy works because the ultimate terms of the period have been invoked. No new nation needs saboteurs and traitors. It is worse when the collusion is with foreigners, especially the ones considered to be enemies. A typical example is seen in *Arrow of God*, where Ezeulu's actions are construed a crime against his society because he is seen to be consorting with the white man whose origin nobody knows. Aristotle, in discussing the type of people one loves or hates, deals with this issue. He observes that we tend to love people who love what we love and vice-versa. We also consider all those who are friends of our friends to be our friends. By the same token, the enemies of our friends are our enemies.[22] For an orator to be seen to be friends with an enemy of the audience is detrimental to persuasion. The general feeling is that foreigners must go and leave the people to manage their affairs. Sam Okoli articulates this feeling clearly in *No Longer at Ease* during the transition period when he says, "I respect the white man although we want them to go"[23] and "White man don go far. We just de shout for nothing.... All the same they must go. This no be them country."[24]   The prime minister who makes this accusation has insured that the finance minister will be hated as an enemy of the Anew nation" (4; ch.1).

At each point that a citizen is accused of collusion, the society reacts vehemently against the accused while, when the sophist—the politician—is accused of corruption, the society reacts against the accuser. That is why Odili watches in trepidation at Chief Nanga's inaugural campaign meeting and agonizes over the obvious reply his accusations will draw if he were to climb the dias and expose Chief Nanga. In Odili's estimation, the people will laugh him to scorn and point out the foolishness in his own part by saying: "What a fool! Whose son is he? Was he not here when white men were eating; what did he do about it?" (139; ch. 13) That Odili exhibits so much fear of the people's reaction shows that he recognizes the fact that the ruling group with its sophistry has the pulse of the people in their hands and knows how to make the people react against their actual saviors. Although the sophistry of this group works against morality, that same sophistry insures the success of the ruling group to the detriment of the well-being of the governed. As Aristotle puts it, "what makes the sophist is not the faculty but the moral purpose."[25]

The use of the media in manipulating the people is a successful rhetorical strategy in the novel. The message about the expert's purported collusion with foreigners is first broadcast over the radio and run in newspaper editorials. The medium of this broadcast message makes dialogue impossible and serves to eliminate a "we-experience" while promoting an "I-experience."[26] The individuals ruminate on the issues individually without the benefits of comparing ideas. Moreover, because the medium is still novel to the people, it keeps them in awe of the product, just as the first coming of the white man kept the people in awe of his wonders. At this point, therefore, anything that comes through this machine has the ring of the truth in it and, like a divine revelation, remains unquestionable. Because there is no face-to-face interaction, the people are denied the chance to ask questions. They are, instead, intimidated by the medium of the message. Marshall McLuhan characterizes the effects of the medium on the message very succinctly when he says that "the medium is the message."[27] Odili, the narrator, testifies to the effectiveness of the use of the radio medium in diseminating the prime miniter's lies on the students; it made them indignant against the prime minister's opponents and made them give their unflinching support to him, the prime minister (4; ch. 1).

Indignation as a rhetorical strategy is a powerful tool when it is used successfully. In making the audience feel indignant against the expert minister of finance, the prime minister has insured sympathy for himself. Aristotle, in discussing emotions and their uses in rhetoric, marks the power of indignation when he makes it an anthithesis of pity. According to Aristotle, indignation comes when one is viewed to have acquired an undeserved good fortune while pity comes when one is seen to have met with an undeserved bad fortune, "for the being pained at undeserved good fortune is in a manner contrary to being pained at undeserved bad fortune... for if we sympathize with and pity those who suffer undeservedly, we ought to be indignant with those who prosper undeservedly."[28] The indignation felt by the populace is manifested in their actions. Odili reveals that the Student Union gave a vote of confidence in the corrupt leader while condemning those that have been dubbed "the miscreants." The people marched and demonstrated in protest of the miscreants' purported deeds (4; ch. 1).

The level of manipulation of truth/knowledge involved in the rhetorical tactics of the governing group can be fully understood through Walter Benjamin's views about the effect of technology on the work of art and the perception of the consumers of the object of art. Benjamin holds that the mode of perception changes with humanity's mode of existence, and social transformations are expressed as a result of these changes. Changes in the medium of perception of the technological age can be comprehended as decay of the aura of artwork, which can now be mass reproduced.[29] The mass-reproduced art object loses its aura because it is detached from its domain of tradition and has substituted plurality for a unique existence.[30] In the same vein, by mass reproduction of speech, the mechanical reproduction substitutes a plurality of "copies" of the orator's voice for the unique experience of oratory before an audience. The result is that mass production of speech robs oratory of its aura while manipulating and controlling the substance of oratory and, thereby, controlling the response to it. Part of the social significance of this state of affairs is, as Benjamin asserts, the "destructive cathartic aspect, that is, the liquidation of the traditional value of the cultural heritage."[31] In the case of *A Man of the People*, it results in the inability to ostracize/root out evil in the society in which the traditional aura of speech has been destroyed. Also as Benjamin sees the effect of reproducibility of the object, things seen by "the unarmed eye"[32] retain more aura than things seen through reproduction because, when seen by the unarmed eye, things retain their uniqueness and permanence while reproduced ones are marked by transitiveness and reproducibility.

In *A Man of the People*, news comes and goes through a medium, either radio or newspaper, not directly from the creator of that news as is the case when the orators in the indigenous society bring information to the citizens. By its nature, news is not permanent; therefore, it does not allow itself to be built on. As in the case of a message on film as against that on canvas, the auditor of a message mechanically reproduced through the radio does not have the time to contemplate and abandon himself or herself to its associations because, as in the moving frame, "[n]o sooner has his eye grasped a scene than it is already changed. It can not be arrested."[33] Thus like Georges Duhamel expresses it when confronted with the changes in Paris, the people "can no longer think what (they) want to think." Their "thoughts have been replaced by moving images"[34] or, should we say, moving sounds. That is partly why, in *A Man of the People*, the people are incapable of taking any action. Also once art lends itself to reproduction, it develops the potential to be manipulated and, therefore, "acquires a hidden political significance." Because art has the potential to stir the viewer, it can be used "to put up signposts..., right ones and wrong ones," with the "directives" becoming "even more explicit and more imperative" causing meaning in some aspects to be prescribed "by the sequence" of a prior message.[35]

The situation in *A Man of the People* can be viewed in the same way. Once the people's mode of receiving messages has become technologized and the message can be massproduced throughe radios and newspapers, it develops the potential to be manipulated in such a way that prior information prescribes subsequent reactions to new information. This is clearly enacted in the tactics used during the gallery incident in which the accused experts are not allowed to speak to the people and are actually shouted down because the people have been conditioned by newspaper and radio messages that have reached them. Prior to the gallery debate, the prime minister had broadcasted to the nation his own side of the story and made serious accusations against his opponents. Moreover, the *Daily Chronicle* had carried an editorial that calls for the extraction of the university-educated men from the body politic of the country (4).

The people who have listened to the radio broadcast and this editorial in the confines of their rooms are influenced by the medium through which the message came to them. The result is that the audience's identification with the message, like an audience's identification with an actor of a film, as Benjamin has discerned,[36] is really an identification with the medium of the message, the camera in the case of a film actor and the radio and the news print in the case of the audience in *A Man of the People*. This is so because actions can be exaggerated by the camera and the radio and the newspaper and can be manipulated to suit the purpose of the producer. This is evident in *Hansard*'s distortion of the minister of finance's gallery speech. Odili tells us that Dr. Makinde, the minister of finance, read a well-repared speech at the debate; however, *Hansard*, another major newspaper in the nation, "carried a garbled version" of Dr. Makinde's speech, which omitted the prime minister's plan to mint money while it portrays Dr. Makinde as a boastful villain who said that "he was 'a brilliant economist whose reputation was universally acclaimed in Europe'" (6-7).

As for the newspaper itself, it is cold print. People react individually without the benefit of shared opinions. The result is also a loss of "we-experience" and a promotion of "I-experience." It is easier to convince the people individually before they have the opportunity to come together and reason collectively. From the onset, the "we-experience" is lacking, especially as the constitution of the country does not allow a "we." Even in a village like Urua, which by its nature is home to an indigenous group, the mode of information is the same. As Odili tells us, the town crier, whose duty it used to be to call people out to make a decision on important matters, announces a decision purported to have been made by the people. Odili wonders: "if the whole people had taken the decision why were they now being told of it?"(136; ch. 13). As noted earlier, reactions to the news of the experts' collusion with the white man serves as one evidence of the effect of the medium of the message on the audience. The Students' Union, a formidable force in early Nigerian politics, condemns the experts whom the politicians have painted as miscreants. The whole country is behind the prime minister as the people march in protest and demonstration, damaging the experts' property, and even physically abusing some of them and seriously injuring one. It suddenly dawns on Odili that the victims of the condemnation "were all university people and highly educated professional men" (4; ch.1).

As the content of the editorial in the *Daily Chronicle* shows, Odili's fear is not paranoia. The *Daily Chronicle* insists that the educated men in the body politic should be extracted like a bad tooth which they have become. This image of the group as detrimental to the health and well-being of the new polity makes it mandatory that the populace will not want to hear the group. The group is also accused of being the white man's stooges versed in textbook economics and aping the white man's mannerism. These are serious accusations meant to evoke an undesirable image of the elites, who are not proud to be Africans and whose education, as the reader has seen in *No Longer at Ease*, has alienated them from their people. The image of the aloof expert, like Christopher in *No Longer at Ease* who embraces scientific proof, is appealed to in this accusation. The image of Obi Okonkwo, who shows ingratitude to the community that educated him, whose education in Britain has made him act as if he were above his people, and who cannot function within the culture of his people, is also brought forward here. Most communities in the novel have had the experience of sending a son to Europe and of ending up alienated from that son because education has formed a barrier between them. The general feeling, as expressed in the *Daily Chronicle* and as has been described in *No Longer at Ease*, is that "expensive university education only alienates an African from his rich and ancient culture and puts him above his people" (4).

By bringing up these images, the prime minister and his group succeed in alienating the minister of finance and his group, causing the populace to identify with the ruling group. Hence the leaders have chosen the best negative symbols for blame in this circumstance. Their choice of symbols makes them desirable because, by implication, they have not become "intoxicated with Oxford, Cambridge, and Harvard degrees" (4). Instead, they speak the language of the people, not only metaphorically but literally: they speak both pidgin and the indigenous languages. The irony here is in the fact that although the speaking of pidgin makes the leaders appear to be communicating at the level of the masses, it also places the leaders above the masses since the leaders use it to coopt, subordinate, and deceive the masses into thinking that the distance between them does not exist. They also use their choice of symbols to induce in the masses the idea that they do not need degrees from Oxford, Cambridge, and Harvard to rule, just as Britain does not need graduates from these institutions to run its affairs (4).

The leaders as consummate sophists appear to be helping the people and for that reason are able to keep the people with them. Chief Nanga, who typifies the politician of this era, constantly hoodwinks the people through his actions and his speech. When, for instance, he is told that his busy schedule is respected, he pretends to dismiss the suggestion of selfless service by saying: "Busy? Nonsense. Don't you know that minister means servant? Busy or not busy he must see his master" (9). By appearing to revere the people, he makes himself appear virtuous. Aristotle prescribes that the rhetorician should be virtuous or at least seem to be.[37] And the "greatest virtues," according to Aristotle, "are necessarily those which are most useful to others, if virtue is the faculty of conferring benefits."[38] Appearing to put precedence on serving the people increases the rating of Chief Nanga's seemingly virtuous disposition. Although Chief Nanga is just playing for effect, he succeeds. The reader is told: "Everybody around applauded and laughed" (9). He praises teachers when speaking to teachers. Although he is committing the rhetorical error of praising "Athenians among Athenians,"[39] the people do not seem to mind the use of this base rhetorical technique. Instead of the people taking him to task on this subject, given the circumstances at the moment when the students are discontented with their lot, they find his lies funny. However, he recognizes his blunder and in feigned seriousness assures the people that he is in support of teachers, having been a teacher himself. By the use of the pronoun "us" in that statement (10), Chief Nanga aims to include himself among members of the audience. This is one way of identifying with his audience and achieving "consubstantiation."

Playing up to the press is another strategy Chief Nanga uses to control knowledge/information. When in the midst of the teachers' fawning at him he turns to a reporter and says, "it is a mammoth crowd" (10), he feeds the public with what he wants them to think and feel the same way that Squealer does in *Animal Farm*. In full view of the press and the villagers, he pretends to be in tune with the custom. He turns to Mr. Nwege, making sure that people hear him, and says "Thank you very much, thank you sir" (10). Of course, he receives the reaction he craves to get even though it is his bodyguard who calls the public's attention to this virtue: "You see wetin I de talk. How many minister fit hanswer *sir* to any Tom, Dick, and Harry wey senior them for age? I hask you how many?" (11). Here the performer pretends to accord age the respect due it. This is one way of making sure he holds fast to the power that comes from his polity. In this culture, as Achebe has demonstrated in *Things Fall Apart*, "age was respected" while "achievement was revered."[40] He has "achieved" but still he demonstrates that he respects. People's negative reaction to Okonkwo in *Things Fall Apart* when he appears to disrespect age explains why Chief Nanga will go to any length to appear respectful to older people. He knows his audience and speaks the pragmatic and opportunistic language of politics. When his paid praise singers heap praises on him, he makes the most of it by gracefully diminishing the praise, thereby elevating himself: "For," as Odili analyzes it, "what is modesty but inverted pride?" (11).

Chief Nanga has demonstrated that he speaks the metaphorical language of the people. He has also, in the same breath, subtly elevated himself above his people since he sees it fit to separate "ministers" from "other people." It is clear that, in his estimation of the societal hierarchy, ministers are not on the same social plane as other people, and he does not want the people to confuse the two and place him at their level. The irony contained in this statement is clearly revealed when one compares the brusque manner in which Chief Nanga treats Mr. Nwege earlier when the chief is being introduced to Odili (8; ch.1). The same Chief Nanga, who addresses Mr. Nwege as "sir," ignores him all through the ceremony because Mr. Nwege takes such a long time making a long-winded speech. In a speech during this visit, Chief Nanga rationalizes to his people his participation in the plunder of the national wealth and practically makes them accomplices in his crime. When inviting Odili to come to the capital and occupy a strategic post, he gives his reason for such a magnanimous gesture in the statement which epitomizes the greedy culture of the period as well as its justification: "our people must press for their share of the national cake" (12; ch.1). Presented thus to the people, the object of Chief Nanga's and others' plunder is construed as a *no-man's* property. Because it belongs to the country as a whole, he is only securing his people's share. Moreover, his seeming magnanimity in inviting a fellow townsman to partake of the national bounty instead of hoarding it to himself is a rhetorical virtue. After all, one of the virtues to exhibit as a rhetorician is magnanimity.[41]

The situation, as Achebe has demonstrated in *A Man of the People*, is what happens when an alien culture/government is imposed on a people who have to operate a system they do not comprehend. Wren also expresses the same sentiment when he says that "what for England has been for centuries the core of national stability became in Nigeria the cause—at least a major cause—of calamity."[42] This explains Achebe's insistent reference to the evils of colonialism, which manifests in his statement, "No one arrogates to himself the right to order the lives of a whole people unless he takes for granted his own superiority over those people."[43] The calamity that follows such arrogation is manifest in the action of the governing group, which is fraught with manipulation, corruption, and outright brigandry, and is demonstrated by people like Chief Nanga, who exploit his "solidarity" with his village to foster his political aggrandizement. Chief Nanga, in making reference to the highland people, is, in effect, evoking and exploiting what Odili has succinctly described as "[p]rimitive loyalty"(7).

Chief Nanga, the accomplished politician, knows that this situation should be exploited by members of the governing group in order for them to insure the support of the governed and in order for them to get votes at elections. This strategy proves very useful later when Odili becomes Chief Nanga's political opponent and starts canvassing for votes. The accusation which Chief Nanga levels against Odili is that he, Chief Nanga, invites him, Odili, to partake of the national bounty, but Odili seeks to send him, Chief Nanga, away from the table. This motif of eating the national cake pervades all the arguments presented by the governing elite: The sacked experts are accused of biting the fingers that feed them; Odili is accused of the same crime. The reader cannot help but notice that no one talks about baking this cake, only about eating it. The metaphor of eating and the right to bring home some of this cake to the villagers becomes part of the governing elites' rhetorical strategy.

The incumbent uses public gallery tactics to intimidate the opponents in argumentation. The public gallery of the house of parliament in *A Man of the People* is the site of the audience of politicians and on-lookers which the governing group exploits to propagate its views. This semblance of the old village square has progressed from what it used to be in *Things Fall Apart* and *Arrow of God*. In these two novels, it is a place where the orators of old aired their views and deliberated fully before a homegeneous audience (although heterogeneity had started rearing its head towards the end of *Things Fall Apart*), giving voice to any who had something to say for the good of the society. This traditional square has now metamorphosed into the Union president's home in *No Longer at Ease* and to the parliament in *A Man of the People* with its public gallery, where a heterogeneous group is brought together to discuss issues of national importance.

The mode of conducting these deliberations has changed along with the venue and the audience. The political use of the gallery in *A Man of the People* exposes the way the governing group insures that all oppositions are squelched through the control of knowledge and through the manipulation of the people themselves, whose interests are not being served at all. In the public gallery, where the two dissenting groups (the country's educated men and the political leaders) come to present their sides of the story to the ruled, the reader sees the experts telling the truth, but no one is listening. First, the incumbent leader has prepared the people's response to the oratory being presented to them by conditioning their disposition towards the group he has already effectively castigated as the "Miscreant Gang" (4; ch.1) in his prior radio broadcasts and the subsequent newspaper editorials.

Second, the prime minister's speech is effective in persuading his audience by virtue of his well-chosen *topoi*. Since he has already conditioned his audience prior to his appearance before them, he has succeeded in controlling the knowledge available to the audience, thereby insuring that the judgment of the audience will depend on its prior knowledge of the situation. By starting his speech with a reiteration of the accusations against the "Miscreant Gang," the prime minister reinforces, in the minds of the audience, the image of these officials as traitors. His chosen images also insure that he carries his audience with him. By ascribing the term "gang" to them, the prime minister has invoked all the connotations of gangsterism—which includes being a criminal, bad guy, mafioso, mobster, racketeer—to their actions. The imagery is truly damaging.

According to the prime minister, the "Miscreant Gang" has been caught "red-handed in their nefarious plot to overthrow the government of the people by the people and for the people with the help of enemies abroad" (5). The catchword in this presentation of the case is "the people." It is the ultimate term of the time, deemed to elicit the most favorable response, and it does. Anybody seen to be protecting the people's interest (even when the people in this case are nonexistent), is seen to be the "god person," deserving "god terms"[44] used in describing the prime minister and of such accolades as are heaped on him: "the Tiger, the Lion, the One and Only, the Sky, the Ocean"(5; ch.1). In Weaver's words, a god term is "that expression about which all other expressions are ranked as subordinate and serving dominations and powers. Its force imparts to the others their lesser degree of force, and fixes the scale by which degrees of comparison are understood." These words used to describe the prime minister, therefore, render him untouchable.

The prime minister also accuses the expert minister for public finance and his group of stabbing the prime minister in the back in spite of his having rescued them from oblivion. This picture of ingratitude dramatizes the height of treachery and appropriately elicits tears from the audience. As noted in Chapter 3, St. Augustine talks about the indispensability of such emotion in persuasion when he says: "I think I have accomplished ... when I see them weep."[45] The prime minister does not stop at drawing tears from his audience. He goes on to push them to the edge of fury when he accuses the "miscreant group" of having "bitten the finger with which their mother fed them." First and foremost, to bite any finger that feeds one is ingratitude that borders on malice; to bite the finger of a mother, whose duty it is not only to feed the offspring once but to continue feeding it until it is able to feed itself, is ingratitude that borders on sacrilege. The feeling which such an image of filial ingratitude calls up can be seen in the feeling which Obi Okonkwo shows in *No Longer at Ease* when a razor he had left in his pocket cut his mother's finger. He felt firmly bound to her.[46]

The emotion which the prime minister evokes at this gathering can be likened to that which Mark Antony invokes when he shows how Caesar was killed, not by the conspirators' knives but by Brutus' ingratitude. Mark Antony's words in that great speech are electrifying:

Through this the well-beloved Brutus stabbed;
And as he plucked his cursed steel away,
Mark how the blood of Caesar followed it,
As rushing out of doors to be resolved
If Brutus so unkindly knocked or no—
For Brutus, as you know, was Caesar's angel.
Judge, O you gods, how dearly Caesar loved him!
This was the most unkindest cut of all.
For when the noble Caesar saw him stab,
Ingratitude, more strong than traitors' arms,
Quite vanquished him. Then burst his mighty heart,...[47]

Like Mark Antony after his powerful and electrifying oration, the prime minister calls for action against the "Miscreant Gang," urging the populace to distrust his Western-educated opponents whom he says are capable of selling their mothers "for a mess of pottage" (6; ch.1). This declaration or call for action evokes the rabble-rousing politicians' manipulation of the rustic and naïve populace demonstrated in two highly political texts, *Julius Caesar* and *Animal Farm*. In *Animal Farm*, for instance, Napoleon uses the same fear of the ousted regime to beat the ruled into submission.

The governing group knows that the worst fear of the ruled is the prospect of going back to an odious colonial subjugation. What they fear most about colonial rule are unjustified taxation, humiliation, and loss of dignity, which they hope will abate with the departure of the colonizers. However, when these do not go away with the inauguration of indiginous rule, the people are driven to cynicism and apathy as is shown in *Animal Farm* and *A Man of the People*. Anyone who opposes a leader like the prime minister or Brutus, who has already been lionized by the people (or Roman mob, respectively), risks the charge of antipopulism, and is condemned even before he or she speaks. For such an opponent to succeed with a conditioned and biased audience and turn the tables on his or her formidable adversaries, he or she must possess the charisma, oratorical skill, and political legerdemain of Mark Antony as well as the aid of the political ineptitude exhibited by Brutus, who arranges to absent himself from the audience when Mark Antony is speaking. However, it is obvious that the expert minister for public finance is no Mark Antony, nor is the prime minister a political fool. Therefore, the mob is not swayed in favor of the "Gang." Instead, from the crowd, one hears such condemnation as "[t]hey deserve to be hanged" (5).

Manipulation of power also dictates control of response to oratory as the prime minister does. Having prepared the minds of the audience, the leader is expected to allow his opponent to speak and present his own side of the story. But that would be acting contrary to the tactics of power monopolization. Because Brutus allows Mark Antony to speak, he loses the Roman mob. Instead, political astuteness demands that the incumbent leader deny the opponent a voice; in this way, he is able to monitor and control the knowledge that gets to the people, thereby controlling the effect of his speech. Hence when the minister of finance comes to speak, the prime minister leads a garrulous crowd, which insures that the minister of finance's words are not heard. The entire house shouts him down, reminding us of that situation between Nwaka and Ezeulu in *Arrow of God* when Nwaka "talks into his [Ezeulu's] talk."[48] As is well known, knowledge is strength, but because the people do not possess knowledge, they are robbed of the strength to act either individually or collectively. In the same way, the people are denied access to dialogue, another source from which they could have obtained knowledge and, therefore, obtain the strength to act.

All in all, one notices the manipulation of knowledge rampant in the situation in *A Man of the People*. Not only does the governing group not allow its opponent a voice, but the group also uses the newspaper to disseminate wrong information to the people, both those present in the house and those who are not able to be there. As I said earlier, the newspaper, *Hansard*, carries a garbled version of the minister of finance's written speech and makes up words that portray the minister as a boastful villain. According to *Hansard*, the minister had said that "he was a brilliant economist whose reputation was universally acclaimed in Europe" (6; ch.1). This tactics successfully alienates him further from the people and confirms the half-truths of the prime minister. By the words attributed to him, he has confirmed that he is educated. He has also admitted that he was trained in Europe. The people, therefore, will conclude that since he has access to Europeans, it is possible for him to have colluded with the Europeans. If so, he could be plotting to take the people back to the rule of the white man. That is undesirable and will elicit the people's ire and condemnation: in a situation echoic of *Animal Farm*, the people will not want Farmer Jones back.

Moreover, the leading group through their sophistry has convinced the members of the society that their interests are represented properly. As members of the society are incapable of forming a homogeneous group, they lack the power to act as a people or see their country as a nation worth protecting. Instead, they are content to protect their nucleus environments, the villages, and to protect their representatation in order to insure their share of the looting of the national coffers. In a situation like this, the leaders, inevitably, have a free hand to manipulate things without fear of retribution. And in a situation as the one in *A Man of the People*, only an outside force can change the trend of events. Achebe brings in the soldiers to sweep the country clean of politicians. The next chapter dealing with *Anthills of the Savannah* will examine the military intervention in politics and its rule by "the Barrel of a Gun,"[49] to use Ruth First's title of a book dealing with the same issue.

NOTES

1.   Achebe, "The Role of the Writer in a New Nation," *Nigeria Magazine* 81 (1964):157.

2.   Claude Ake, "Why Is Africa Not Developing?" *West Africa* (June 17, 1985):1213.

3.   Aigbe, *The Theory of Social Involvement*, 122.

4.   Achebe, *Morning Yet*, 144.

5.   Wayne C. Booth, *A Rhetoric of Irony* (Chicago: University of Chicago Press, 1974), 238.

6.   Perelman and Olbrechts-Tyteca, *The New Rhetoric*, 21.

7.   Malcolm Muggeridge, intro. to George Orwell, *Animal Farm* (New York: Time Life Books, 1965), IX.

8.   Robert Lee, *Orwell's Fiction* (Notre Dame, IN: University of Notre Dame Press, 1970), 12.

9.   Perelman and Olbrechts-Tyteca, *The New Rhetoric*, 203-205.

10.   Achebe, *Arrow of God*, 144; Ch. 13.

11.   Michael Crowder, *The Story of Nigeria* (London: Faber and Faber, 1962), 267.

12. Alan Burns, *Principles of Native Administration and Their Application* (Lagos: 1934). Quoted in Crowder, *The Story of Nigeria*, 267-268.

13. Achebe, *No Longer at Ease*, 62; Ch. 7.

14. John S. Ostheimer, *Nigerian Politics* (New York: Harper and Row, 1973), 27. Quoted in Sunday Aigbe, *Theory of Social Involvement*, 122.

15. Ibid., 437. (Emphasis added by Aigbe who also contends the same.)

16. Flora Shaw, "Nigeria," *The Times* (London: June 8, 1897) 6. Quoted in Aigbe, *Theory of Social Involvement*, 2.

17. Akin L. Mabogunje, "Nigeria: Physical and Social Geography," in *Africa South of the Sahara* (London: Europa Publications, 1986), 723-724. Quoted in Aigbe, *Theory of Social Involvement* 2.

18. Wren, *Achebe's World*, 133.

19. Aristotle, *Rhetoric*, II.i.6.

20. Burke, *A Rhetoric of Motives*, 20.

21. Weaver, "The Phaedrus and the Nature of Rhetoric" discusses the calamity that visits such a rhetorician as the minister of finance is shown to be. That rhetorician needs truth plus its artful presentation in order to succeed. *Ethics of Rhetoric*, 15.

22. Aristotle, *Rhetoric*, II.iii.7.

23. Achebe, *No Longer at Ease*, 61; Ch. 7.

24. Ibid., 62; Ch. 7.

25. Aristotle, *Rhetoric*, I.ii.3.

26. Mikhail Bakhtin, *Marxism and the Philosophy of Language*, trans. Ladislav Matejka and I. R.Titunik, in Bizzell and Herzberg, eds., *The Rhetorical Tradition*, 932.

27. Marshal McLuhan, *The Medium Is the Message* (San Francisco: Hardwired, 1996), 8.

28. Aristotle, *Rhetoric*, II. ix. 1.

29. Walter Benjamin,."The Work of Art in the Age of Mechanical Reproduction," *Illuminations* (New York: Harcourt, Brace and World, Inc., 1968), 224.

30. Ibid., 223.

31. Ibid.

32. Ibid., 225.

33. Ibid., 240.

34. Georges Duhamel, *Scènes de la vie future* (Paris: 1930), 52. Quoted in Benjamin, *Illuminations*, 240.

35. Benjamin, *Illuminations* 228

36. Ibid., 230

37. Aristotle, *Rhetoric* I. ix.1-7.

38. Ibid., I. ix. 6.

39. Ibid., I. ix. 30. Aristotle is against this tactic since he tells us "to consider in whose presence we praise ... it is not difficult to praise Athenians among Athenians."

40. Achebe, *Thing Fall Apart*, 8; Ch. 1.

41. Aristotle, *Rhetoric*, I.ix.6.

42. Wren, *Achebe's World*, 135.

43. Achebe, *Morning Yet*, 139.

44. Weaver discusses the use of god terms in persuasion in *The Ethics of Rhetoric*, 212.

45. St. Augustine, *De Doctrina Christiana*, Bk IV, see note 44, Chapter 3 of this book.

46. Achebe, *No Longer at Ease*, 68; Ch.7.

47. Shakespeare, *Julius Caesar*, Act IV, 1: 174-184.

48. Achebe, *Arrow of God*, 142; Ch 13.

49. Ruth First, *The Barrel of a Gun: Political Power in Africa and the Coup d'État*, (London: Penguin, 1970).

Chapter 6

The Rhetoric of Military Intervention in Politics: *Anthills of the Savannah*

TO EVERYONE HIS DUE

Anthills of the Savannah, like *Things Fall Apart*, responds to rhetorical analysis when seen as argumentation. As in *Things Fall Apart*, the argument in *Anthills of the Savannah* is superbly handled. In this novel, Achebe first argues that everyone deserves his due. A society that ignores the wisdom contained in this maxim faces chaos. Central to the novel is a speech by the elderly leader of the Abazonians, An analysis of his speech should make clear Achebe's argument.

The old man has just come to Bassa to meet with the president, who has refused to visit Abazon and who has stopped progress on the pipe-borne water project going on in Abazon. As the leader of the delegation from Abazon, the old man is received by a member of the cabinet, a politician, actually a professor of political science, Dr. Okong. The old man is made to understand that, much as the president would want to meet with the delegation, he is occupied with matters of international importance. This is a politician talking to a politician. They speak the same language. They both understand that the refusal to see him and his entourage has nothing to do with international politics. However, the refusal is subtly handled and no one loses face or feels affronted. Ikem Osodi, in his capacity as a press man and as a native of Abazon, meets with the group. At this meeting, the president of the Abazonians residing in Bassa expresses his discontent at the fact that Ikem has never before attended their meeting. We have seen the authority of such meetings and the power of their presidents in *No Longer at Ease*, where such a group is instrumental to Obi Okonkwo's obtaining of Western education and where such a group dictates the moral conduct expected of its members. His observation is, therefore, an admonition to Ikem for neglecting the group to which he belongs and portends a threat as to what happens to an individual who is not seen to be in the fold. The individual relinquishes all claims to group solidarity in times of adversity. The observation also serves as the cue for the the the old man's speech in which he deals with the issue of division of duties in a society and the issue of the punishment the Abazon people are suffering because of their previous, unguided political choice.

The white-bearded elder starts his speech by thanking his audience for their show of camaraderie. The Abazonians in Bassa had accompanied the leaders to the Presidential Palace. That support the old man and his entourage appreciate. The gesture shows respect and support for the delegation, and it also shows that Abazonians are a formidable force. By thanking the audience, the old man displays a sense of appreciation, a virtue that insures further gratification. It is also a virtue that puts the audience in a right frame of mind to listen to the speech that will follow. Since the crux of the old man's speech is that every individual should be accorded his or her due, his recognizing the efforts of the Abazonians in Bassa is a good rhetorical move because he will be seen to be acting what he is preaching. Thus, his exordium is appropriate.

His next move is to settle a rift he foresees among the people of Abazon that, as he knows, might bring rancor and divide the house if not dispensed with. This is a good political/rhetorical move because if the Abazonians intend to remain a formidable force, they need to be united. It also shows the old man to further exhibit goodwill towards his audience by interceding in what he sees as a future impediment to his audience's progress. He turns to the man who remonstrates Ikem Osodi for not joining their gathering and gives a speech on the importance of division of labor. Ikem Osodi is dealing with a national issue which benefits them, the Abazonians, in two major ways: by his actions he shows that someone from amongst them is trying to rescue the whole country, and that in helping the whole country, he is also helping them, the Abazonians.

This type of logic is inherent in the proverb that when one finger touches oil it smears the rest. Even though this proverb is negative in that it deals with the individual committing a crime which has a retribution that affects all, the name-taking practice of *ozo* people, which Romanus Egudu describes in his analysis of the Ojebe poetry, indicates the positive side of the concept of this proverb. The *ozo* men are reminded of their fathers' past marvellous and heroic activities which they inherit. This idea is expressed as "'Ani-na-efu-Ngwu', ... 'The-Land-That-Breeds-The-*Ngwu*-Tree.'"[1] According to Egudu, the "Ngwu tree is sacred and mystic; it is a symbol of supernatural power." The type of feat the *ozo* man has performed brings social dignity to his people and "[a]s the Ngwu trees are very important ones, the land that breeds them is highly regarded."[2]

By the same token, Ikem is the *Ngwu* that has sprouted among his people. The land that has bred him enjoys social prestige and recognition. What Ikem does affects them all and the benefit of his action with it. And if they expect him to do a job that brings such tremendous honor to them and expect him also to attend their meetings, they will be asking for far more than he can handle. For "our wise men have said that ...a man who answers every summons by the town-crier will not plant corn in his fields" (112; ch. 9 the quotes in this chapter are from the 1989 Doubleday edition of Anthills of the Savannah). In the old man's view, although the Abazonian meetings are also important, Ikem should be left alone to deal with the task of national importance that occupies his days or this task will suffer. In quoting the wise men of Abazon, the old man is calling on the wisdom of the ancients for witness and support to his claim. The choice of the source of witness is strong and lends authority to his claim. It also insures acquiescence and adherence to his advice. The cockerel proverb the old man uses in his illustration succeeds in elevating Ikem's chosen duty to his community and in making the people feel part of Ikem's achievement. In the old man's view, all of the members of the Umuofia Union are beneficiaries of whatever causes Ikem's absence from their village meeting. In making these people benficiaries, the old man has made sure that there will not be any rancor against Ikem, whom they will now see in a new and better light. Where before they felt snubbed by his absence, now they will feel proud to have him as part of them. This argument hinges on the fact that more is better than less.[3] If the people gain more from Ikem's absence, chances are they will prefer his absence from their meeting to the paltry gain of his presence. His absence takes their town into the limelight while his presence just makes them benefit from his wisdom, which they can benefit from whether he is present or not.

The writer tells us that "[t]here was such compelling power and magic in his voice that even the MC who had voiced the complaints was now beginning to nod his head, like everybody else, in agreement" (112). The old man is a politician and knows how to use words and how to modulate his voice to carry the desired emotion. There is evidence that he has achieved "consubstantiation."

The next segment of the old man's speech reiterates his first. However, he gets down to specifics of Ikem's accomplishments in order to buttress his argument that Ikem should be left alone to deal with higher issues. He, the old man, has heard how Ikem fights for the poor. Again, Aristotle's more-or-less *topos* comes into play here. If Ikem fights for the poor in general, he will surely fight more for the poor in his hometown. Ikem is gifted in that area and should be allowed to realize his potentials. Hence the Abazon people have the saying "[t]o everyone his due" (113). Our fathers fashioned this practice in which if one has a multitude to greet one just says "[t]o everyone his due." By invoking the fathers of the land, the old man is buttressing the authenticity and is ensuring the legitimacy of his claim. He also points out the wisdom behind that saying: "We can all see how that handful of words can save us from the ache of four hundred handshakes and the headache of remembering a like multitude of praise-names" (113).

However, "that handful of words" has another dimension to it. This dimension is the thesis of Achebe's argument. According to the elder, every member of the Kangan society deserves to be accorded respect and appreciation, no matter how minimal the person's contribution to the society seems. He uses the job the bush fowl performs every morning to illustrate this point (113). This is a good transition for the old man to delve into the real issue at stake here: that is the inability of the powers that be to recognize that different people are imbued with different gifts. Therefore, they refuse to listen to Ikem Osodi, the symbolic bushfowl that is making the wake-up call. The government does not only ask him to shut up but later kills the bushfowl so that it does not disturb its conscience by calling attention to its dereliction of duty to the masses. This segment of the old man's oratory also points a finger at the intellectuals for not recognizing their shortcomings in the field of politics.

"To everyone his due," therefore, encapsulates the merit accorded to each member of a society. Everyone has a task to perform in a society. That is how the world has been fashioned. Some people have the gift of uttering the word and inducing actions; others act while others recount the story of the action (112-113). By this logic, we are made to see that Chris, the commisioner for information, calls for action; Sam, the soldier, acts; Ikem, the editor of the national news medium, tells the story and analyzes the issues for the people. While the new generation, like Sam's regime, and the young intellectuals, represented by Ikem and Chris, believe that war is the greatest remedy, the old generation, represented by the old man who is the leader of the Abazon delegation to the Presidential Palace, believes that the story is supreme, for "only the story can continue beyond the war and the warrior" (114). The story charts the way for a people and directs the people's footsteps in order to guide them safely through its journey. That is why the people of Abazon "give the name Nkolika to their daughters—Recalling-Is-Greatest"(114). By extension, it points to the fact that survival is esteemed. If nobody survives in a society, there will not be anybody to tell the story of what happened. Not only will that society be extinct, but the society's name will also be lost for ever. This reasoning marks political astuteness. A politician like Professor Okong, a political science teacher, plays this survival game very well as is seen in his activities in and out of the cabinet. Any attempt to control the story leads to calamity befalling the controller (114). The thrust of the old man's oratory is that if Sam, Chris, and Ikem play their parts together and harmoniously they would produce a well-blended choral epic and keep the body of the Kangan state healthy and insure the continuity of the society. The moment one of the three starts encroaching on the other's territory there is bound to be discordant and cacophonic rhythm, which will make the state sick.

INCOMPETENT SAVIOR

Achebe's next argument is that the military is incapable of taking up political leadership because the military has turned out to be a monstrous version of the civilian politicians. He demonstrates that the military is incompetent in its efforts to save the country. The story of this novel is quite simple. But when examined, the reader sees more than this simple plot enfolding. The reader sees Achebe arguing against, among other things, the intrusion of the army in the political life of a nation. The army regards itself as the custodian of the polity and the ultimate political arbiter. In its view, its intervention in the country's politics is for the purpose of preserving the country's unity and stability when the conditions for democracy were on the verge of collapse, "when," as Achebe has articulated it, "our civilian politicians finally got what they had coming to them and landed unloved and unmourned on the rubbish heap" (11; ch. 1). Therefore, the military wants the polity to believe that its members are first and foremost patriots, dedicated to the defense of the nation, who have been forced into a governing role, not by design but by the need to prevent anarchy. Hence, the army does everything it can to represent itself as a group convinced of its righteous cause. The words of the soldiers expose their conviction on the righteousness of their mission.

However, the reader witnesses violations of human rights which Achebe condemns through his chosen *topoi*. The reader also watches, like Chris, with trepidation as the ideological concerns of the people are frustrated and trampled upon because the actors have taken on a different garb; corruption has acquired a different strength: it not only tries to control knowledge, it now has a gun, and it demands absolute obedience. The state itself has ceased to be based on a consensus, as people are no longer part of the country by choice but by subjugation. National consciousness has become undesirable and a threat. Oppression and domination are from within not from without, and therefore, difficult to contend. Sam's regime ends up repressing rather than succoring human freedom. The whole experience is as confusing to the masses as it is to Chris, and it induces a state of inertia and initially robs them of the strength to react against the new hegemony. Chris wonders why he is a part of the whole deceitful and decadent government. He concludes by convincing himself that he is in the Cabinet just as an observer. By the end of *Anthills of the Savannah*, Achebe uses Sam's actions to expose the military rhetoric of rescue as unpersuasive and Chris' claim of taking an observatory stance as delusional..

Perelman and Olbrechts-Tyteca prescribe that a rhetorician choose a presence around which to build his case. Achebe chooses Sam as one of the *foci* of his arguments in this novel. Sam is not ethical enough to propagate a moral purpose for the army. Sam is not involved in the coup that brought him into power. His ascent to power is pure chance. As Ikem lets us know, Chris has a theory about such soldiers like Sam: "military life attracts two different kinds of men: the truly strong who are very rare, and the rest who would be strong" (43; ch 4). While those in the first group make excellent soldiers, those in the second group go into soldiering for the power it accords them. In Ikem's estimation, Sam belongs to the second group. He is neither strong enough nor smart enough to rule the nation, and that is why Ikem believes that Sam needs Chris' and Ikem's services. As Ikem discerns the situation, "[i]f Sam were stronger or brighter he probably wouldn't need our offices; but then he probably wouldn't have become His Excellency in the first place. Only half-wits can stumble into such enormities" (42).

Although Sam's initial policies win him broad popular support and his decisiveness elevates him, when he decides to subvert the army's desire to be only a temporary caretaker government, he retires his military counterparts from his cabinet and replaces them with civilians. This is a wrong political strategy and an obstacle to his future ability to persuade his military support, because as Achebe shows the reader, Sam succeeds in incurring enemies both among his military colleagues as' well as among his civilian friends.   Both kinds of enemies are detrimental to the success of his regime. Since his colleagues naturally have friends among the serving officers, he has created room for the subversion of his role as their agent. Also since his values as a soldier are different from the values of his civilian friends, he has given room to the fulfillment of the cliché that too much familiarity breeds contempt. He ends up having the type of division within the house that the old man advises against in his oratory. The result is that some soldiers work against his system while his old friends hold him in contempt and exhibit gross insubordination.   The masses he seeks to persuade of his ability to rule are unpersuaded because if he cannot move his immediate audience, it is impossible for him to persuade his remote audience. This argument hinges on the flip side of the more-and-less *topos*. As Aristotle puts it, "a man who beats his father also beats his neighbours."4 Sam is seen to deal unfairly with his close friends and colleagues. Therefore, the masses will be right in thinking that he will not deal fairly with them.

Moreover, Sam makes the civilian cabinet, which he has created, secondary to the real echelons of power. This action renders his cabinet members powerless. Achebe argues that their powerlessness is part of what turns them into clowns and Sam into a monster. As Ikem describes the situation, these members become part of "the many petty interests salaaming around him [Sam] all day, like that shyster of Attorney-General" (42). Achebe begins the story with an examination of the activity at a cabinet meeting. The reactions of the members of the cabinet show a nervous group. Chris perceives their apprehension as he surveys the room: "I could read in the silence of their minds, as we sat stiffly around the mahogany table, words like: *Well, this is going to be another of those days.* Meaning a bad day. Days are good or bad for us now according to how his excellency gets out of bed in the morning" (2; ch. 1).

From Chris' description, the reader realizes that the commissioner for education's uneasiness at this meeting is typical. The members are both comical and nervous and, as a result, try to protect themselves by selling each other out or by acting absurdly. Chris muses about the predicament of the intellectuals in the cabinet given Sam's treatment of them: "I am not thinking so much about him as about my colleagues, eleven intelligent, educated men who let this happen to them, who actually went out of their way to invite it, and who even at this hour have seen and learnt nothing, the cream of our society and the hope of the black race" (2). The commisioner's actions are the most comical, if not ludicrous. According to Chris, the honourable commissioner for education, who is "far the most frightened" of the whole cabinet, acts in a manner that shows his acute fright. He tries a desperate but futile disappearing act, gathers his papers as if he were going to disappear with his file, spreads out his papers again, all the while emitting acute nervousnes and fear (3). The moment His Excellency's mood changes, the cabinet's follows. The moment he speaks in an "almost friendly and conciliatory" manner, "the day changes" for the members of the cabinet: "The fiery sun retires temporarily behind a cloud"; the members feel "reprieved and" find themselves "immediately celebrating" (3). This meeting as seen through the eyewitness account of Chris is both powerful and authentic. The use of eyewitness as a means of proof is a strong rhetorical weapon.

The result of this type of situation is the various moves for survival among the members, as, for example, Professor Okong's attempt to sacrifice Chris and Ikem in order to gain political favor from Sam. Professor Okong's manipulation of Sam during his interview with Sam on the Abazon visit exposes Professor Okong's nervousness, which emanates from his attempt at self-preservation at the expense of his colleagues. Professor Okong is a politician of questionable educational background and, therefore, has a great need to protect his position and to uproot any source of disruption of a system that insures his high position in the country. He needs to be seen as Sam's loyal servant. At this interview, Professor Okong accuses Chris and Ikem of conniving behind Sam's back. The dialogue between Sam and Professor Okong at this interview attests to the intimidating tactics that elicit this nervousness among the members.

Professor Okong is obviously intimidated throughout this interview. Sam himself makes him uneasy in spite of the supposedly valuable information Okong is bearing. The moment Sam gets the information, Sam reduces Okong by stripping him of his title. Professor Okong becomes "Mr. Okong" (18; ch. 2). Although Sam dismisses Professor Okong's accusations as gossip devoid of facts and treats Okong like a child, he [Sam] uses these accusations when he finds them expedient and useful to get rid of Ikem. Sam's radio broadcast to the nation accuses Ikem of conspiring with the Abazonians to invade the presidential palace. Achebe is, in effect, saying that the Okongs of this era make it possible for an unqualified president to turn into a monster because the actions of such people allow him to see the immensity of his power and make him lose his fear of the power of the masses. It is amazing to watch Sam's metamorphosis from a needy president to a monstrous one. Chris' eyewitness account is relevant here. According to Chris, Sam is reduced to a state of panic at the thought of public demonstration and is flustered by the Abazonian visit to his headquarters. These accounts show the reader how much fear the presence of the masses used to bring to this "baby monster" created by Chris and his fellow members of the Kangan cabinet who have now turned out to be so fearful that Professor Okong and some of his colleagues behave like nonentities before him.

Also, Sam appropriates the national newspaper and broadcasting stations, seizing the voice of the people. As a result, instead of being an admirable character, he becomes a monster who, whether present or not, instils fear in friends and colleagues. He enjoys seeing them cower before him as is seen in his conduct with Chris, Beatrice, Professor Okong, the secretary of the cabinet, and the attorney-general. Therefore, Sam elicits indignation from his peers, and indignation is detrimental to fostering ideology. Sam believes that he bears the military might and the miltary ideology and wants to project it no matter what, but some people within the army are not ready to help foster his hegemony, which they rightly perceive is mixed up with his private pursuits and ambition. Thus he loses his ethos among his colleagues. He strives to control the story and, as the old man has predicted, the story swallows him up.

By extrapolating the idea of the makeup of a society as shown to us by the old man from Abazon, Achebe insists that the military is not politically equipped to rule a nation. Its purview is not large enough to encompass a whole way of life. Rather it projects a fraction of the society's view of the world. They and their leader lack ethical merit, and possession of ethical merit is one of the ingredients of persuasion. The army lacks cohesion; the soldiers are divided among themselves. The military can use armed power, which, as has been shown by history, can only succeed in maiming the flesh and not the spirit. The spirit is supreme in every human being. When one cannot control the spirit, one has failed to master the "person," the real human being. The Bible says "[d]on't be afraid of those who can kill only your bodies—but can't touch your soul. Fear only God who can destroy both soul and body in hell."[5] In Shakespeare's *Julius Ceasar*, Casca attests to this lack of power of the man who is in control of the body when he says

every bondman in his own hand bears
The power to cancel his captivity.[6]

Stories of revolutions throughout history have incidents in which the bearer of arms has failed to subjugate the masses completely. In *Things Fall Apart*, Okonkwo refuses to submit his spirit and commits suicide. That is why religion wins where pacification fails.

In *Anthills of the Savannah*, the people manifest the freedom of their spirits when they help Chris to elude Sam in spite of the death penalty such acts will incur. The soldiers are dealing with a people that have developed what Aigbe describes as "a strong and undiminishing will to survive."[7] This will to survive is embodied in the soldier-trader encounter in which the civilian trader refuses to acknowledge the threat to his existence contained in the soldier's utterance: "If I kill you I kill dog"

(44; ch. 4). The disregard for the people which Achebe describes in this encounter shows the soldiers exhibiting symptons of lack of feeling for the people and total disregard for the life and safety of the same people to whom they had presented themselves as their Messiah. Having nearly run down the trader, the soldier shows no compunction. Instead, he rubs in the helpessness of the civilian trader by that utterance. But the seller refuses to admit to the nothingness depicted by the comparison that the act of killing him is like the act of killing a dog. He would rather be comfortable with seeing the action as being chronological, in which he is higher up in the hierarchy of the perpetration of the two undesirable actions. The soldier's callousness is as disturbing as the trader's denial. Although the soldier's utterance implies that the trader is nothing, the trader refuses to recognize the implication of the soldier's utterance, which declares the nothingness of the trader's being as is shown in the dialogues witnessed by Ikem. Once again, Achebe uses an eyewitness account to support his claim. He frowns at the idea that the same public that welcomed the soldiers and hoped that they would bring to an end the wanton killing, the corruption, and the disregard for the people is thrown into a state of shock that makes them deny the atrocities they witness. As has been shown in *A Man of the People*, the situation in which the people do not feel as if they belong to a nation brings about a nonchalance concerning events in the state and a situation in which groups take care of the nucleus group, abandoning the larger group.

After all, the military believes it is on a salvific mission. Sam's seeking to make himself president for life robs the military regime of the required *ethos* to maintain its pose as a temporary measure for returning peace and abolishing corruption. Achebe exposes the irony in the military argument through Sam's utterance: "When we turn affairs of state back to you and return to the barracks, that will be the time to resume your civilian tricks" (4; ch. 1). Here the reader is supposed to believe that the military really intends to hand over power. But the reader is also shown Sam's maneuvers to become the president of Kangan for life and his anger when the Abazonians' refusal to endorse him botches his plan. He has never intended to hand over power.

Moreover, the army does not want to be perceived as using force to advance its hegemony. That will be criticized by the outside world. But Sam has lost his *ethos* on this front too. He has come to a stage in which his pretenses no longer serve him. When he feels slighted by his friends, he engages in armed subjugation, thereby going against the group's view of his hegemony. He is not ready to make sacrifices in the interest of the army group, which as the leader and the bearer of its hegemony it is his duty to make. Instead, Sam employs intimidation as a technique for persuasion. He not only pursues his personal interest in going after Chris, but also he misuses the group's machinery to track down his personal enemies; he is guilty of abuse of office; he is an embarrassment and has to be dispensed with in order to restore life to the group body. The military, in order to retain its credibility, dissociates itself from Sam's actions by toppling him. However, Achebe seems to be saying that although Sam has gone to excesses in pursuing his vendetta, he is a military man and is actually manifesting the characteristics of the military ethos as rulers.

The military men are humans and like all human beings, once in power, they find it difficult to give up that power; power exerts unforseen influence on the holder. Hence Sam's metamorphosis into monster, which takes Chris by surprise, makes Sam human too. The army itself does not abdicate the throne of the government, seeing what one of them has done with the power vested in him. Instead, another soldier, having deposed Sam, takes over the mantle of leadership. This is an indication that such will be the order of things: one soldier will misuse power and another will take over, and "La luta continua"[8] as Ngugi Wa Thiong'o, the foremost Kenyan novelist, characterizes the vicious cycle in his novel, *Petals of Blood*.

The reader discerns that the rhetoric of the miltary is not very different from that of the politicians. In fact, Achebe seems to argue through the episodes of the plot that the military is a monstrous version of the civilian politician. As Bale Onimode succinctly puts it while analyzing the reason for underdevelopment in Nigeria, "[t]he military is the same as the politicians. Both are "members of Nigerian budding petty-bourgeois."[9] The only difference, however, is that the military has the arms to enforce its views and to insist on persuasion. Just as Chief Nanga in *A Man of the People*, Sam retaliates on opponents whether real or apparent. He denies the Abazonians of the much-craved presidential visit, which like the much-promised visitation of the messiah, is expected to restore life to the impoverished region. He has also ordered the closure of the water bore-holes being dug in the region in order to teach the Abazonians a lesson because the Abazonians have refused to sign the referendum urging the people to vote for him to become president for life. First he agrees to visit Abazon to see the problems drought is causing in the area. Then he refuses to visit them without giving any reason for his change of mind and without even informing his commisioner for information. When the Abazon elders come to his palace to be heard, he refuses them audience.

At the beginning of the novel, the president's reply to the proposition urging him to pay a visit to Abazon shows that there is a difference of opinion on the issue and that he is unrelenting in his reply to the suit before him. He reminds the reader of Caesar saying no to a suit in the capitol just before he is murdered. Hence this scene causes apprehension in the reader and the reader is poised, waiting for this drama to unfold and aware that it is a distressing drama.

Sam's methods of persuading Ikem, Chris, and Beatrice reminds us of Chief Nanga's method of persuading Odili in *A Man of the People*. The only difference is that while Chief Nanga tries first to persuade through words and distortion of information before resorting to the use of thugs, Sam exhibits a sterner approach towards persuading his opponents. He uses his efficient tool, the Director of State Research Council (SRC), Major Ossai. Beatrice's perception of Major Ossai reveals an unpleasant servant of a ruthless master. The director of SRC is handsome but "strong in a vaguely disagreeable way." He has "enormous hands...

like a wrestler's which struck you at once as being oversize even for a man as big as he" (70; ch. 6). He is not only the attentive servant, he is also a torture machine, the man who uses a paper-stapler as an instrument of torture. What he does is "place the hand where the paper should be—palm up or down doesn't really matter—and bang. The truth jumps out surprisingly fast, even from the hardest cases" (97; ch.7). Chris also gives the reader a chilling description of this director's capabilities when he says, "[t]here were unconfirmed rumours of unrest, secret trials and executions in the barracks" (13; ch. 2).

In the case of getting rid of Ikem Osodi, Achebe shows that Major Ossai proves invaluable. He makes sure that Ikem's movements and meeting with the Abazon leaders are recorded officially through Ikem's stage-managed encounter with a traffic policeman. In this encounter, Ikem comes out of the Harmoney Hotel, where he has been meeting with the delegates from Abazon, only to find a traffic policeman by his parked car. The policeman books Ikem for not leaving his parking lights on. When the charge for plotting against the government is fabricated against Ikem, this incident is cited as proof of Ikem consorting with the Abazonians to storm the presidential palace. Sam, his excellency, makes these accusations while urging Chris to suspend Ikem as the editor of the *National Gazette* (132; ch. 11).

Sam's accusations of Ikem contain some base rhetorical strategies in them as the accusations of the politicians in *A Man of the People* do. In the accusations, the use of [i]ntelligence reports" as the source of Sam's information is equivocal. Instead of mentioning the real source of the information, Major Ossai, Sam couches the source in passive terms, thereby ascribing the source to no particular person and also lending both anonymity and lack of self-interest to it. Had he mentioned it as Major Ossai, the report would not have had any credibilty. Therefore, Sam shrouds the source in mystery. Mystifying as a tactic invokes authenticity and objectivity. He goes further to say that this report "established" something against Ikem. The choice of the term "established" is an appeal to the conclusiveness of the finding. Then Ikem is accused of "planning the recent march on this Palace." The reader notes that the march is recent; therefore, the consequence is yet to be dealt with. And to plan against the presidential palace is to plan against established order. A palace is the abode of a king, and a king is inviolable. Hence, a plan against the palace is a plan against the crown. The consequence is a charge of treasonable felony which has its punishment as death.

The delegates from Abazon are called "agitators." The name chosen for them reduces their prestige and removes their legitimacy, thereby making them vulnerable to Sam's punishment. If their mission is called a delegation, it will have a positive image, but if it is called an agitation, it will have a negative image. Sam needs the delegates to be seen in a negative light. He further removes the legitimacy of the group by saying that they *claim* to have come from Abazon. Severing them from their place is a move that insures that Sam does not incur the wrath of the region they represent and also that Sam is not indicted for not listening to a representation of a section of the country. He can claim not to have believed in their mission and in this case the burden of proof is on the delegates to show that they really represent the people they claim to represent. Having reduced the status of the delegation to that of agitators, Sam has created a clear way for reducing Ikem's activity from its legitimate status as a press man and an indigene. To support his claim, Sam evokes what he calls "incontrovertible evidence" that Ikem was in contact with this group. That Ikem has contact with the group does not prove anything. He definitely has not planned the visit. Sam is using "seeming" to represent reality. Because he places Ikem at the scene of the march, he has used faulty enthymematic reasoning to accuse him of subversion.

On the basis of this faulty argument, Major Ossai seems in the right when he sends people to arrest Ikem at night and shoot him on a trumped-up charge of resisting arrest. He also seems to be in the right when he arrests the elders from Abazon on false charges of plotting against the government and planning to kill the President. The accusations against Ikem before he is murdered also expose Sam's use of the same rhetorical technique as the ousted politicians. As with the politicians in *A Man of the People*, the media is one avenue of spreading calumny against an opponent. The accusations transmitted over the radio are made in such a way as to put Sam in a positive light and portray Ikem negatively. The choice of the euphemistic term, "State Research Council," the name of the government organ headed by Major Ossai, instead of calling it accurately the secret police, is a good rhetorical move deployed basely. The members of this organ, in their research, have "uncovered a plot." Of course, they should be commended for uncovering this plot if indeed there were a plot. This plot also is said to be hatched by "unpatriotic elements in Kangan." If these people referred to as "elements" are found to be unpatriotic, it goes without saying that they deserve any punishment meted out to them. The worst thing said about the crime of these "elements" is that they are consorting with "certain foreign adventurers." As has been shown in the previous chapters, the act of colluding with an outsider is viewed more seriously than the act of committing any solitary crime against the state. And to make the act worse, these foreigners are adventurers and, therefore, neither reputable nor responsible. By dubbing these foreigners "adventurers," Sam has separated them from other foreigners and has implied that other foreigners are not bad for the state. Hence, he still assures the foreigners in Kangan of his friendship, and insures that these foreigners will support him.

The next evidence that the broadcast message uses for support is "[i]nvestigations by top security officers." This evidence asks the populace to reason that if this investigation is carried out by top security officers, it must have credibility. Also notable is the organization's initials "SRC" used at this point. This tactic removes immediate connection of the organization to Major Ossai and removes attention from him. Rather, it focuses attention on the outcome of the investigation. That is, that Ikem Osodi, who has already been dismissed as the editor of the *National Gazette*, has "master-minded" a "dastardly plot" to "destabilize the lawful government of this country." Many images are used in this part of the accusation to insure that Ikem is portrayed as a criminal. He is ascribed a motive for the action of which he is accused; he has been dismissed by this government. He is shown to possess the ability to carry out this action. He was the editor of the *National Gazette*. Here Sam is using Ikem's talent to make negative arguments against him. The masses know that as the editor of the *National Gazette*, he has performed creditably and has exhibited a great analytical mind. The people have read his analysis of events. The same people would believe that he has the mental capability to master-mind any plot if he chooses to do so. Also, by connecting Ikem's crime to the activities of the people he called "unpatriotic chiefs in the Province of Abazon," Sam is evoking the feeling some segments of the country have against the Abazonians as well as using the force of ethnic rivalry that is rife in the country to insure that he has the support of the other provinces. He squarely locates Ikem in his region while dissociating him from the work he has done for the masses.

At this point, Ikem is no longer the cock that is crowing for the public. He is the owner's cock. This strategy insures that the public does not identify with Ikem and decide to right the wrong done to him. It may even remind the populace of the demerits of the region from which Ikem comes, and by association, Ikem may be dubbed a trouble-maker, all his fights for the benefit of the masses forgotten. Moreover, it may even whip up envy in some region that does not have someone of Ikem's caliber to boast of. Professor Okong's comment about the Abazon visit shows the reader the type of ethnic rivalry and ethnic sentiment Sam is exploiting. The scene between Sam and Professor Okong in which Professor Okong calls attention to the disaffection people feel towards the Abazonians gives the reader an insight into the complex rivalries.

Ikem's public lecture is another avenue for indictment. According to the radio broadcast, he has committed three acts against the state: he helped the plotters further their aim, he incited the students of a university to rebel against the government and the president, and he threatened the peace and security of the state. These three charges, thus outlined in a crescendo-like manner are aimed at effecting a climax. Also if he has to carry out these action under a disguise, then his actions must have been premeditated. The use of the date of the action is meant to make the accusation seem like a fact. Then the accusation of leading students astray is serious because students are the future generation of the country and anybody found guilty of leading them astray should be made to suffer. In Plato's "Apology" in which the same accusation is made against Socrates, the Athenians voted for his execution.[10] Ikem is also executed in *Anthills of the Savannah*. His crime seems even worse because the people he is accused of trying to lead astray are university students whom I have shown in the previous chapter to be a formidable force in the politics of Nigeria. In emphasizing that leading these students astray threatens the peace and the security of the state, Sam is using the most powerful argument of blame for condemning Ikem.

Therefore, Sam, who carries the soldiers' ideology, is a performer like Chief

Nanga, the epitome of the politicians' persona in *A Man of the People*. Where Sam is worse is that he is ruthless under the guise of a redeemer. Sam likes to point out that he is not a politician. "You all seem to forget that I am still a soldier, not a politician" (4; ch. 1). Achebe employs a scathing irony here to counteract Sam's claim by devoting the next sentence and, actually the entire paragraph following this assertion, to revealing how much the man of action is emulating the ousted politicians. Sam wears mufti very often, especially the embroidered *danshiki* that the outed politicians were fond of wearing. As in *Animal Farm*, the pig is emulating Farmer Jones more and more. He also wants people to believe that "[s]oldiers are plain and blunt" and that the civilians play tricks. However, Sam is becoming more and more like the ousted politicians not only in his cravings but also in playing tricks. He secretly enjoys little services, like the positioning of his shoes under the table, which are done for him by the civilian cabinet secretary. However, he lacks one of the admirable attributes of the politicians—tolerance. He does not have tolerance for and patience with the opposition because he has the weapon to instill total submission. He does not use words; actually, he may not have thought that he needs words. As such, he shuns the need for one of the greatest assets and the greatest ally of a politician like Chief Nanga. He has the gun in addition to having the means of disseminating his version of information, the broadcasting media. Any suasory effort that the verbal medium starts but is unable to effect, the weapon, as the ultimate persuasive instrument, finishes off effectively. In other words, what Sam does not achieve by controlling the ideas that reach the people, he achieves by inflicting physical pain. Yet he pretends to respect the people as the reader sees by his interpretation of whatever Chris has asked him to do during one of their arguments: "you are telling me to insult the intelligence of these people," he says, "his tone mollified and rather superior" (4). At this moment, he is playing on the cabinet's intelligence and has no respect for the people as later events show.

Because there is no correlation between the words of the soldiers and their actions, their argument fails to persuade the people and they are forced to operate against the soldiers. The people help reveal Sam's action when Ikem is killed. Ikem's neighbors disclose that Ikem was in handcuffs when he was led away, indicating that Ikem could not have been resisting arrest when he was shot. He was murdered. The people also help Chris to elude Sam. The fact that they are ready to go through any difficulty to prevent Sam from catching Chris shows that the army has lost its credibility and has been unsuccessful in inculcating its ideology. The taxi driver who aids Chris' escape is willing to sleep on the floor in a neighbor's house just so that Chris will sleep in his bed. Even Sam's fellow army officers are not persuaded by the military rhetoric; therefore, they subvert the usual hierarchical army system. The officer whose duty it is to track down Chris shows reluctance in carrying out his duty when he divulges information that helps Beatrice to relocate Chris each time Major Ossai's officers are closing in on Chris. He calls himself a horse lover and makes sure that the horse, Chris, is never found. All in all, both the masses and the soldiers are found to be working against the system.

Just like Chief Nanga in *A Man of the People*, Sam is ready to squander the nation's resources (to use what Udumukwu has rightly identified as Althusser's "Repressive State Apparatus"[11] to carry out a personal vendetta) just to arrest Chris and just to show how powerful he is, thus carrying out personal intentions at the expense of the country and its people. The use of Major Ossai, the chief of security of Kangan, to carry out a personal vendetta is both irresponsible and criminal. The reader is told that the surprising and disturbing visit of the Abazonian is "swiftly assuaged by his (Sam's) young, brilliant and aggressive Director of the State Research Council" (13; ch. 2). He also uses the nation's resources to kill Ikem. He not only wastes the nation's manpower but also jeopardizes the nation's peace. Major Ossai uses all the government machinery to hunt Chris as if he were a common criminal. Here as in other cases, Achebe demonstrates that these are the same methods that the politicians in *A Man of the People* used. Chief Nanga makes Odili and his father suffer and even attempts to dispose of Odili. The politicians in *A Man of the People* also trumped up charges against their opponents. The only difference is that they do not have the means of mounting roadblocks as Sam has.

Although Major Ossai is not successful in getting rid of Chris when it becomes expedient for Sam to do so, Major Ossai makes life uncomfortable and terrifying for Chris during the time Chris is hiding from the government. The cold efficiency with which Ossai discharges these duties and controls the information reaching the public sends shivers down the reader's spine. The skill with which he twists every innocent occurrence and utterance of his victims leaves the reader aghast, wondering how Sam the president could permit Major Ossai to operate in his name. Where the politician withdraws his largesse temporarily until the people obey, Sam witholds his forever. Sam is worse than the ousted politician because he is more unscrupulous. Chief Nanga first tries to compromise and co-opt his opponent, Odili Samalu. There are indications that had Odili accepted Nanga's bribe he would have been spared. But Sam fights right away and is unrelenting in unleashing his pogrom even after he has put his opponent into a tight corner. The slightest opposition irks him since he favors monologue. Hence he expects absolute obedience and is ready to engage in combat with whoever shows the slightest sign of not towing his line. Evidently, dialogue, which has been receding, starting from the end of *Things Fall Apart*, has disappeared totally in the discourse of Sam, the ruler, in *Anthills of the Savannah*. Achebe makes a strong *tu quoque* argument using this picture of Sam acting like the ousted politicians.

Intimidations also manifest in the language of the military, which is brusque and efficient so much that there is no room for connotations and resonance. It is as clear and decisive as the user's actions. It carries a message which celebrates raw force. This can be seen in the traffic policeman's encounter with Ikem, the sergeant's verbal abuse towards Beatrice as he is trampling on everything in her house, in the name of searching for the fugitive, Chris, and the soldier's brutal reply to the trader he nearly runs down.

Torture as a means of persuasion is also greatly practiced in the rhetoric of the military. Torture can be inflicted physically as well as emotionally. Sam tortures Ikem and the Abazon people physically and tortures Chris and Beatrice emotionally. Major Ossai, Sam's chosen instrument, is portrayed as beastly, physically as well as emotionally. He is the epitome of the brutality and incisive actions of the military. His method is revolting. After all, as I pointed out earlier, he "invented the simplest of tortures for preliminary interrogations" (97; ch.7),

ACADEMIC ARROGANCE

Achebe argues that the arrogance and the indignation felt by the intellectuals and the political ineptitude that they exhibit impede their efforts at leadership. He demontrates that the academicians' arrogance impedes their ability to persuade. In *Nichomachean Ethics*, *Politics*, and *Rhetoric*, Aristotle discusses how people react to newly acquired riches or power and how those who acquire power or riches regard their new acquisition.[12] Generally, he contends, there is preference for the old over the new. Although these preferences rest on illusions rather than reality, there is some element of truth contained in the perception of the characters of the people who are new to riches or power. There is also some element of truth contained in the perception that those who have to endure the attitude of the newly rich or powerful often exhibit indignation. In discussing indignation, Aristotle shows that indignation comes as a result of one's feeling that the other's good fortune is unmerited. Cassius' indignation at Caesar is an example to this type of feeling. While trying to persuade Brutus to join the conspiracy against Caesar, Cassius shows his utter indignation of Caeser's unmerited power when he exclaims:

Ye gods, it doth amaze me
A man of such a feeble temper should
So get the start of the majestic world,
And bear the palm alone![13]

In *Nichomachean Ethics*, as well as in *Politics*, Aristotle describes the moral principle that demands distributive justice.[14] This principle insists that goods of fortune, such as power and wealth should go to worthy men. If an unworthy man happens to receive one of these, the moral sense is assaulted, and the person who has to endure the fact that fortune is bestowed on an unworthy fellow can be driven to indignation. This situation is played out in *Anthills of the Savannah*. The intellectuals, represented by Ikem and Chris, consider themselves the academic betters of the soldiers, yet the soldiers rule them because the soldiers have stumbled into power. Just as Caesar is reported to have been weak in his youth, Sam, the bearer of the army ideology, was the least brilliant when he, Ikem, and Chris were high school peers. Therefore, as Cassius finds it difficult to accept Caesar's rulership, so do Chris and Ikem find it difficult to accept Sam as their president. The newly wealthy and the newly powerful provoke such indignation because the evolution of the newly wealthy from rags to riches or from fear and powerlessness to powerfulness is evident to the observer. Chris and Ikem are witnesses to Sam's metamorphosis; therefore, they are indignant.

Chris, the first witness in *Anthills of the Savannah*, tells us that he is part of the process that has created the monster, Sam. Therefore, it is unnatural for him to bend to Sam's rule. In such a situation, just as in *Julius Caesar*, a civil strife is inevitable. Sam, like Caesar, has an inferiority complex, which also clouds his vision and creates the need to subdue and subjugate his betters. Achebe uses Sam as the stereotypical military head of state and Chris and Ikem as the typical educated elite, especially those trained in Britain. They find it difficult to believe that these soldiers who were weak academically "should," like Caesar, "[s]o get the start of the majestic world, And bear the palm alone!"[15] He shows the immense power the military wields viciously and unrighteously and the pitiful state of the educated elite who play second fiddle to an inferior.

Ikem exhibits extreme insurbordination towards Sam. Yet Ikem is inept as a leader. He is too idealistic and operates in a philosophical realm. His assessment of Sam as a weak man exposes his error of judgement, which makes him inadequate as a leader and even costs him his life. He believes that Sam is neither strong enough nor smart enough to rule the nation, and that is why Sam needs his and Chris' services. Ikem erroneously and arrogantly believes that he and Chris have the duty of "letting [Sam] glimpse a little light now and again through chinks in his solid wall of court jesters" (42; ch. 4). He feels that by virtue of the length of friendship he and Chris enjoy with Sam, it is not necessary to compete with the other members of Sam's cabinet for Sam's favor. This attitude evokes Ezeulu's and Winterbottom's attitudes in *Arrow of God*, and like Ezeulu and Winterbottom, Ikem and Chris are accused of subversion, and they lose Sam's trust and friendship (42). Not only are Chris and Ikem seen to have exhibited pride and arrogance where prudence is required, but also they have exhibited absolute ignorance of human nature. Because of this error in judgment Ikem is unable to recognize that he has outlived his usefulness to Sam. Instead, he keeps believing that Sam needs to be saved before his sycophants turn him into a monster. Ikem especially underestimates Sam, whom he regards as a "half-wit." (42).

From Ikem's remarks about Sam, the reader realizes that Ikem holds Sam in contempt and shows it in his actions, too. Contempt breeds contempt. Therefore, it is natural for Sam to find Ikem contemptible. Ikem is too impractical to make a leader. His reasoning belongs to the realm of platonic philosophy in which the quest for absolute truth overrides the quest for inducing belief through probability and received wisdom. He writes a "Hymn to the Sun" that reveals his Platonic tendency in its extreme (28-30; ch 3). Both the ethical and pathetical appeals in that poem are more spiritually uplifting than rooted in reality. He first admonishes the sun and then arrogantly implores the sun to have mercy in the interest of its own survival. In his reasoning, the sun risks extinguishing itself by meting out punishment to the lesser being. One can assume that Ikem meant Sam in the image of the sun. However, instead of appealing to Sam in person, he appeals to the spirit in a solitary rendition meant to purge him, Ikem, of his personal anguish at the turn of the events in the country.

Ikem's insurbordination also causes turmoil in the cabinet. Although Ikem is absent most of the time he is discussed, his aura pervades the entire cabinet. The Abazon issue revolves around him. When he does not advise his people to endorse Sam's referendum, his people, the Abazonians rightly discern, "cunning had entered that talk" (116; ch. 9). The result is that the Abazonians refuse to endorse Sam as president for life. No wonder Sam is rankled.

Ikem erroneously believes that he voices the people's opinion. He believes that he is closer to them than Sam is. He tries to tell the story his own way. However, the commoners are not willing to admit him among them. Ikem is rejected as a pretender when he tries to align himself with the downtrodden. He has acquired the status that sets him apart from the poor, a European education. Dressing in poor clothes and driving a dilapidated car cannot make him a poor man. He is incapable of functioning in their world because he does not share the worldview of the poor. He can speak their language, but it is a language devoid of the life experience embodied in being poor; it is merely the autography, lacking the nuances of the language. Even his people, the Abazonians, are not happy with him because he absents himself from their gathering. Therefore, he is alienated from his people. Although the old man tries to patch up things between Ikem and his people living in Bassa, the reader sees from the old man's speech that Ikem is partly to blame for his people's political choice. In the instance of the president's referendum, Ikem has failed his people. He hides behind silence when confronted with a major political decision. Because his people do not know his stand, they have chosen imprudently although morally. Therefore, Ikem is actually the cause of the adversity they are facing. As the old man has said, his people waited for him to come home and advise them. When he did not come, they concluded that the referendum was a deceit. His people then decide to rescind their words. In not guiding them correctly, Ikem has not only lost his *ethos*, but has also exposed his people to danger. He is politically irresponsible.

Chris also is irresponsible in his failure to discharge his duty. He is the minister for information who does not possess or disseminate information. He cannot even persuade his president and his fellow cabinet members. He lacks the art of communicating and achieving "consubstantiation." He, too, tries to control Ikem and the story, but the story insists on being told correctly. His activities during one of the cabinet meetings also help to spur Sam on. He constantly gets into combat with Sam and causes Sam to seek to reestablish his authority before the cabinet. On one occasion, Chris dangerously engages Sam in an eye duel in the cabinet meeting. This eye duel pervades the whole story and the history of the state and even Nigeria, which obviously is the butt of this criticism. Two very important persons, who are piloting the nation, are here busy carrying out a childish squabble, like the proverbial fool who chases rats while his house is burning. The house, Nigeria, is in flames because of ethnic squabbles, nepotism, corruption, and even back-biting, and these two giants, one a civilian and the other a soldier, are busy chasing the rat of childhood competition. These constant battles between Chris and Sam and Chris and Ikem go to show how flexing muscles is more important to the trio than saving the country is. The ultimate result is that the country itself, like Ikem Osodi's neglected "unswept and unlit stairs," becomes "the goat owned in common which dies of hunger" (33; ch.4).

Because Chris is busy flexing his muscle with Sam, he unwittingly aids such manipulators as Professor Okong, the attorney-general, and the commissioner for education, in their efforts to influence Sam against his best friends. The scenes during the cabinet meeting and in the crucial episode of the visit of the elders from Abazon arouse the reader's wonder at the irresponsibility of Chris seeking to prove that he is not afraid of Sam instead of considering the larger picture. Chris becomes clinically disinterested in the proceedings and indulges in inanities and self-amusement at the expense of his colleagues, the country, and the president. In spite of the tension between Chris and Sam at this meeting, Chris pulls expensive pranks. He corrects the attorney-general on his mispronunciation of the word "flout," which he pronounces as "flaunt" and uses sensitive words in a way that heightens his colleagues' suspense and trepidation (5; ch. 1). At this meeting, the attorney-general, who obviously is a sycophant, tries to assuage Sam's guilty conscience on the issue of breaking his word to the Abazon people and accuses the absent Ikem of being "a self-seeking saboteur" (5). As Chris says, "Your Excellency I wish to dissociate myself from the Attorney-General's reference to a saboteur and appeal to my colleagues not to make such statements against public servants who are not present to defend themselves" (5), the reader is aware that Chris's concern is not to defend Ikem but to exhibit his unbridled temerity, designed to jolt both Sam and his colleagues. And he relishes the effect his utterance has on them. Chris says, AI like the look of terror on my colleagues' faces when I used the word *dissociate* and the relaxation that followed when they realized that I was not saying what they feared I was saying. Even His Excellency was thrown off his poise momentarily" (5). Thus Achebe shows that Chris' and Ikem's indignation and arrogance make them irresponsibile and impede their efforts to be convincing leaders.

From the foregoing, it can be seen that the military rhetoric of intervention is not successful. The military came to power terrified of and unprepared for political leadership and was intelligent enough to elicit the help of the educated intelligentsia in forming a cabinet and in running the country. But the power has made the military seek more power and demand obeisance from former classmates, academic betters, and friends like Chris and Ikem. Seeking to subjugate these friends becomes an obsession that is carried to the national level and to the level of throwing the whole country into confusion, jettisoning the interest of the country to the personal interest of controlling these peers. Sam, the representative of army hegemony, goes through a journey which spans from being a good officer to becoming a monster. In this journey, several factors play important roles. His peers to whom he goes for help are not ready to obey him like the other members of the populace. Their arrogance and irresponsibility sometimes get in the way. The country's intelligentsia that make up the cabinet are cowardly, inept, and malicious, seeking to destroy one another in order to belong to the power circle in their scramble to align with new power. They put their personal interest above that of the country. The masses lack the kind of leadership that will prevent a ruler from taking advantage of them. They are equally guilty. The power structure is fluid because the power Sam has is yet to crystalize since it has not been long in existence.

Aigbe analyzes the predicament of the Nigerian situation clearly in his book, *The Theory of Social Involvement*. As he sees it, early years of each decade in Nigerian history seem to indicate a paradigm shift, a revitalized economy, and goodwill of the people and government which are shattered as time goes on; Nigeria lacks a committed leadership; religion and tribal identity take their toll on the fate of the state, generating instability.[16] The shift makes the ruler see the immensity of his power over the scrambling intelligentsia, and since he has not been used to such power, he misuses it. This shift also makes the power seekers act comically in their bid to outshine each other, as seen in the cabinet meeting where the members are tripping over each other in order to get closer to Sam, closer to power.

Aigbe succinctly articulates the situation, "The military has tasted power and wanted more of it."[17] After all, absolute power corrupts absolutely. Corruption and nepotism were rife, leading the country into drifting, giving rise to coup and counter coup, cracking down on the press, violating human rights, and being confrontational with the masses. Thus, it alienates itself from the public and loses public support and even the support of some military officers. Chief Francis Arthur Nzeribe describes the same situation under some military regimes in Nigeria when he says, "those the military government cannot buy over, they try to intimidate"[18] After analyzing the trouble with Nigeria, to borrow Achebe's title dealing with the issue of leadership in Nigeria, Aigbe asks: can these cycles be broken?[19]

Achebe shows that the cycle of bad leadership can be broken, but that it requires the concerted efforts of all—the public, the storyteller, the soldier, the politician—who must all become good leaders in their individual spheres. In the end, the reader is shown that military coups are not capable of providing solutions to fundamental contradictions in Achebe's society, given that history has played a tragic game with the society whose people are diverse and are very much aware of this diversity, both in their actions and in their speech. The military is not able to understand and help the nation because it has to contend with ethnic squabbles and the insubordination of the intelligentsia, and, above all, the military has the urge to keep state power forever, as is manifested in Sam seeking to be made president for life. Achebe seems to be saying the same thing Aigbe has said: "If both the military and the civilian political authorities are part of the national problems, then it follows that we look elsewhere for a more articulating yet neutral institution full of life and hope to break the tie."[20] Aigbe sees the solution in the church. However, Achebe suggests that putting aside religious differences, political differences, ethnic differences, gender differences, and class differences and facing the task of nursing this newly born child symbolized by Ikem's and Elewa's procreativeness will insure hope. The scene at Beatrice's house during the naming of Elewa's child (where the true nation is born, giving the parents, the supporters, and the situation the ultimate sacrifice paid for by its parents) suggests this fully. In his prayer over the kolanut brought in honor of Elewa's newborn child, Elewa's uncle says what the narrator wants for the new nation:

What brings us here is the child you sent us. May her path be straight ...

.... .

What happened to her father, may it not happen again.

.... .

When I asked who named her they told me All of Us. May this child be the daughter of all of us (211; ch.18).

Sam has turned into that rampaging power symbolized by the Idemili. Like the Idemili diety that terrorizes its worshippers, Sam needs to be bridled with moral sense to bring together power and the morality that was in the culture before the erosion of the autochthonous culture, the separation of which causes chaos. Since he does not acquire this moral sense, he is removed from office. Achebe has shown the process of this erosion of the moral sense in his preceding novels.[21] The fact that Ikem's and Elewa's child is a daughter signifies the gentleness that will bridle the rampaging power signified by the Idemili myth. The military man, the politician, the student union president, the Jehovah's Witness, the agnostic Beatrice, the traditional Elewa, her mother, and her uncle gather to equip this newly born child (Nigeria) for the journey of life.

NOTES

1. Romanus Egudu, "Ojebe Poetry," in *Introduction to African Literature: An Anthology of Critical Writing*, ed. Ulli Beier (Essex: Longman, 1967), 59.

2. Ibid., 60.

3. Aristotle notes the power of this *topos* in *Rhetoric*, II. xxiii.4.

4. Ibid.

5. *The Catholic Living Bible*, Matthew 10. verse 28.

6. Shakespeare, *Julius Caesar*, Act 1, sc. 3, 100-101.

7. Aigbe, *The Theory of Social Involvement* 139.

8. Ngugi wa Thion'go, *Petals of Blood* (London: Heinemann, 1978), Part Four.

9. Bale Onimode, *Imperialism and Underdevelopment in Nigeria* (London: Zed, 1982), 199.

10. Plato, "Apology (The Defence of Socrates)," trans., W.H.D. Rouse, eds. Eric H. Warmington and Philip G. Rouse, *Great Dialogues of Plato* (New York: Penguin, 1984), 423-446.

11. Louis Althusser, *Lenin and Philosophy and Other Essays*, 2nd ed., trans. Ben

Brewster (New York: Monthly Review Press, 1977) 149-150. First published as *Lénine et la Philisophie* (Paris: Maspero, 1969). Quoted in Onyemaechi Udumukwu, "Achebe and the Negation of Independence," *Modern Fiction Studies*, 37 (Autumn, 1991): 475.

    12. Aristotle *Ethics*, Bk. II. 1131a, 24-32; *Politics* Trans. T.A. Sinclair; Revd. Trevor J. Sanders (Harmondsworth: Penguin, 1981),1281a, 2-10.

    13. Shakespeare, *Julius Caesar*, Act 1, sc. 2, 130-134.

    14. Aristotle, *Ethics*, 1131a, 24-32; *Politics*, 1281a, 2-10.

    15. Shakespeare, *Julius Caesar*, Act 1, sc. 2. 132-133.

    16. Aigbe, *The Theory of Social Involvement,* 139.

    17. Ibid., 126.

    18. Francis Arthur Nzeribe, *Nigeria: Another Hope Betrayed* (London: Kilimanjero, 1985) 78.

    19. Aigbe, *The Theory of Social Involvement,* 139.

    20. Ibid., 139-40.

    21. Aigbe, *The Theory of Social Involvement,* also discusses the relationship of power and morality in the Igbo culture.

Conclusion

The preceding chapters have shown how Achebe has harnessed the epistemic power of oratory to reveal how his society has responded to the exigencies of its encounter with the West. In each of the novels discussed, oratory is used to advance the theme of the novels and to make arguments in order to achieve an educational purpose. Thus oratory becomes epistemic, creating knowledge of the people and their practices, their fears, and their realities and exposes the temper of the ruling regime, be it the autochthonous rulership or the colonizing invaders' or the indigenes as the pilots of their affairs after a period of subjugation. Achebe has also depicted other rhetorical media and persuasive elements exploited in the African milieu: print and broadcast media, symbols, threat of force, the auras of the military, the politician and the educated elite. In other words, Achebe has used the novel form to argue how and by whom traditional society was brought to an end, who or what accelerated the change, what groups are involved in bringing about the biggest change, and what responsibility should be assigned to the Africans for their predicament.

Achebe employs techniques that can be found in the classical rhetoric of Aristotle, Cicero, and Quintilian, and their adaptations in Chaim Perelman and Lucie Olbrechts-Tyteca, Richard Weaver, Kenneth Burke, and Mikhail Bakhtin in carrrying out his objectives. Through the oratorical situations in the novels, the reader discerns that the principles of oratorical performance that obtained in classical Greek society as well as in modern European societies are similar to those found in Achebe's society: the moral grounding for a good speech is similar, these societies have similar criteria for judging a good speech, their audiences have similar expectations of accomplished orators. Achebe thus uses the role of the audience to advance his argument that colonialism destroyed what was good in his culture and to assert that this society had culture and dignity. He weaves the argument through a presence as prescribed by Perelman and Olbrechts-Tyteca. In *Things Fall Apart*, the reader sees the attributes of a good orator as is manifested in Ogbuefi Ezeugo. Umuofia society, which I have likened to the classsical Greek society, shows that they know a good speaker too. There is no confusion when Ogbuefi Ezeugo speaks to a homogenous Umofia as there is when Okika speaks to a heterogenous Umuofia. Aristotle's view of the relationship between poetics, rhetoric, and dialectics, its adaptation in Weaver's view of the duty of rhetoric, and Cicero's and Quintilian's concept of an orator to explore the theme that a society which has no orator to guide it when making crucial political decisions is in jeopardy are all at work in these novels. Thus Ezeulu, in *Arrow of God*, faces the dilemma a philosopher faces if he or she does not know how to achieve consubstantiaton with the society he is seeking to direct. Umuaro suffers the consequence of not having a real orator, "a good man skilled in speaking" as Quintilian has defined him. In *No Longer at Ease*, Achebe uses the effect of locale on argumentation to explore the exigences of a society in transition. In *A Man of the People*, he uses irony as a master trope to examine a group's argument of governance. He also uses *tu-quoque* argument to explore another group's claim to leadership. He exposes some sophistic practices in the oratorical situations in these novels, such as the use of negative symbols to castigate an opponent. In *Arrow of God, A Man of the People,* and *Anthills of the Savannah*, the philosophers who are accused of subverting the system are always accused to have done so with the aid of a foreigner. Therefore, the persuaders tap into the people's fear of subjugation to identify themselves with the masses.

The use of the media to control both knowledge and information and to condition the masses prior to oratorical occasions in order to portray opponents as subverting officially recognized values is rampant. According to Perelman and Olbrechts-Tyteca, "group leaders will regard any attack on the officially recognized values as a revolutionary act, and, by the use of such measures as censorship, an index, and control over all means of communicating ideas, they will try to make it difficult, if not impossible, for their opponents to achieve the conditions preliminary to any argumentation."[1] Denial of voice, then, is one way the politicians insure that their opponents' views are not heard. In this case, the politicians either boo their opponents out of the arena, thereby ensuring that their opponents do not meet the minimum condition preliminary for argumentation to take place, or they show contempt for their opponents by talking while their opponents are delivering their speeches. Or the a third option is for the politicians to kill them. The Western society on which Perelman based his insight is similar to the society that Achebe depicts in his post-independence novels. They exhibit similar responses to similar stimuli. Thus I opine that the evolution of the society affects rhetorical strategies in Achebe's society as it does in Western societies as can be seen in the modern rhetorical theorists' prescriptions and the rhetorical strategies employed in Achebe's novels.

Achebe's assertion that Africans need to know where the rain began to beat them in order to know where to dry their bodies sums up his vision of how to deal with the predicament of his people, which resulted from the encounter with colonialism.   The dichotomy between the West and the rest of us, to use Chinweizu's title of a book dealing with the same issue of Africa's colonial encounter,[2] is such that even after the West is no longer physically present in the African soil, the Africans still suffer the effect of the encounter, either through the choices the Western invaders made during the years of subjugating Africans and/or the incomprehensible culture left in the wake of European subjugation. The novels under study here have used rhetorical devices in one way or the other to articulate these thoughts.

Achebe uses *Things Fall Apart* to argue that his society had culture and dignity before the arrival of the colonialists and that the encounter with the West, though beneficial in certain respects, destroyed the best in his culture. His argument rests on what Perelman and Olbrechts-Tyteca maintain—that the audience is the pivot of argumentation. His choice of materials and his arrangement of them shows clearly who his primary audience is, the Nigerian schoolboy who has suffered years of denigration and who has even begun to denigrate himself. He is teaching this schoolboy to appreciate his culture. Achebe uses oratory effectively to portray how language shifts in the face of a changing society and to expose the fact that the contact of an alien culture with an indigenous culture causes the language of the indigenous culture to undergo flux, thus causing miscommunication and confusion in a once homogeneous and united society. He also uses the orator effectively to show the movement from a homogenous though restless society to a society that has been infiltrated, and whose values have been compromised and adulterated. Two oratorical pieces have been analyzed to expose the extent to which oratory changes to meet with the demands of a changing audience.

Achebe works out another of Nigeria's problems in *Arrow of God*. He shows the calamity that befalls a society that does not have politicians with an understanding of the rhetorical art to guide it in a crucial time of its history. As I have pointed out in Chapter 3, Plato rightly condemns rhetoric precisely because of its susceptibility to being misused and abused. Aristotle also recognizes that rhetoric, like all good things, could be used to do good as well as bad, "for as these, rightly used, may be of greatest benefit, so, wrongly used, they may do an equal amount of harm."[3] Rhetoric is thus a tool that can be manipulated by an adept rhetor. One, then, needs to ask if any of the people seeking to direct the people of Umuaro at a critical conjuncture in their cultural-political history has used the tool of rhetoric to the benefit of the people of Umuaro. Achebe does not answer this question. He leaves the reading audience to draw its own conclusions.

However, the reader comes out of reading *Arrow of God* wondering about the nature and function (and use) of rhetoric as an instrument of persuasion. If one has the truth but either will not or cannot convey it properly, he is as guilty as the one who speaks eloquently for a bad cause. In the case of this society, Ezeulu, the man elected to lead the people, fails them through his inept oratory. Nwaka's rhetoric—

or sophism—leads the people astray and to loss of lives. On reflection, one wishes that Nwaka did not possess such power of eloquence that pushes his people to make all the wrong choices. One also wishes that Ezeulu, who has the discerning power to realize that the presence of the white man has created a new order of hierarchy, a new level of reality at which the people should be ordering and evaluating ideas, would be imbued with the power of eloquence which Nwaka has. This way Ezeulu will have been able to persuade his people to make the right choices. Both Nwaka and Ezeulu fail because they lack one or more of the ingredients of rhetoric: *logos, ethos,* and *pathos.* The British administration also fails because it lacks an understanding of the power of *pathos.* The Christian religion succeeds in winning the souls of Umuaro because the representative, Mr. Goodcountry, uses rhetoric full of matter and manner. Although his subject matter is not discovered through invention, it has *ethos, pathos,* and *logos* taken from God as a source of authority. All in all, *Arrow of God* demonstrates the effectiveness of the use of dialectic as a complement of rhetoric in persuasion in a political situation.

In *No Longer at Ease,* Achebe demonstrates the inadequacy of the European education that is given to African elites, and he explores the uneasy relationship between the outgoing colonial masters and the African budding elite seeking to replace them. The education given to the chosen few creates a situation in which those who have come back from acquiring European education have to operate in a society that has changed in their absence. Obi Okonkwo, the literary man, appeals mostly to the passion without regard for ethical and logical merits of his argument. Christopher, the economist, couches his argument dialectically but does not attempt to use either *pathos* or *ethos* in seeking to persuade. Both fail woefully in dealing with the changes they have met on return to Africa because they do not understand the reality of their time and because they lack some ingredients of persuasion. They fail to achieve rapport with the people and, therefore, do not inherit the mantle of leadership when the masters leave.

There is a tension emanating from the situation in which these elites, who are educated in what Geertz terms "a tradition of exogenous inspiration," and the masses, who are still in the indigenous cultures are forced to co-exist.[4] The elites in their nationalistic temper seek to elevate the "dignity of their traditional culture and their standing in the world" but are impeded by the fact of having to use a foreign language, with its inherent derogation of the indigenous language and culture. One of the conditions preliminary to achieving what Perelman and Olbrechts-Tyteca call contact of minds is that the speaker and the audience speak the same language.[5] In the heterogeneous setting of *No Longer at Ease,* different ethnic groups are forced to use the foreign language, English, to communicate. The result is that words lose their moral implications and are often used too lightly, without regard to meaning. Arguers exploit this condition. Even in the indigenous locale, the conflict of two values seeking to dominate each other causes language and its meaning to shift, thereby rendering persuasion impossible. As Geertz sees such a situation, there is a tendency for the existence of "discreet collectivities—ethnic, communal, caste, religious or linguistic—that have little sense of identity with one another or with the national whole."[6] When this occurs, rhetoric constantly breaks down because the two people engaged in a persuasive venture are not speaking the same language. Language here implies Bahktin's concept of inner-speech, the presence of which Bahktin asserts aids successful dialogue and persuasion.[7] Hence, the returnee finds it difficult to operate in the milieu in which he finds himself and either goes crazy, as in Ayi Kwei Armah's *Fragments*[8] or succumbs to the temptations in his society, as Obi Okonkwo does.

Also, in *No Longer at Ease*, the joint administration of the colonial master and the emerging black elite comes under scrutiny. Achebe shows that the marriage between these two is uneasy because neither trusts the motives of the other. This also leads to inability to achieve contact of minds because distrust is detrimental to persuasion. He also shows that the emerging elite not only has to grapple with the outrage of being diminished in his fatherland but also has to answer to two masters because of the preparation given to him by colonial education. He has to satisfy the tenets and the ethics of that foreign education as well as satisfy the social, political, and religious expectations of the autochthonous culture.

A Man of the People examines the effect of the ethnic characteristics of a fictional country like Nigeria (that has not attained the status of a nation) even though it has gained political independence. As is seen developing earlier *in No Longer at Ease*, primordial attachments prevent the maintaining of affection for the larger body in a *A Man of the People*. E. Shils, in his essay "Primordial, Personal, Sacred and Civil Ties," explains how ties to blood, religion, or race have strong coerciveness that result in supporting one's kin no matter what.[9] It is this tie that politicians like Chief Nanga invoke in *A Man of the People*. It is this tie also which Achebe exploits through his use of sophistic techniques of argumentation.

However, the biggest problem Achebe presents in *A Man of the People* is that Nigeria is unable to congeal as an entity and form a nation because many disparate nations are yanked together. If the country is not qualified to be a nation, any appeal made to its status as a nation becomes fallacious. Rupert Emerson, in his book, *From Empire to Nation*, defines a nation as "the largest community which, when the chips are down, effectively commands men's loyalty, overriding the claims both of the lesser communities within it and those which cut across it or potentially enfold it within a still greater society."[10] From this definiton, one can see that the ingredients for forming a nation are lacking in the conglomerate society Achebe shows us budding in *No Longer at Ease* and which comes into full operation in *A Man of the People*. Geertz, while pointing out the implication of Emerson's definition—some countries like Nigeria may not be nations—makes the crucial point that one of the attributes of a new state is the people's "desire to be recognized as responsible agents whose wishes, acts, hopes and opinions 'matter,' and the desire to build an efficient, dynamic modern state."[11] When people have these two desires, they are propelled to strive to achieve a nation. What also strengthens this urge to achieve a nation is when the people's sense of self is bound by blood ties, race, language, locality, religion, or tradition. When these ties are not there, individuality among the different entities sets in. Such individuality is measured against the multifarious conditions, be they religion, race, or language, leading to the detriment of, insurbordination to, and lack of general commitment to an order that is both alien and incomprehensible.

Different entities in the new nation fear the action of surbordination to the overarching order because the sense of autonomy of the smaller groups is threatened as the smaller groups fear being swallowed up by the "culturally undifferentiated mass" or worse, being dominated by "some other, rival ethnic, racial or linguistic community that is able to imbue that order with the temper of its own personality."[12] The politicians' pathetic appeals to this situation win them followers. This explains the rat race of the different ethnic groups in the earlier novel, *No Longer at Ease*. They strain to have one of their own in the civil service and attribute every hitch to the handiwork of the other ethnic groups. This is what Chief Nanga exploits in making the people believe that he is in politics to bring his people their share of the national cake. This also explains why the different ethnic groups in *A Man of the People* watch while their representatives loot the nation. The result is that the individual ethnic groups in the country decide to foster individual interests. However, as Geertz states, almost all members of such societies in which there is tension between ethnic, religious, or race allegiance and the overarching order "are at least dimly aware—and their leaders are acutely aware—that the possibilities for social reform and material progress they so intensely desire and are so determined to achieve rest with increasing weight on their being enclosed in a reasonably large, independent, powerful, well-ordered polity."[13] Hence Chief Nanga in *A Man of the People* is representative of such leaders. He wants to steal from the larger body and, at the same time, wants the larger body to still exist. For only when the larger body is still in existence can he find the wealth to loot. By the end of the novel, the culmination of nepotistic politics, material aggrandizement, and corruption has forced the military to seize power from the politicians. Therefore, they appear to be the messiah, trying to save the country tottering before a chasm.

Following his practice of using oratory to express the people's historical predicament, in *Anthills of the Savannah*, Achebe extends his theme of negation of independence. He exposes the temper of the military regime and its unconvincing argument of being the people's messiah. In *The Trouble with Nigeria*, Achebe observes that Nigeria has not been blessed with good leadership.[14] In that work, as Onyemaechi Udumukwu points out, Achebe is preoccupied with the leaderships' "correlative abuse of power"[15] as he is in all his post independence writing. Achebe's view is that the true leader "must put the people and the country first before his own interest."[16] However, in the last novel of the series, as Udumukwu has stated, "state power is removed from its public domain and made the instrument of struggle between the members of the dominant social group."[17] This group comprises the army and the intellectuals. Achebe examines the military's rescue attempt in order to assess its effectiveness. The result is a great argument against the intrusion of the military and the intellectuals in the political arena of the society of Kangan in the novel. Achebe contends that politicians should be allowed to do the business they know how to do best—that is, running a country. He believes that the military is useful in what it does, the intellectuals are useful in what they do, but once they leave what they do well and dabble in politics they are risking their heads. Thus the core of Achebe's argument hinges on the saying "[t]o everyone his due."[18]

Although in *A Man of the People* the military is portrayed as the redeemer and the people are relieved and herald the military intervention in *Anthills of the Savannah*, the people's perception of the military changes drastically. Achebe uses the novel to argue that after mopping up the atrocities of the politicians, the military has outstayed its welcome. It has acted just as civilians did. It has taken the shape of the ousted regime, making it difficult for the ruled to distinguish the pig from the human. Finally he argues that the intellectuals lack the political and interpersonal skills to become leaders. In the end he proposes a solution that power bridled with morality will save the postindependent African nations from disintegrating.

The analysis of the novels in this study serves to elucidate Achebe's intentions and disclose the variety of rhetorical methods he has used to carry out his program of reform, methods which have, heretofore, not been explored. I have here uncovered some fundamental Nigerian rhetorical practices as exhibited in Achebe's craftsmanship. I believe that this study provides a foundation or a model for further investigation of indigenous rhetoric in West African literature and will also help other researchers who seek to tap into the interelationship between rhetoric and literature in the general quest to expose the richness of West African literature.

As part of the discussion in this book I have shown the historical trajectory of rhetoric and literature in order to explain the role of persuasion in Achebe's novels (see Appendix I). Besides the classical and modern rhetorical theorists who have shed light on the elements of persuasion in these novels, Bakhtin's theory of language offers indispensable aid in our interpretation: *Things Fall Apart* ends with the incipient destruction of the we-experience, the cohesion and solidarity of Umuofia, symbolized by the hanging body of Okonkwo, solitary and deserted by his kinsmen. *No Longer At Ease* enacts the impossibility of collective, group action in a new, strange locale and the displacement of the we-experience by the I-experience. *Arrow of God* demonstrates how the attempted merger of the spiritual with the political, exemplified by Winterbottom's offer of kingship (under colonialism) to Ezeulu (high priest of Ulu), drives a wedge through the social order of Umuaro, making mockery of group solidarity and cohesion, the we-consciousness, without which inner speech cannot be effectively deployed. *A Man of the People* illustrates the sad irony of couching I-interests in a we-idiom. *Anthills of the Savannah* exposes the falsity of military rhetoric which, like that of *A Man of the People*, pretends to altruism while, actually, the dictators are saviors only to themselves and of their interests. The movement has thus been from the inner speech, we-experience, double-voicedness, and dialogism of *Things Fall Apart*, through individualism, I-experience, and polyglossia of *A Man of the People* and *Anthills of the Savannah*. Cohesion and we-ness have fled while the monologism of the radio and the newspaper has replaced dialogue. Polyglossia becomes coterminous with cacophony. Rhetoric finally breaks down.

When Achebe creates fictive scenes to portray the very real predicaments of his people, he echoes Aristotle's advice in the *Poetics* to emphasize action. While ordinarily the realm of poetics and rhetoric are different—the former concerning a universal truth of the human experience in the particular and the latter attending to the particular case of a particular time—Aristotle advises creators of poetry to turn to rhetoric for guidance in depicting oratory and persuasive arguments, thus drawing the powerful tool of oratory into the mimetic process. Achebe made oratory a powerful force in his novel because he knows that this reflected the traditional praxis of the society he represented.

NOTES

1.   Perelman and Olbrechts-Tyteca, *The New Rhetoric*, 55.

2.   Chinweizu, *The West and the Rest of Us* (New York: Random House, 1975).

3.   Aristotle, *Rhetoric*, I.i.13.

4.   Clifford Geertz, "The Integrative Revolution: Primordial Sentiments and Civil Politics in the New States," in *Old Societies and New States: The Quest for Modernity in Asia and Africa*, ed. Clifford Geertz (New York: The Free Press, 1963), 2.

5.   Perelman and Olbrechts-Tyteca, *The New Rhetoric*, 55.

6.   Geertz, "The Integrative Revolution," 2.

7.   Bakhtin, "The Problem of Speech Genres," *Speech Genres & Other Late Essays*, 86.

8.   Ayi kwei Armah, *Fragments* (London: Heinemann, 1974).

9.   E. Shils, "Primordial, Personal, Sacred and Civil Ties," *British Journal of Sociology* (June 1957). Quoted in Geertz, *Old Societies and New States*, 109.

10.   Rupert Emerson, *From Empire to Nation* (Cambridge, MA: Harvard University Press, 1962), 95-96.

11.   Geertz, "The Integrative Revolution," 108.

12.   Ibid., 109.

13.   Ibid.

14.   Chinua Achebe, *The Trouble with Nigeria* (Enugu, Nigeria: Fourth Dimension, 1983), 11.

15.   Onyemaechi Udumukwu, "Achebe and the Negation of Independence," *Modern Fiction Studies* 3 (Autumn, 1991), 473.

16.   Bernth Lindfors et al. eds., *Palaver: Interviews with Five African Writers in Texas* (Austin: African and Afro-American Research Institute, University Texas Press, 1972), 4-12. Also quoted in Udumukwu, "Achebe and the Negation of Independence," 473.

17.   Udumukwu, "Achebe and the Negation of Independence," 473.

18.   Achebe, *Anthills of the Savannah*, 113; Ch. 9.

Appendix I:
Historical Trajectory

Literature and rhetoric have shared interrelatedness from the time both came into being. Etymologically, a rhetorician is a public speaker whose art involves addressing an audience, whether in a court of law or in a popular audience setting where he aims to influence, persuade, exhort, and instruct through manipulation of language. Rhetoric has featured in literature since ancient times. Homer's *Iliad* and *Odyssey* contain rhetoric. Aristotle's *Rhetoric* codified the art of rhetoric, and rhetorical prowess became an art in politics. Later, some writers, especially the Roman rhetoricians, equated rhetoric to literary style and gave attention to figures and tropes.[1] Cicero, for instance, saw close affinity between rhetoric and literature. In *De Oratore* Book I, he asserts that both poets and orators are related not just because both can speak on any subject but because "the poet is a very near kinsman of orator ... in the use of many sorts of ornament he is his ally and almost his counterpart, in one respect at all events something like identity exists."[2] Although political rhetoric lost importance, rhetoric's role in education, literature, and even literary criticism remained central in the Hellenistic period. Many poets received this form of education; as a result, rhetors were regarded as poets and poets were regarded as rhetors. Thus rhetoric merged with poetics so much that a rhetorician like Quintilian talked of rhetorical ornamentation in literature and even advised orators to read the great poets in order to enrich their speeches with figures.[3] Cicero says that the function of rhetoric is to instruct, please, and move.[4] Poetry is also mandated to instruct and delight according to Horace.[5] In the Medieval period, St. Augustine advocated the propagation of the word of God through the use of figures to teach and delight.[6] He also notes the characteristic of rhetoric to teach and delight. Thus literature and rhetoric come together in these eminent scholars' prescriptions.

In modern times, theorists have also sought to relate rhetoric to literature. Hence, rhetorical criticism has become one of the avenues of revealing the richness of a literary work. Some twentieth-century theorists believe that literature yields more if it is examined in terms of its effect on the reader. Ivor A. Richards redefines rhetoric as the study of verbal understanding and misunderstanding.[7] His definition implies that rhetorical analysis covers all the techniques by which a writer establishes rapport with his readers and by which the writer elicits and guides the readers' responses to a work. Kenneth Burke believes that the study of rhetoric facilitates understanding the effects of all forms of discourse, including literature.[8] To Burke, every use of language is rhetorical.[9] In "Lexicon Rhetoricae" he asserts: "effective literature could be nothing else but rhetoric. ... [E]ffects on readers is what matters. Therefore, the study of rhetoric is needed to understand the effect of literature and all other forms of discourse."[10] Richard Weaver asserts that the rhetorician makes use of the moving power of literary presentation to induce in his hearers an attitude or decision that is political in the the broadest sense. Therefore, rhetoric must be viewed as operating at that point where literature and politics meet. [11]

Wayne C. Booth's *The Rhetoric of Fiction* sees rhetoric as the author's means of controlling his readers.[12] Booth believes that because language plays a very important role in rhetoric and literature, it establishes a common ground for the two. Poetry or literature has always emphasized the use of words to achieve maximum force and expression. Therefore, rhetoric has been taken to refer to the techniques of style and patterns of words that display an author's verbal skill and resourcefulness. In *The Rhetoric of Fiction*, Booth rejects the idea that good fiction should be "pure," devoid of rhetoric. As he sees it, "if recognizable appeals to the reader are a sign of imperfection, perfect literature is impossible to find."[13] His argument is that fiction has a rhetorical function whether it is overtly persuasive or not. According to Booth, although an author can choose to hide himself in his work, he cannot choose to disappear, as he is always either "showing" or "telling," always attempting to advance a viewpoint in some form. He sees authors as always using such rhetorical devices as distance, irony, sympathy. He recognizes that great literature and drama work rhetorically to build and strengthen communities.[14]

Wilbur Samuel Howell insists that literary theory comprises poetics, rhetoric, and logic. He asserts that poetics alone can not bear all the burden of literary theory because it cannot account for certain tendencies in some great works. In Howell's opinion,

poetics, if left to stand by itself for all of literary theory, cannot undertake to explain and evaluate many eminent literary works which by long-standing agreement lie outside the traditional realm of poetry, yet belong by long-standing agreement to the traditional realm of one of the two other disciplines.[15]

Howell does not believe that poetry should be limited to an aesthetic function because poetry is an instrument of communication, instruction, and persuasion as well as delight.[16] He points out that in *Lectures on Rhetoric and Belles Lettres*, Adam Smith declared that amusement and entertainment were the distinguishing aims of poetry, and that the other branches of literature were variously engaged in instruction, conviction, and persuasion.[17] This view is also limiting because, according to Howell, it excludes delight from the other forms of literature while excluding instruction and persuasion from poetry. Instead, he supports Horace's dictum that poetry both delights and teaches and Burke's thesis in *Counter Statement* which locates the central focus of the theory of literature in the mechanisms by which literary works produce effects upon their readers and hearers.[18] He laments that modern criticism has sustained a deep loss by severing the genuine and deep instruction of the ancient discipline of rhetoric from the practice of modern literary theory and by deemphasizing the interrelations of rhetoric with logic and poetics.[19] To buttress his view, Howell points out that Horace's *Ars Poetica* represents the rhetorical approach to literature because, for Horace, poetry is mandated to please or to be useful or both and to instruct. He refers to Aristotle's definition of rhetoric and poetics and shows that persuasion in rhetoric is equivalent to catharsis in literature. Shifting then to the Renaissance, Howell shows how Sir Phillip Sidney's *In Defense of Poetry* brings out the relationship of rhetoric and literature when Sidney tells a story exemplifying the notion of the belief "that the poet and the story-teller are one and the same person, and that the story may have on occasion a greater persuasive effect than the oration or the argument, without becoming in the light of that particular result any less a poem."[20] In Howell's view, any literary work that shows the kind of sensitivity Sidney thus advocates must be admired for its depth, its sophistication, and its ultimate wisdom. He concludes that didacticism, persuasiveness, a concern for audience, thought content, and style should not be regarded as purely rhetorical. They must be regarded as the common properties of rhetoric and poetics.[21]

Terry Eagleton has also argued that distinctions between literature and rhetoric are not possible to establish and that a comprehensive poetics should coincide with the classical conception of rhetoric as a broadly based consideration of the stylistic, formal, psychological, social, political, and cultural elements of discourse.[22] As Eagleton sees it, since literature is an illusion because of its political baggage, literary theory is equally an illusion. Therefore, Michel Foucault's view of "discursive practice" is apt as a substitute for literary theory. On the other hand, rhetoric, the oldest form of literary criticism, which "examined the way discourses are constructed in order to achieve certain effects," must be effectively engaged in literary criticism.[23]

The philosopher Chaim Perelman and his colleague Lucie Olbrechts-Tyteca have also attempted to redefine and expand the scope of rhetorical analysis and to apply it to all forms of language use. In their view, the epidictic genre of oratory has the closest connection with literary discourse, and therefore, its features have, most often, been consigned to the literary genre. For Perelman and Olbrechts-Tyteca, "epidictic oratory forms a central part of the art of persuasion" as it seeks to promote adherence to common values.[24] Since epidictic rhetoric features so prominently in the literature, literary discourse can use argumentation for its enhancement, especially if the literary work is one with a clearly suasive purpose. In this case, as the authors point out, the writer, while trying to establish a sense of communion centered upon particular values recognized by the audience, uses the whole range of means available to the rhetorician and every device of literary art, "[F]or it is a matter of combining all the factors that can promote this communion of the audience."[25] In effect, poetics uses rhetoric as part of the elements of an effective composition. More important, literary artists have, sometimes, used their fiction as a forum for defending their theses.

NOTES

1. Cicero, *De Inventione*, trans. H. M. Hubbel, ed. G. P. Goold (Cambridge, MA: Harvard University Press, 1976); *Ad Herennium*.

2. Cicero, *De Oratore*, I. xv. 70-71. He reiterates this relationship in *De Oratore*, III. Vii. 27.

3. Quintilian, *Institutio Oratorium*, Bk VIII.iii 24-27. Quintilian commends Virgil's ornament which he says Agive our style a venerable and majestic air.

4. Cicero, *De Optimo Genere Oratorum*, I. 3.

5. Quintus Horatius Flaccus (Horace), *On the Art of Poetry*, trans. T. S. Dorsch *Aristotle/Horace/Longinus:Classical Literary Criticism* (London: Penguin, 1965), 90.

6. St. Augustine, *De Doctrina Christiana*, Bk IV, 381-416.

7. Richards, "The Aims of Discourse and Types of Context," in *The Philosophy of Rhetoric*, 23.

8. Burke, *A Rhetoric of Motives*, 43.

9. Ibid.

10. Burke, *Counter Statement*, quoted in Bizzell and Herzberg, *The Rhetorical Tradition*, 989.

11. Richard M. Weaver, "Language Is Sermonic," in Edward P. J. Corbett, James L. Golden and Goodwin F. Berquist, eds. *Essays on the Rhetoric of Western Thought*, 4th ed. (Dubuque, IA: Kendall/Hunt, 1984), 315-317.

12. Booth, *The Rhetoric of Fiction*, 15.

13. Ibid., 99.

14. Ibid. 17.

15. Samuel Wilbur Howell, *Poetics, Rhetoric, and Logic: Studies in The Basic Disciplines of Criticism* (Ithaca, NY: Cornell University Press, 1980), 35.

16. Ibid., 35

17. Ibid., 33.

18. Ibid., 37.

19. Ibid., 43.

20. Ibid., 91.

21. Ibid., 105.

22. Terry Eagleton, *Literary Theory: An Introduction* (Minneapolis: University of Minnesota Press, 1995), 206.

23. Ibid., 205.
24. Perelman and Lucie Olbrtechs-Tyteca, *The New Rhetoric*, 49.
25. Ibid., 51.

Appendix II:
Critical Appraisal of
Chinua Achebe's Novels

Achebe has often been called the foremost novelist of African literature.[1] As a result, his novels have attracted a a great deal of critical attention, especially his conscious indigenization of the novel for educational purposes. Some of the criticisms have been glowing while others have been adverse. Early critics devoted attention mostly to the historical, anthropological, and psychological dimensions of the novels and, especially, to Achebe's mission of using the novel form as a means of education. However, critics have noted the artistic qualities of the novels, comparing them to the novels of Thomas Hardy[2] and to works by T.S. Eliot[3] and W. B. Yeats.[4] Simon Gikandi has examined the structural elements of the novels to expose how they carried the novels' ideologies.[5] Robert Wren has posited the novels against Achebe's world.[6] Lekan Oyeleye has even applied sophisticated linguistic theories in analyzing some of the novels.[7]

Eustace Palmer, one of the critics who have paid much attention to the sociological relevance of Achebe's novels, concentrates his evaluation of these novels on Achebe's "perception of the social forces at work in an ancient and proud society."[8] He remarks on Achebe's "great skill in evoking his society as it used to be; ..."[9] thereby showing Umuofia society in *Things Fall Apart* as a "proud, dignified and stable society governed by a complicated system of customs and traditions, extending from birth, through marriage to death."[10] Palmer has an appropriate response to those critics who charge *Things Fall Apart* with being riddled with an inordinate proportion of sociological information which, they claim, makes the reading tedious as well as making the writer ignore the fact that the novel form ought to exist in its own right, not as a sociological document, but as a medium for the treatment of personal relationships. His answer is that

> *Things Fall Apart* does rely on sociology, but it is neither didactic nor tedious.What according to all rules, should have been a dull work, is actually a powerfully achieved work of art. The solution of the mystery lies in the relevance of sociological information to the themes of the novel and the way in which this information is handled by the author. Traditional society is regarded almost as a character in its own right since what we are witnessing is the destruction of an entire way of life.[11]

Lloyd W. Brown, another proponent of Achebe's method, which he claims is both artistic and socially relevant, discusses Achebe's use of the colonizer's language to speak back to the colonizer and the colonized, not just as a means of communication but as a total cultural experience. In his opinion, Achebe exploits the colonizer's cultural criteria to project the merits of his own culture and debunk the colonizer's claim to being the sole repository of culture and history. In his masterly explication of Achebe's *Things Fall Apart* and *No Longer at Ease,* he marks the close affinity of these works to Yeats' and Eliot's visions in "The Second Coming" and in "Journey of the Magi" respectively. He also comments on *A Man of the People* showing how the European ignorance of the Africans' norms and culture makes them misinterpret gestures and actions.[12]

Kalu Uka sees the use of the novel form to teach as laudable. According to him, Achebe "denotes the generic qualities of creative literature as an imaginativeness whose function is practically to educate, edify, and challenge the audience .... The writer must direct the vision and sharpen the awareness of his people. These are incontrovertible propositions."[13]

Adrian Roscoe lauds Achebe's use of the earlier novels, *Things Fall Apart, No Longer At Ease*, and *Arrow of God* to teach his people but thinks that the use of *A Man of the People* to satirize them was a failure. He asserts that while Achebe's desire to teach through the novel form is not new, there are special implications of the choice for his style and method. According to Roscoe, the African oral tradition and the nature of the African writers' audience make it easy to teach through the novel form because an indigenous audience dictates the use of indigenous modes and practice. In Achebe's novels "characteristics of traditional African literary art and the present need for good pedagogy meet because a docile audience must be taught by lessons that have a strong central line and little sidetracking." Roscoe believes that Achebe maintained a simple narrative plot with one central figure and few digressions, a species of language that is clear and familiar, "which stirs the emotions and drops anchors in the memory."[14] Achebe also employs proverbs profusely in this teaching mission because the proverb by its nature is an effective pedagogical tool. According to Roscoe, however, Achebe is inept as a satirist. Achebe's use of the first-person narrator in *A Man of the People* "introduced problems that had marred the novel—reduced it to the job of radio, TV and journalism."[15] In Roscoe's view, the use of a *persona* can be very effective in assuring the author's detachment, as writers such as Swift, Conrad, Salinger, and Waterhouse demonstrate. However, in Achebe' hands, "the technique is a failure" because it seems that the "zeal displayed...was politically rather than artistically directed." As Roscoe sees it, "Righteous indignation with corrupt political elite is well enough; but as a primary aim in writing, it is more in line with the tradition of the political tract than with the tradition of fiction."[16] Arthur Ravenscroft treats the political aspect of the novel and concludes that Achebe has gone beyond dealing with the theme of the negation of independence which is the subject of *A Man of The People* and has proposed a solution in *Anthills of the Savannah*.[17]

Simon Gikandi discusses, in depth, Achebe's political vision in his novels. In his assessment, all Achebe's novels "can be read as one continuous quest for the meaning of Nigerian nation in particular and the African experience in general." He strongly believes that reading Achebe reveals a great depth in the study of personal motives and politics as a game. Personal motives permeate the political situations which Achebe dissects in these novels as the political situations themselves dictate individual's reactions and dictate a person's ability to cope with issues of life, rulership, and subjugation.[18] In discussing why Achebe chose the novel form, Gikandi states that Achebe recognized the function of the novel, not solely as a mode of representing reality, but one which had limitless possibilities for inventing a new national community. This attention to the historical and the anthropological aspects of the novels, Gikandi asserts, very often focuses on Achebe's use of the novel form to educate.[19]

Among critics who have argued adversely against Achebe's use of the novel form to educate is Kolawole Ogungbesan, who thinks that authors should separate literature from politics.[20] Ogungbesan argues that although the writer should not ignore the social and political issues of the day, "it is a betrayal of art for the writer to put his writing in the service of a cause even if it is such a laudable and uncontroversial cause as the 'education' of the people."[21] Sunday Anozie also attacks Achebe's idea of the novelist as a teacher when he says:

No doubt the thrill of actualized prophecy can sometimes lead poets particularly in the young countries to confuse their role with that of seers and novelists to see themselves as teachers. Whatever the social, psychological, political and economic basis for it in present-day Africa, this interchangeability of role between the creative writer and the prophet appears to be a specific phenomenon of underdevelopment and therefore, like it also, a passing or ephemeral phase.[22]

Sam Asein also frowns at the use of the novel form to educate. He quotes extensively from an interview with Christopher Okigbo in 1965 in which he rejected the idea of teaching through the novel form. In that interview, Okigbo had said:

I don't, in fact, think that it is necessary for the writer to assume a particular function as the messiah or anything like that. As an individual, he could assume this sort of role, but I don't think that the fact that he's a writer should entitle him to assume a particular role as an educator. If he wants to educate people he should write text books.[23]

Some other critics rank Achebe's novels according to artistic merit. In Abiola Irele's view, the treatment of tragedy is better handled both in *Things Fall Apart* and *Arrow of God* than in *No Longer at Ease* because in *No Longer at Ease,* unlike in *Arrow of God,* the hero has an inadequate stature, the situations are sketchily treated, and events are unrelated.[24]

Although Eustace Palmer gives a measure of support to Achebe's innovative use of the novel form, he too yields to the temptation to rank Achebe's novels. According to Palmer, *Things Fall Apart* treats the same themes as *No Longer at Ease,* but *No Longer at Ease* is greatly inferior to *Things Fall Apart* because the hero is weak and insufficiently realized. He finds, also, an imperfect blending of two themes and sees the novel as melodramatic and too episodic, with some of the scenes being not just transposable, but also irrelevant.[25] In addition, some important events are not given the weight they deserve. In *A Man of the People,* Palmer goes on to assert, Achebe achieves "stylistic virtuosity through the use of Odili as his eyes" while at the same time using Odili as a means of deconstructing Odili himself.[26] He also shows consumate skill in the use of irony. However, *A Man of the People* is "an inadequately structured artistic whole" and is weak because there are digressions that affect "the internal unity of individual scenes" so much that they constitute distractions,[27] and the novel is so didactic that it fails to show "situations, characters and plot which can convincingly carry the message."[28]

Recently, critics have started looking into the art that formed the novels of Achebe. Some critics refute the apparent simplicity of the plots, which they assert is deceptive and masks a complex and subtle interplay of values and attitudes artistically embedded in the works. Solomon Iyasere[29] and David Carroll[30] have focused on the narrative technique while Bu-Buakai Jabbi,[31] and Donald J. Weinstock, and Cathy Ramadan[32] have treated particular images and symbols in the novels. M. J. C. Echeruo discusses Achebe's artistic prowess in marrying the novel tradition with traditional norms of story telling. He asserts:

Achebe's rhetorical strength lies in the ease of his performance, the total absence of a straining after an effect or a manner. It is as if, because he is completely aware of his hearers and understands them thoroughly, he can afford to devote his energies fully to his art, that is to the modulation of his effects and to the establishment of his meaning.[33]

Echeruo rejects the simplistic impression that Achebe's novels are merely novels of culture conflict. In his opinion, Achebe was demonstrating that "our very troubled present and anxious future could best be understood by looking at the experiences through which the African has passed in the last century."[34] To Echeruo, Achebe has a control of history, is aware of his reader as a collaborating but discriminating intelligence, and exhibits a shrewd sense of literary style which could both be listened to and read. All these made Achebe "the simplest and still the most technically competent of Nigerian novelists."[35] As for *A Man of the People*, which some critics have condemned for what they take to be its flaws, Echeruo believes that the flaw is not in the novel but in the moral character of the world of that novel.[36]

In his insightful essay, "Chinua Achebe and the Possibility of Modern Tragedy," Alastair Niven describes Achebe's gift as a tragedian, focusing on Achebe's depiction of modern tragedy as achievable. According to Niven, although tragedy has been grossly abused in modern works, in Achebe's novels, where man is constantly pitted against social forces, Achebe has achieved a balance between the individual, the society, and the gods. Niven strongly states: "Achebe demonstrates an essentially tragic view of human action whereby we cannot easily determine our own destiny or even understand the pattern of it, much as we may plan to do so."[37] He has used a sophisticated narrative structure, especially in *Anthills of the Savannah*. He notes that Achebe advocates knowledge as a way of getting out of the tragic quagmire in which his society has found itself. Hence, in Niven's assessment, Achebe's call in "The Novelist as Teacher" is not just a "clarion call to his African readers to remember their heritage but ... an even larger statement about the perpetual urgency for human beings to attain maximum knowledge in their search for a way out of their tragic spiral."[38] He points out that the Africa portrayed in Achebe's novels is "politically tragic in much of its destiny to date, but culturally and humanly so rich that the underside of tragedy, which is self-knowledge and eventual accession to a better future, was inevitable."[39]

Gikandi also examines the structures of Achebe's *Things Fall Apart* and *No Longer at Ease* in depth, focusing on the effect of space and time on the treatment of the themes in these novels. He notes that, hitherto, time and historicity have been the focus of literary criticism of Achebe's novels for two reasons: Achebe's work seems to have followed those emphases in its evolution, thereby forcing critics to view his novels along those lines. The critical tradition, which insists on explicating history and development of novels in temporal terms, still dictates our response to critical works. In his opinion, while the first part of *Things Fall Apart* promotes progressive narrative, the second part "negates the temporal process." When the reader resists the temptation of following the plot linearly and focuses "attention on the juxtaposition of different spatial configurations and the uncanny ways in which the hierarchy of social spaces that emplaces Okonkwo in Umuofia is also responsible for his displacement," the reader is bound to recognize that Achebe weaves a complicated relationship between the emplacement of the hero of *Things Fall Apart* and the negation the structure of the novel suggests.[40] *No Longer at Ease,* according to Gikandi, takes up the question of the exact authority of custom and what spaces sustain it, given the challenge posed by the forces of colonialism, which is seeking to share the society's space with the autochthonous culture.[41] As a result of this contest between the forces of colonialism and the authority of the indigenous custom, Obi, the protagonist, constantly struggles to define himself in the two contending spaces, the schizophrenic inherited space in Umuofia and "his transplanted locale," Lagos, which is fully under the hegemony of colonialism. In negotiating his way through these spaces, Obi is faced with options which Gikandi sees as "not real options."[42]

Other critical theories, although not helpful to my purpose but should be noted in appraising the variety of critical responses to Achebe abound. Madhusaudan Pati uses *Things Fall Apart* as illustrative material for testing "the critical legitimacy of classical Indian poetics as an interpretive tool in the context of 'alien' literary texts."[43] In this essay, the writer uses rasa criticism to analyze *Things Fall Apart* in spite of the fact that *Things Fall Apart* is not in the Sanskrit tradition. Nelson Chidi Okonkwo's essay insightfully examines the effect destruction of the rural culture had on the emerged society. He uses the concept of the cosmic force on the cyclical nature of the order of the universe in which death depicts a return to the womb which in turn leads to a rebirth.[44] Lekan Oyeleye examines how transference of meaning in *Things Fall Apart* and *Arrow of God* is used to achieve literary excellence. He asserts that Achebe uses transference to overcome the limitation imposed on him by the language medium, English, when he tries to convey an African culture. Tranference in the hands of Achebe becomes a process in the domestication and Africanization of English.[45] Clement Okafor examines how Achebe has used his environment to his advantage in his novels: taking advantage of his Igbo oral tradition and the adopted English novel tradition.[46] Adeleke Adeeko asserts: "Achebe's fiction provides strong tools for unearthing the relationship of language and power in colonial societies."[47] Govind Narain Sharma examines the role of Christianity in colonialism.[48]

One aspect of the novel that always claims attention is Achebe's innovative use of the English language. Adrian Roscoe, in spite of his quarrel with Achebe for employing the novel genre in the service of education, recognizes the effectiveness of the use of proverbs in the novels. According to Roscoe:

one of the most useful devices which Achebe has employed to achieve his aim has been the African proverb. This, one suspects, is why the rich vein of proverbs and proverbial allusion that appears to be simply a happy coup d'essay in his first book, *Things Fall Apart*, (1958), becomes an important feature of style in the two novels which follow, *No Longer At Ease* (1960) and *Arrow of God* (1964).[49]

As Roscoe sees it, the proverbs represent a "versatile device" used to guide conduct, to instruct, and to keep people united. They are also used as weapons of debate and as a buttress for oratory.[50]

In chapter 1 of this book, I have presented an overview of Achebe's writing and examined his published interviews and essays to throw light on his intentions in the novels, and on his views about African literature with respect to its mission, its practice, and its audience. Here I have examined the critical appraisals of Achebe's novels in order to expose the debate in critical literature about Achebe's use of the novel genre to educate as well as the artistic merits of the novels. In Appendix I, I have also shown the interrelationship of literature and rhetoric which makes it possible for such a craftsman as Achebe to use the novel genre to persuade. Hopefully, those still new to Achebe scholarship will find in these explications a useful base for approaching the reading of Achebe's novels.

NOTES

1. Catherine L. Innes and Bernth Lindfors, eds. *Critical Perspectives on Chinua Achebe* (London: Heinemann, 1979), 2.

2. John Povey, "Novels of Chinua Achebe," Bruce King, ed. *Introduction to Nigerian Literature* (London: Heinemann 1971), 97 - 111.

3. Lloyd W. Brown, "Cultural Norms and Modes of Perception in Achebe's Fiction," Innes and Lindfors, *Critical Perspectives on Chinua Achebe*, 25-26.

4. A. G. Stock, "Yeats and Achebe," in Innes and Lindfors, *Critical Perspectives on Chinua Achebe*, 87.

5. Simon Gikandi, *Reading Chinua Achebe*. Also in "Chinua Achebe and the Poetics of Location: The Use of Space in *Things Fall Apart* and *No Longer at Ease*," Abdulrazak Gurnah, ed., *Essays on African Writng: A re-evaluation* (Portsmouth, NH: Heinemann, 1993).

6. Robert M. Wren, *Achebe's World: The Historical and Cultural Context of the Novels* (Washington, D.C.: Three Continents Press, 1980).

7. Lekan Oyeleye, "Transference as a Stylistic Strategy," *Odu*, 32: (July 1987).

8. Eustace Palmer, *Introduction to the African Novel* (London: Heinemann, 1972), 48.

9. Ibid., 48.

10. Ibid., 49.

11. Ibid., 60.

12. Brown, "Cultural Norms and Modes of Perception in Achebe's Fiction," in Innes and Lindfors, *Critical Perspectives on Chinua Achebe*, 23-24.

13. Kalu Uka, "From Commitment To Essence," Donatus I. Nwoga, ed. *Literature and Modern West African Culture* (Benin City, Nigeria: Ethiope, 1978), 20.

14. Adrian Roscoe, *Mother Is Gold* (London: Cambridge University Press, 1971), 123.

15. Ibid., 130.

16. Ibid.

17. Arthur Ravenscroft, "Recent Fiction From Africa: Chinua Achebe's *Anthills of the Savannah*," *The Literary Criterion*, 23, 1-2 (1991), 172-175.

18. Simon Gikandi, *Reading Chinua Achebe: Language and Ideology in Fiction* (London: Heinemann, 1991), 126.

19. Ibid., 3.

20. Kolawole Ogungbesan, "Politics and the African Writer," in Innes and Linfors, eds. *Critical Perpectives on Chinua Achebe*, 7.

21. Ogungbesan, "The Modern Writer and Commitment," in Nwoga, ed. *Literature and Modern West African Culture*, 7.

22. Sunday Anozie, *Christopher Okigbo: Creative Rhetoric* (New York: Evans, 1992) 17.

23. Sam O. Asein quoted Christopher Okigbo in his essay, "Literature as History: Crisis, Violence and Strategies of Commitment in Nigerian Writing," in Nwoga, ed. *Literature and Modern West African Culture*, 105.

24. Abiola Irele, "The Tragic Conflict in the Novels of Achebe," in Innes and Lindfors, eds. *Critical Perspective on Chinua Achebe.*

25. Palmer, *Introduction to the African Novel*, 70.

26. Ibid., 73.

27. Ibid., 83.

28. Ibid., 84.

29. Solomon Iyasere, "Narrative Techniques in *Things Fall Apart*," in Innes and Linfors eds. *Critical Perspectives on Chinua Achebe.*

30. David Carroll, "*A Man of The People*," in Ibid.

31. Bu-Buakei Jabbi, " Fire and Transition in *Things Fall Apart*," in Ibid.

32. Donald Weinstock and Cathy Ramadan, "Symbolic Structure in *Things Fall Apart*," in Ibid.

33. Micheal Echeruo, "Chinua Achebe," in Bruce King and Kolawole Ogungbesan eds. *A Celebration of Black And African Writing* (London: Oxford, 1978), 152.

34. Ibid., 152-153.

35. Ibid., 157.

36. Ibid., 161.

37. Alistair Niven, "Chinua Achebe and the Possibility of Modern Tragedy," Kirsten Holst Petersen and Anna Rutherford, eds. *Chinua Achebe: A Celebration* (Oxford: Heinemann,1990), 45.

38. Ibid., 46.

39. Ibid, 47.

40. Gikandi, "Chinua Achebe and the Poetics of Location," in Gurnah, ed. *Essays on African Writng*, 4.

41. Ibid., 9.

42. Ibid., 11.

43. Madhusudan Pati,"*Things Fall Apart*: An Enquiry Into Rasa-Configuration," *The Literary Criterion*, 26(1: 1991).

44. Nelson Chidi Okonkwo, "Chaos and Cosmos: The Colonial Encounter as Rite of Passage in the African Novel," *Landfall* 44, 4 (Dec. 1990), 461-475.

45. Lekan Oyeleye, "Transference as a Stylistic Strategy," *Odu*, 32 (July 1987): 160-169.

46. Clement Okafor, "Chinua Achebe: His Novels and the Environment," *College Languages Association Journal*, 32, 4, (June 1989), 433-442.

47. Adeleke Adeeko. "Contest of Text and Context in Chinua Achebe's *Arrow of God*," *Ariel*, 23, 2 (April 1992), 21.

48. Govind Narain Sharma, "The Christian Dynamics in the Fictional World of Chinua Achebe," *Ariel* 24, 2 (1993), 85-99.

49. Adrian Roscoe, *Mother Is Gold*, 123.

50. Ibid., 124.

Bibliography

PRIMARY MATERIAL

Achebe, Chinua. *Anthills of the Savannah*. New York: Doubleday, 1988 .
—. *Arrow of God*. New York: Doubleday, 1967.
—. *A Man of the People*. New York: Doubleday, 1989.
—. *No Longer at Ease*. New York: Anchor Books, 1960.
—. *Things Fall Apart*. New York: Doubleday, 1994.

SECONDARY MATERIAL

Achebe, Chinua. In "African Literature as Restoration of Celebration." *Chinua Achebe: A Celebration*. Kirsten Holst Peterson and Anna Rutherford, eds. Oxford: Heinemann; 1990.
—. "The Black Writer's Burden," *Presence Africaine*, 31, 59 (1966): 135-141.
—. *Chike and the River*. Cambridge: Cambridge University Press, 1966.
—. *Girls At War and Other Stories*. New York: Doubleday, 1972.
—. *Hopes and Impediments: Selected Essays*. New York: Doubleday, 1989.
—. *Morning Yet on Creation Day*. New York: Doubleday, 1975.
—. "The Role of the Writer in a New Nation." *Nigeria Magazine*, 81 (1964): 156-162.
—. *The Trouble with Nigeria*. London: Heinemann, 1983.
—. "The Writer's Role in Society." *African Concord*, 20 (October, 1987).
Adeeko, Adeleke. "Contests of Text and Context in Chinua Achebe's *Arrow of God.*" *Ariel: A Review of International English Literature*, 23, 2 (April 1992): 7-22.
Aidoo, Ama Atta. *No Sweetness Here: A Collection of Short Stories*. London: Longman, 1970.
Aigbe, Sunday A. *The Theory of Social Involvement: A Case Study of the Anthropology of Religion, State, and Society*. Lanham, MD: University Press of America, 1993.
Ake, Claude, "Why Is Africa Not Developing?" *West Africa* (June 17, 1985): 1212-1214.

Akindele, F. "Dialogue and Discourse in Nigerian English Fiction." In *Approaches to the Analysis of Literary Discourse*, ed. E. Ventola. Turko: Abo Akad, 1991.

Althusser, Louis. *Lenin and Philosophy and Other Essays*, 2nd ed., trans. Ben Brewster. New York: Monthly Review Press, 1977. First published as *Lénine et la Philosophie*. Paris: Maspero, 1969.

Amuta, Chidi. *The Theory of African Literature*. London: Zed, 1989.

Anhart, Larry. *Aristotle on Political Reasoning: A Commentary on the Rhetoric*. De Kalb: Northern Illinois University Press, 1981.

Anozie, Sunday. *Christopher Okigbo: Creative Rhetoric*. New York: Evans, 1992.

Aristotle. *Art of Rhetoric*, trans. J. H. Freese. Cambridge, MA: Harvard University Press, 1991.

—. *Nicomachean Ethics*, Bk II. *Aristotle's Selected Works*, 3rd ed., trans. Hippocrates G. Apostle and Lloyd Gearson. Grinnell, IA: The Peripatetic Press, 1991.

—. *The Politics*, trans. T.A. Sinclair, rev'd. Trevor J. Saunders. Harmondsworth: Penguin, 1981.

—. *Posterior Analytics. Aristotles Selected Works*, 3rd ed., trans. Hippocrates G. Apostle and Lloyd Gearson. Grinnell, IA: The Peripatetic Press, 1991.

Armah, Ayi Kwei. *Fragments*. London: Heinemann, 1974.

Asein, Samuel Omo, ed. *Comparative Approaches to Modern African Literature*. Ibadan: Ibadan University Press, 1982.

—. "Literature as History: Crisis, Violence and Strategies of Commitment in Nigerian Writing." In *Literature and Modern West African Culture*, ed. Donatus I. Nwoga. Benin, Nigeria: Ethiope, 1978.

Augustine, St. *De Doctrina Christiana* Bk IV., trans. Thèrèsa Sullivan. In *The Rhetorical Tradition: Reading from Classical Times to the Present*. Eds. Patricia Bizzell and Bruce Herzberg. New York: St. Martin's Press, 1990.

Bakhtin, Mikhail M. *The Dialogic Imagination*, ed. Michael Holquist, trans. Carl Emerson and Michael Holoquist. Austin: University of Texas Press, 1981.

—. *Problems of Dostoevsky's Poetics*, Trans. and ed. Carl Emerson, Minneapolis: University of Minnesota Press, 1987.

—. "The Problem of Speech Genres." In *Speech Genres and Other Late Essays*. trans. Vern W. McGee, eds. Carl Emerson and Michael Holquist, Austin: University of Texas Press, 1987.

—. "Verbal Interaction." From *Marxism and the Philosophy of Language*, part II, Ch.3. In *The Rhetorical Tradition: Readings from Classical Times to the Present*, eds. Patricia Bizzell and Bruce Herzberg. New York: St Martin's Press, 1990.

Baldwin, Charles Sears. *Medieval Rhetoric and Poetics*. New York: Macmillan, 1928.

Beier, Ulli, ed. *Introduction to African Literature*. Essex: Longman, 1967.

Benjamin, Walter. *Illuminations*. New York: Harcourt, Brace and World, 1968.

Bhabha, Homi K. *The Location of Culture*. London: Routledge, 1994.

Bizzell, Patricia and Bruce Herzberg eds., *The Rhetorical Tradition: Readings from Classical Times to the Present*. New York: St Martin's Press, 1990.

Booth, Wayne C. *The Rhetoric of Fiction*, 2nd ed. Chicago: University of Chicago Press, 1983.

—. *A Rhetoric of Irony*. Chicago: University of Chicago Press, 1974.

Bowker, V. "Textuality and Worldliness: Crossing the Boundaries: A Post-Modernist Reading of Achebe, Conrad and Lessing." *Journal of Literary Studies*, 1 (1989): 55-86.

Brown, David Maughan. "*Anthills of the Savannah*: Achebe's Solutions to the 'Trouble with

Nigeria.'" In *Critical Approaches to Anthills of the Savannah*, ed. Holger G. Ehling. Atlanta: Rodopi, 1991.

Brown, Lloyd W. "Cultural Norms and Modes of Perception in Achebe's Fiction." In *Critical Perspectives on Chinua Achebe*, eds. Catherine Innes and Bernth Lindfors. London: Heinemann, 1979.

Burke, Kenneth. *Language as a Symbolic Action: Essays on Life, Literature, and Method*. Berkeley: University of California Press, 1966.

—. *On Symbols and Society*, ed. Joseph R. Gusfield. Chicago: University of Chicago Press, 1987.

—. *A Rhetoric of Motives*. Berkeley: University of California Press, 1969. Campbell, George. "The Nature and Foundation of Eloquence." In *The Rhetoric of Blair, Campbell, and Whately*, eds. James L. Golden and Edward P. J. Corbett. Carbondale: Southern Illinois University Press, 1990.

Carroll, David. "*A Man of the People*." In *Critical Perspectives on Chinua Achebe*, eds. Catherine Innes and Bernth Lindfors. London: Heinemann, 1979.

Catholic Living Bible,The. Wheaton, IL: Tyndale House Publishers, 1971.

Chinweizu. *The West and the Rest of Us*. New York: Random House, 1975.

Chinweizu et al. *Toward the Decolonization of African Literature*. Enugu, Nigeria: Fourth Dimension, 1980.

Cicero, Marcus Tullius. *Ad Herennium*, trans. H. Caplan. Cambridge MA: Harvard University Press, 1991.

—. *De Inventione*, trans. H. M. Hubbell. Cambridge: Harvard University Press, 1976.

—. *De Optimo Genere Oratorum*, trans. H. M. Hubell, ed. G. P. Goold. Cambridge, Mass: Harvard University Press, 1976.

—. *De Oratore* Bks. I and II, trans. E. W. Sutton, ed. T. E. Page. Cambridge, MA: Harvard University Press, 1976.

—. *De Oratore* Bk. III, trans. H. Rackham. Cambridge, MA: Harvard University Press, 1976.

Crossley-Holland, Kevin, trans "Beowulf," In *Literature of the Western World*. eds. Brian Wilkie and James Hurt New York: Macmillan, 1992.

Crowder, Michael. *The Story of Nigeria*. London: Faber and Faber, 1962.

Curtin, Philip D. *The Image of Africa: British Ideas and Actions*. Madison: University of Wisconsin Press, 1964.

Davidson, Basil. *The Blackman's Burden: Africa and the Curse of Nation-State*. New York: Random House, 1992.

Davis and Hena Macs-Jelinck, eds. *Crisis and Creativity in the New Literatures in English. Cross/Cultures*. Atlanta: Rodopi, 1990.

Dorsch, T. S., trans. *Classical Literary Criticism: Aristotle: On the Art of Poetry, Horace: On the Art of Poetry, and Longinus: On the Sublime*. Harmondsworth, England: Penguin, 1965.

Eagleton, Terry. *Literary Theory: An Introduction*. Minneapolis: University of Minnesota Press, 1995.

Echeruo, Michael. "Chinua Achebe." In *A Celebration of Black and African Writing*, eds. Bruce King and Kolawole Ogungbesan. London: Oxford University Press, 1978.

Egudu, Romanus. "Ojebe Poetry." In *Introduction to African Literature: An Anthology of Critical Writing*, ed. Ulli Beier. Essex: Longman, 1967.

Eliot, Thomas Stearns. "The Journey of the Magi." In *Literature: Reading, Reacting, Writng*, 3rd ed., eds. Laurie G. Kirzner and Stephen R. Mandell. New York: Harcourt

Brace, 1997, 924-925.

Emenyonu, Earnest N., ed. *Black Culture and Black Consciousness in Literature*. London: Heinemann, 1987.

—, ed. *Critical Theory and African Literature*. London: Heinemann, 1987.

—, ed. *Literature and Society: Selected Essays on African Literature*. Calabar, Nigeria: University of Calabar, 1986.

Emerson, Rupert. *From Empire to Nation: The Rise to Self-assertion of Asian and African Peoples*. Cambridge, MA: Harvard University Press, 1962.

Enos, Theresa and Stuart C. Brown, eds. *Professing the New Rhetoric: A Source Book*. Englewood Cliffs, NJ: Prentice Hall, 1994.

Fabian, Johannes. *Language and Colonial Power: The Appropriation of Swahili in the Former Belgium Congo 1880 - 1938*. Berkeley: University of California Press, 1986.

—. *Time and the Other: How Anthropology Makes Its Object*. New York: Columbia University Press, 1983.

First, Ruth. *The Barrel of a Gun: Political Power in Africa and the Coup d'État*. London: Penguin, 1970.

Fisher, W. R. *Rhetoric: A Tradition in Transition*. Michigan: Michigan State University Press, 1974.

Geertz, Clifford, ed. *Old Societies and New States: The Quest for Modernity in Asia and Africa*. New York: The Free Press, 1963.

Gikandi, Simon. *Reading Chinua Achebe: Language and Ideology in Fiction*. London: James Curry, 1991.

Gurnah, Abdulrazak, ed. *Essays on African Writing: A Re-evaluation*. Portsmouth, NH: Heinemann, 1993.

Hardin, C. *Shakespeare*. Evanston, IL: Scott, Foresman, 1958.

Harrison, G. B. *Introducing Shakespeare*. Harmondsworth: Penguin, 1966.

Howell, Samuel Wilbur. *Poetics, Rhetoric, and Logic: Studies in the Basic Disciplines of Criticism*. Ithaca, NY: Cornell University Press, 1980.

Ikegami, R. "Knowledge and Power, the Story and the Storyteller: Achebe's *Anthills of the Savannah*." *Modern Fiction Studies* 3 (Autumn 1991): 493-507.

Innes, Catherine Lynette. *Chinua Achebe*. London: Cambridge University Press, 1990.

Innes, Catherine Lynette and Bernth Lindfors, eds. *Critical Perspectives on Chinua Achebe*. London: Heinemann, 1979.

Irele, Abiola. "The Tragic Conflict in the Novels of Achebe." In *Critical Perspectives on Chinua Achebe*, eds. Catherine Innes and Bernth Lindfors. London: Heinemann, 1979.

Isocrates. *Antidosis*, trans. George Norlin, ed. G. P. Goold. Cambridge, MA: Harvard University Press, 1982.

Iyasere, Solomon. "Narrative Techniques in *Things Fall Apart*." In *Critical Perspectives on Chinua Achebe*, eds. Catherine Innes and Bernth Lindfors. London: Heinemann, 1979.

Jabbi, Bu-Buakei. "Fire and Transition in *Things Fall Apart*." In *Critical Perspectives on Chinua Achebe*. eds. Catherine Innes and Bernth Lindfors. London: Heinemann, 1979.

Kennedy, George A. *The Art of Rhetoric in The Roman World*. Princeton, NJ: Princeton University Press, 1972.

King, Bruce and Kola Ogungbesan, eds. *A Celebration of Black and African Writing*. London: Oxford University Press, 1978.

Lear, Jonathan. *Arstotle: The Desire to Understand*. Cambridge: Cambridge University Press, 1988.

Lee, Robert. *Orwell's Fiction*. Notre Dame, IN: University of Notre Dame Press, 1970.

Mabogunje, Akin L. "Nigeria: Physical and Social Geography," In *Africa South of the Sahara*. London: Europa Publications, 1986.

McLuhan, Marshal. *The Medium Is the Message*, San Francisco: Hardwired, 1996.

Mboya, Tom. *The Challenge of Nationhood: A Collection of Speeches and Writings*. New York: Praeger, 1970.

Minogue, K. R. *Nationalism*. New York: Basic Books, 1967.

Moore, Gerald H. *Twelve African Writers*. London: Hutchinson, 1980.

Muggeridge, Malcolm. "Introduction" to George Orwell, *Animal Farm*. New York: Time Life Books, 1965.

Narasimhaiah, C. D. "Where Angels Fear to Tread: Chinua Achebe and Wole Soyinka as Critics of the African Scene." *Literary Criterion*, 1-2 (1988): 222-236.

Nauman, M. "The Semantic Structure of Chinua Achebe's *Anthills of the Savannah*" *Commonwealth Essays and Studies* 1 (Autumn 1990): 112-116.

Niven, Alastair. "Achebe and Okri: Contrasts in Response to Civil War." In *Short Fiction in the New Literatures in English: Proceedings of the Nice Conference of the European Association Commonwealth Literature and Language Studies*, ed. J. Bardolph. Nice: Faculties des Lettres et Sciences Humaines, 1989.

—. "Chinua Achebe and the Possibility of Modern Tragedy." In *Chinua Achebe: A Celebration*, eds. Kirsten Holst Petersen and Anna Rutherford, (Oxford: Heinemann, 1990), 45.

Nkosi, Lewis. *Tasks and Masks: Themes and Styles of African Literature*. Essex: Longman, 1981.

Nkosi, Lewis, Cosmos Pieterse, and Dennis Duerden, eds. *African Writers Talking: A Collection of Radio Interviews*. London: Heinemann, 1972.

Nwoga, Donatus I., ed. *Literature and Modern West African Culture*. Benin, Nigeria: Ethiope, 1978.

Obiechina, Emmanuel N. *Culture, Tradition and Society in the West African Novel*. London: Cambridge University Press, 1975.

Odinga, Ajuma Oginga. *Not Yet Uhuru:The Autobiography of Oginga Odinga*. New York: Hill and Wang, 1967.

Ogungbesan, Kolawole, "The Modern Writer and Commitment." In *Literature and Modern West African Culture*, ed. Donatus I. Nwoga. Benin, Nigeria: Ethiope, 1978.

—, ed. *New West African Literature*. London: Heinemann, 1979.

—. "Politics and the African Writer." In *Critical Perspectives on Chinua Achebe*, eds. Catherine Innes and Bernth Lindfors. London: Heinemann, 1979.

Okafor, Clement Abiaziem. "Chinua Achebe: His Novels and the Environment," *College Language Association Journal*, 32, 4 (June 1989): 433-442.

Okonkwo, Nelson Chidi. "Chaos and Cosmos: The Colonial Encounter as Rite of Passage in the African Novel." *Landfall: A New Zealand Quarterly*, 44, 4 (Dec. 1990): 461-475.

Ola, Vincent U. "Pessimism and Commitment in the Works of Achebe and Armah: Comment." In *Literature of Africa and the African Continuum*. eds. J. A. Peters, M. P. Mortimer, and R. V. Linnenman. Washington, DC: Three Continents Press and African Literature Association, 1989.

Onimade, Bale. *Imperialism and Underdevelopment in Nigeria*. London: Zed, 1982.

Orwell, George. *Animal Farm*. New York: Time Life Books, 1965.

—. *A Collection of Essays*. Garden City, NY: Doubleday, 1957.

Ostheimer, John S. *Nigerian Politics*. New York: Harper and Row, 1973.

Owusu, K. "The Politics of Interpretation: The Novels of Chinua Achebe." *Modern Fiction Studies*, 30 (Autumn 1991): 459-470.

Oyeleye, Lekan. "Transference as a Stylistic Strategy: An Inquiry into the Language of Achebe's *Things Fall Apart* and *No Longer at Ease*." *Odu: A Journal of West African Studies* 32 (July 1987):160-169.

Palmer, Eustace. *The Growth of the African Novel*. London: Heinemann, 1979.

—. *An Introduction to the African Novel*. London: Heinemann, 1972.

Pati, Madhusudan. *"Things Fall Apart*: An Enquiry into Rasa-Configuration." *The Literary Criterion*, 26,1 (1991): 40-53.

Peiterse, Cosmos and David Munro, eds. *African Writers Talking*. London: Heinemann, 1972.

Perelman, Chaim and Lucie Olbrechts-Tyteca. *The New Rhetoric: A Treatise on Argumentation*, trans. John Wilkinson and Purcell Weaver. London: University of Notre Dame Press, 1969.

Petersen, Kirsten Holst and Anna Rutherford, eds. *Chinua Achebe: A Celebration*. Oxford: Heinemann, 1990.

Plato. "Apology (The Defence of Socrates)." In *Great Dialogues of Plato*. trans W. H. D. Rouse, eds. Eric H. Warmington and Philip G. Rouse. New York: Penguin, 1984.

—. "Phaedrus." In *Plato: Complete Works*. trans. Alexander Nehamas and Paul Woodruff, ed. J. M. Cooper, Indianapolis: Hackett Publishing Company, 1997.

Povey, John. "Novels of Chinua Achebe." In *Introduction to Nigerian Literature*, ed. Bruce King. London: Heinemann, 1971.

Quintilian. *Institutio Oratoria* I and III. trans. H. E. Butler. Cambridge, MA: Harvard University Press, 1991.

Ravenscroft, Arthur. "Recent Fiction from Africa: Chinua Achebe's *Anthills of the Savannah*—a Note." *The Literary Criterion*, 23, 1-2 (1988): 172-175.

Richards, Ivor, A. *The Philosophy of Rhetoric*. New York: Oxford University Press, 1936.

Richter, David H., ed. *The Critical Tradition: Classic Texts and Contemporary Trends*. New York: St. Martin's Press, 1989.

Roscoe, Adrian. *Mother Is Gold: A Study in West African Literature*. London: Cambridge, 1971.

—. *Uhuru's Fire: African Literature East to South*. London: Cambridge University Press, 1977.

Rutherford, Anna. "Interview with Chinua Achebe," *Kunapipi*. Denmark: Dangaroo Press, 1979.

Shakespeare, William. *The Tragedy of Julius Caesar*, eds. Stanley Wells and Gary Taylor. In *The Complete Oxford Shakespeare III. Tragedies*. London: Guild Publishing, 1989.

Sharma, G. N. "The Christian Dynamic in the Fictional World of Chinua Achebe," *Ariel: A Review of International English Literature*, 24, 2 (April 1993): 85-99.

Shils, E. "Primordial, Personal, Sacred and Civil Ties." *British Journal of Sociology* (June 1957). Quoted in *Old Societies and New States: The Quest for Modernity in Asia and Africa*, ed. Clifford Geertz. New York: The Free Press, 1963.

Sinha, A. K. "The Satire in Chinua Achebe's *A Man of the People."* In *Modern Studies and Other Essays in Honour of Dr. R. K. Sinha*, eds. R. C. Prasad and A. K. Sharma. New Delhi: Vikas, 1987.

Stock, A. G. "Yeats and Achebe." In *Critical Perspectives on Chinua Achebe*, eds. Catherine Innes and Bernth Lindfors. London: Heinemann, 1979.

Taiwo, Oladele. *Culture and the Nigerian Novel*. London: Macmillan, 1976.

Thion'go, Ngugi Wa. *Petals of Blood*. London: Heinemann, 1978.

Thompson, James. *Models of Values: Eighteenth-Century Political Economy and the Novel*. Durham, NC: Duke University Press, 1962.

Turkington, Kate. *Chinua Achebe: Things Fall Apart*. London: Edward Arnold, 1977.

Udumukwu, Onyemaechi. "Achebe and the Negation of Independence." *Modern Fiction Studies*, 37 (Autumn 1991): 471-491.

Uka, Kalu. "From Commitment to Essence." In *Literature and Modern West African Culture*, ed. Donatus I. Nwoga. Benin, Nigeria: Ethiope, 1978.

Vickers, Brian. *Classical Rhetoric in English Poetry*. Carbondale: Southern Illinois University Press, 1989.

Walton, Douglas. *The Place of Emotion in Argument*. University Park: Pennsylvania State University Press, 1992.

Weaver, Richard M. *The Ethics of Rhetoric*. Davis, CA: Hermogoras Press, 1985.

—. *Ideas Have Consequences*. Chicago: University of Chicago Press, 1948.

—. "Language Is Sermonic." In *The Rhetoric of Western Thought*, 4th ed., eds. James L. Golden et al. Dubuque, IA: Kendall/Hunt, 1984.

—, "Nature of Culture." In *Contemporary Perspectives on Rhetoric*, 2nd ed., eds. Sonja K. Foss, Karen A. Foss, and Robert Trapp. Prospect Heights, IL: Waveland Press, 1991.

—. *Visions of Order: The Cultural Crisis of Our Time*. Baton Rouge: Louisiana State University Press, 1964.

Weinstock, Donald and Kathy Ramadan. "Symbolic Structure in *Things Fall Apart*." In *Critical Perspectives on Chinua Achebe*, eds. Catherine Innes and Bernth Lindfors. London: Heinemann, 1979.

Wren, Robert M. *Achebe's World: The Historical and Cultural Context of the Novels*. Washington, DC: Three Continents Press, 1980.

Zubus, Chantal. "The Logos-Eater: The Igbo Ethno-Text" In *Chinua Achebe: A Celebration*. Kirsten Holst Petersen and Anna Rutherford, eds. Oxford: Heinemann, 1990.

Index

About the Author

CHINWE CHRISTIANA OKECHUKWU is a Professor in the Department of Reading and English as a Second Language, Foreign Languages, and Philosophy at the Rockville campus of Montgomery College.